IMAGES
of America

ROYSE CITY

On the Cover: In this c. 1910 image, citizens of Royse City gather on Main Street in front of the Woodmen of the World (WOW) building. WOW was founded in Omaha, Nebraska, in 1890 as a fraternal organization that provides life insurance to its members. The building has been restored and now houses the police department. (Courtesy of David Smith.)

IMAGES
of America

ROYSE CITY

Sheri Stodghill Fowler

ARCADIA
PUBLISHING

Copyright © 2012 by Sheri Stodghill Fowler
ISBN 978-0-7385-9678-5

Published by Arcadia Publishing
Charleston, South Carolina

Printed in the United States of America

Library of Congress Control Number: 2012949904

For all general information, please contact Arcadia Publishing:
Telephone 843-853-2070
Fax 843-853-0044
E-mail sales@arcadiapublishing.com
For customer service and orders:
Toll-Free 1-888-313-2665

Visit us on the Internet at www.arcadiapublishing.com

In memory of my grandfather Woodrow Stodghill, who often took me to Royse City when he needed to do business at the bank and always managed to make time for a trip to the candy store, and for my nephew Dashiell Woodrow Stodghill, who shares both his great-grandfather's name and his birthday.

CONTENTS

Acknowledgments

To be honest, the true guru of Royse City history is Deloris Cross Ballard. There might be other lifelong residents who know as much about the city, but as the museum assistant for the Zaner Robison Historical Museum, she dedicates much of her time to preserving the photographs, documents, memories, and memorabilia of Royse City's history. I want to offer a heartfelt thanks to Deloris for the countless hours she spent schooling me in Royse City history and for allowing me to use her personal recollections. From the moment I met her, it was obvious she has a passion for preserving the history of her community.

I would also like to thank Ann Cornelius for helping me gather photographs and written histories at the start of this project and the Royse City officials—particularly Jerrell Baley—who blessed this project and allowed me access to the archives of the city's Zaner Robison Historical Museum.

In addition, I would like to thank Carolyn Francisco and the board of directors of the Rockwall County Historical Foundation (RCHF). Since I began chronicling the history of Rockwall County, the RCHF has been generous in allowing me access to their photograph archives and their written histories.

Individuals whose family photographs appear in this book include Florelle Cookston Burks, Lucille Cross Bell, Mary and David Vervalin, and David Smith. I cannot thank them enough for their efforts on my behalf. A special thanks to David Smith, who asked many of his relatives for Royse City photographs and provided the photograph that appears on the cover.

All of the photographs in this book are courtesy of either the Zaner Robison Historical Museum or the RCHF.

I want to thank my mother, from whom I inherited my love of writing, and my father, who loved history and passed on that love to me. When I moved back to Rockwall County in 2000, one of the first things my father did was pay my membership dues for the Rockwall County Historical Foundation. He knew me well.

I would like to thank my children, Jake and Grace. They are the joys of my life. Jake has patiently shared many of my historical journeys and has even acknowledged that history can be kind of cool. Without doubt, Grace shares my love of our family's Rockwall County heritage, including my overwhelming desire to preserve our family home in Heath.

Finally, no list of acknowledgments would be complete without mentioning the love of my life, Stacy Parks. He is patient, loving, generous, and kind. He has driven me thousands of miles around this country so I could explore history and never once complained. He makes me smile each and every day.

INTRODUCTION

With Texas becoming a state in 1845 and the blackland prairies of northern Texas offering unlimited opportunities, pioneer visionaries began to settle into a number of communities that would one day be a part of Rockwall County. Although there may have been settlers in the area as early as 1841, the first documented family to settle in what is now Royse City arrived around 1849. Nancy McCasland, a widow, and three of her sons obtained the title to a large tract and began a life of farming and living off of the land.

Throughout the following decades, families from Kentucky, Arkansas, Illinois, Kansas, and other states made their way to Texas as part of a massive westward expansion. The McCasland family was joined by dozens of other settlers, including members of the Royse family. Garrett Burgess Griffin Royse, commonly known as Byrd Royse, was a Confederate veteran who was born in Kentucky. In 1880, Byrd Royse married Nan McCasland, granddaughter of Nancy McCasland. Six years later, in 1886, Royse platted a town site. He sold the first lot to Alf Reese and Al Royse, his nephew, and they built the first store in the community.

In the early 1880s, a major economic shift was on its way to the small community as the Missouri-Kansas-Texas Railroad began plans to lay tracks through the area. Train service would mean easier shipping (at the time, farmers wanting to ship crops by rail had to haul them by the wagonload to either Terrell or Dallas), better access to transportation, and increased ease for merchants and families bringing goods into the community. Byrd Royse knew what a rail line would mean to his small community, and he was instrumental in making sure the route between Greenville and Dallas passed through his newly platted town. The common belief passed down through the Royse family is that Byrd Royse offered to donate the land for the train station in exchange for the city being named after him. Regardless of how it transpired, Byrd Royse was the official founder of the small, north Texas town of Royse City.

Following the railroad's arrival in town, Royse City experienced a period of steady growth and expansion. A post office, a drugstore, a newspaper, and the first city school all opened within a few years. By 1890, the community had a population of 1,000 and boasted two cotton gins, a gristmill, and 20 businesses. Some of these businesses had been moved from the town of Fate (sometimes referred to as "Old Fate"), which was bypassed by the railroad. Fate residents foresaw the devastating effect of this on their community, and most chose to move to either Barnes or Royse City, which were both on the direct path of the railroad. (Barnes was eventually renamed Fate, and the community still exists by this name today.) One of the first businesses that relocated from Old Fate to Royse City was a general store—owners N.B. Jouett and R.E. Yeager literally loaded their store building on rollers and used four oxen to pull the store to its new location. Houses were moved into the community in the same way, with families remaining inside the dwellings as the homes were transported across the open blackland.

In 1891, Royse City incorporated. Businesses included a hotel, a blacksmith, a livery stable, and numerous stores selling hardware, dry goods, and general merchandise. The community was growing but suffered a setback in 1893, when a fire destroyed the majority of the south side of the business district. Owners worked to rebuild, and civic improvements, including sidewalks (wooden planks laid end-to-end), were evident by 1895. In 1898, the local school system employed four teachers to instruct 204 students. By 1900, Royse City had a population of 1,245—just slightly higher than that of nearby Rockwall—making it, for a short period of time, the largest city in Rockwall County. In 1902, the city's incorporation was voted out, but it was reinstated in 1906.

Royse City, like its surrounding communities, thrived on farming and the ancillary businesses it created. Cotton growing, cotton ginning, and cottonseed oil manufacturing were all prevalent for many, many decades. Corn and grain were also common crops. Merchants, lawyers, and doctors also did a steady business through the first part of the 20th century. Local residents from this era recall multiple banks, grocery stores, garages, churches, and furniture stores, as well as a Woodmen of the World lodge, a doctors' and lawyers' professional building, a hotel, a movie theater, and a Coca-Cola bottling works. Opportunities for family recreation included an annual oyster supper and a large Fourth of July celebration at the picnic ground, which contained a bandstand. The local train depot also supplied entertainment, as residents often spent time just watching the arrivals and departures of the trains.

By 1914, Royse City had 40 businesses and a population of 1,300. Although the population remained near 1,000 during the 1920s and 1930s, the Depression hit the area hard. Falling prices for farm products resulted in some families moving away from the community in order take jobs in larger cities. Despite the hardships, the population remained fairly stable for many decades. In the late 1960s, when Lake Ray Hubbard was built along Interstate 30 leading to Royse City, all of Rockwall County began a gradual transformation into a suburban bedroom community. From 2000 to 2008, City-Data.com rated Royse City at no. 42 on its nationwide "Top 100 Fastest Growing Cities" list. The population has risen from 2,957 in the year 2000 to a population of approximately 11,000 citizens in 2012. Retail, manufacturing, and construction top the list of Royse City's most common industries.

Although major chain businesses operate along the I-30 corridor, Royse City's current city staff and elected officials are dedicated to the preservation of the historic downtown business district. In 2008, Royse City was designated a Texas Main Street community and has remained a part of the statewide preservation program. The Texas Main Street program encourages revitalization of historic buildings and districts throughout the state, as well as local and visitor involvement in the area through events such as festivals, parades, and celebrations.

Royse City's earliest settlers probably never envisioned their agrarian railroad town as part of a sprawling metroplex filled with small, suburban communities; however, with just one glimpse at the present-day Royse City, they would instantly recognize the community's ongoing commitment to its families, schools, businesses, and churches. The small-town feeling the early settlers experienced still thrives today in the historic Texas town of Royse City.

One

Early Settlement and the Arrival of the Railroad

The Royse City of the late 1800s could easily have been plucked from the pages of a Louis L'Amour novel or the frames of a John Wayne western, with dusty streets, wooden clapboard buildings, and a population dedicated to the growth of their thriving community. When Rockwall County was formed in 1873, Royse City found itself situated in the northeast corner. Although it extended into both Collin and Hunt Counties, Royse City was very much a Rockwall County town playing an active role in the economy and politics of the county as a whole.

When word reached Royse City that the Missouri-Kansas-Texas Railroad was building a line from Greenville to Dallas, city founder G.B. "Byrd" Royse lobbied extensively for the line to travel directly through his newly platted city. In 1886, this became a reality, and Royse City began to transform from a dusty prairie town to a thriving city with a growing population and business district. Brick buildings replaced the wooden ones, and Royse City experienced an extended period of growth and economic prosperity.

In 1892, Royse City citizens found themselves in the middle of a countywide controversy. The Rockwall County Courthouse had been destroyed by fire, and the citizens of Fate (located between Rockwall and Royse City), faced with construction of a new courthouse, spearheaded an effort to move the county seat from Rockwall to Fate. An election was scheduled for April 19, 1892, and community lore has it that the citizens of Royse City were the sway votes. In the heat of the election, prominent Rockwall businessmen convinced prominent Royse City businessmen that moving the county seat to Fate would prove disastrous for both cities. After all, with Fate located between the two, business would most certainly be redirected to the new county seat. Minutes from the commissioners' court reflect that there were 372 votes "For Removal to Fate" and 760 votes "For Remaining at Rockwall." Royse City—Rockwall's chief rival in baseball and, eventually, football—had saved the day for that city and set the stage for its own steady growth through the first part of the 20th century.

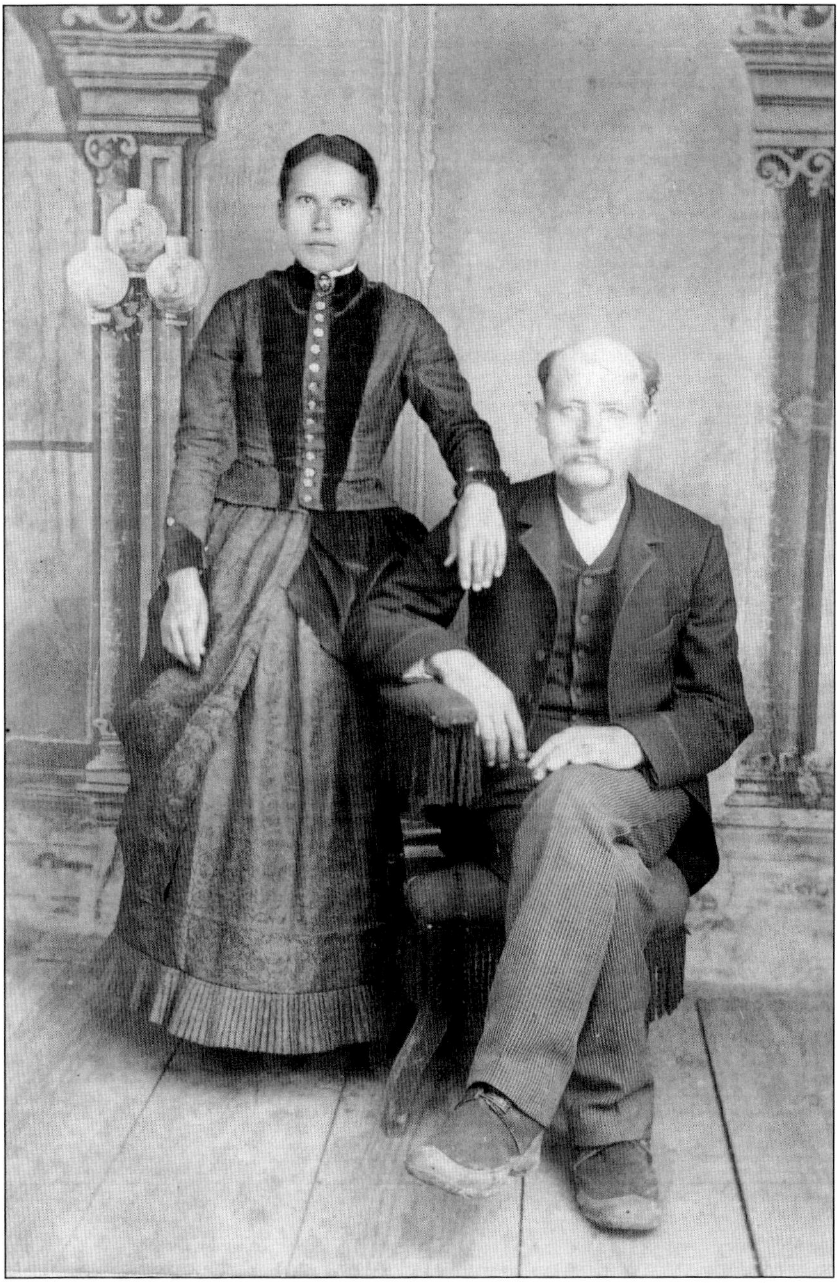

In 1880, town founder G.B. "Byrd" Royse married Nan McCasland, granddaughter of pioneer settler Nancy McCasland. Her dowry was 181 prime acres of blackland prairie. Royse, the seventh of 14 children, was born in Kentucky in 1838. He was a Confederate veteran who served with the 19th Regiment, Missouri Infantry. After his marriage to Nancy, he built a home at what is now 207 North Houston Street, and in 1886, he platted the town site for the city that would bear his name. He sold the first lot to Alf Reese and Albert Royse, his nephew. Byrd and Nan only stayed in Royse City until 1893, when they headed to Oklahoma during the land rush; they resided in Custer County, Oklahoma, for the rest of their lives. Byrd Royse died in 1928; Nan Royse passed away seven years later. They are both buried in the Stafford Cemetery near Foss, Oklahoma.

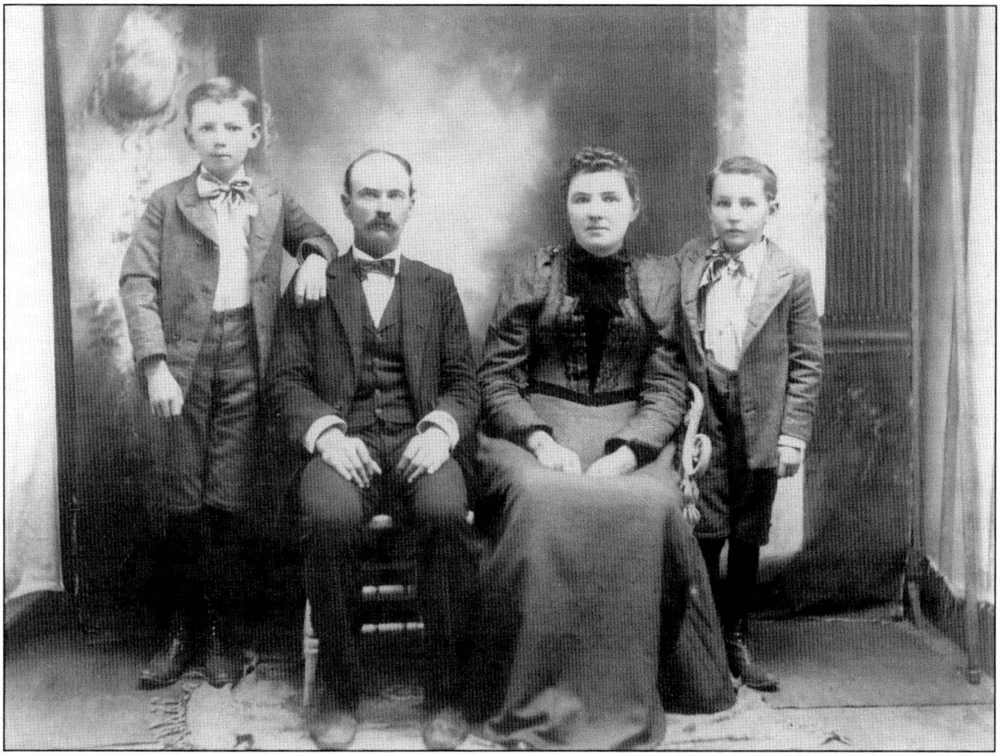

Albert G. Royse, in partnership with Alf Reese, built the first store in the newly platted town of Royse City. Pictured here around 1899 are, from left to right, Charles J. Royse (1891–1912), Albert G. Royse (1864–1939), Bella A. Royse (1870–1949), and Frank A. Royse (1893–1969). Albert was the nephew of city founder Byrd Royse.

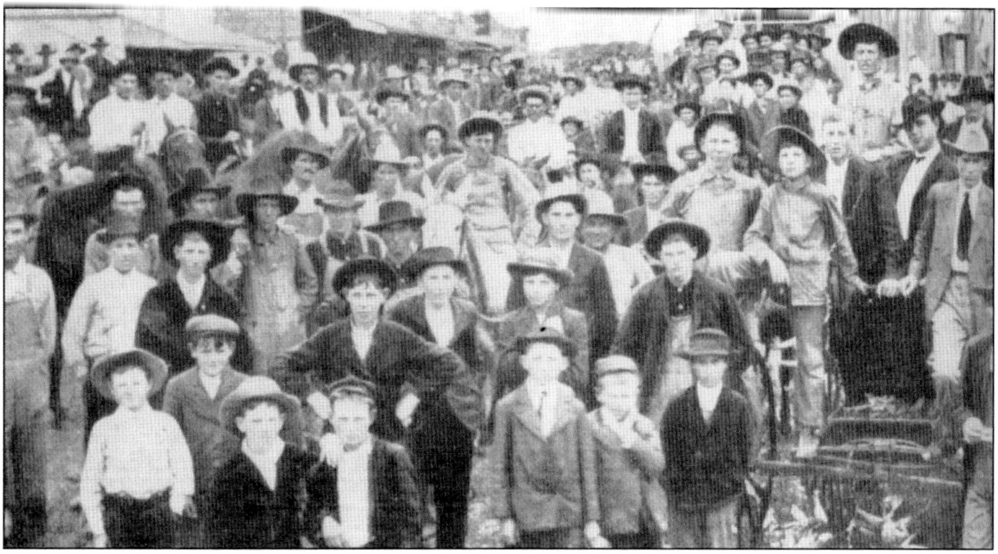

Prior to the late 1880s, businesses along Royse City's Main Street had clapboard storefronts and included general merchandise, hardware, sundries, and dry goods stores. The first brick buildings were constructed by the Miller brothers before the start of the 20th century. This group of Royse City men was gathered on Main Street.

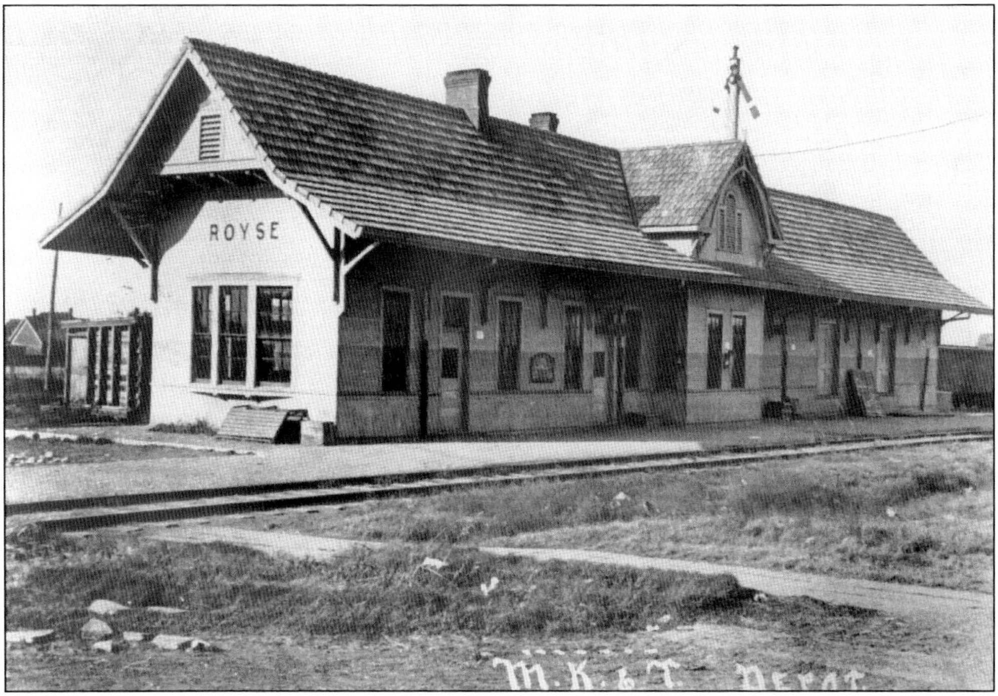

The construction of the Missouri-Kansas-Texas (MKT) Railroad through Royse City in 1886 marked a significant shift in the city's economy as people, crops, and merchandise could come and go with greater ease. Accounts from the Sorrells family, early settlers to the area, recount the first train that ran through Royse City: "We all donned our best Sunday clothes and went along long before time. All the people of the town were there lined up on each side of the track, all anxious, tense, waiting to see the first train." During the peak of its operation, the MKT ran up to eight passenger trains and five freight trains daily through the Royse City, Fate, and Rockwall depots. Above is the exterior of Royse City's MKT Depot; the interior of the depot is pictured below.

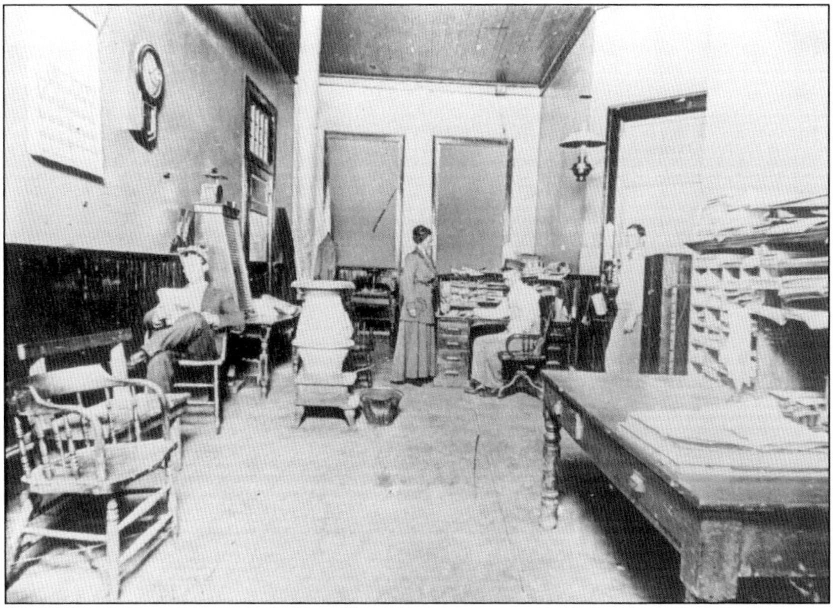

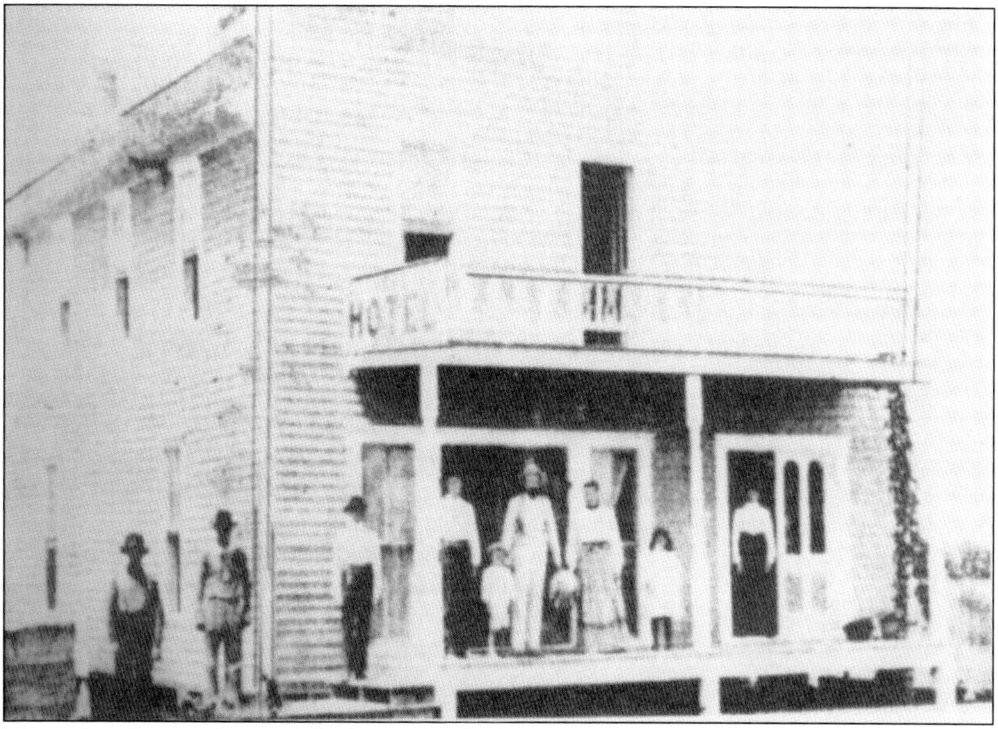

The railroad's arrival provided a boom for the business district as it became easier to travel to and from Royse City. The Commercial Hotel is pictured here around 1900. It was built by Jed Vervalin (pictured, with beard, in the center of the porch) in the years following the Civil War. The Vervalin family also owned a drugstore.

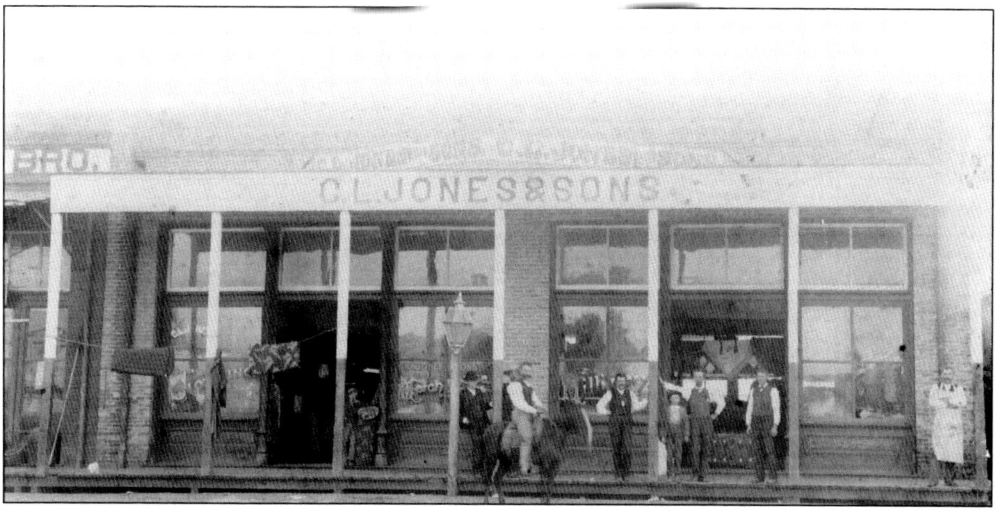

The C.L. Jones & Sons general merchandise store was located on Main Street and was one of the few businesses in town to escape an 1893 fire that destroyed most of the south side of downtown. Jones was a well-known businessman who also had a store in Rockwall. In 1873, Jones rode to Austin on horseback with John Summerfield Griffith to obtain the original charter for Rockwall County.

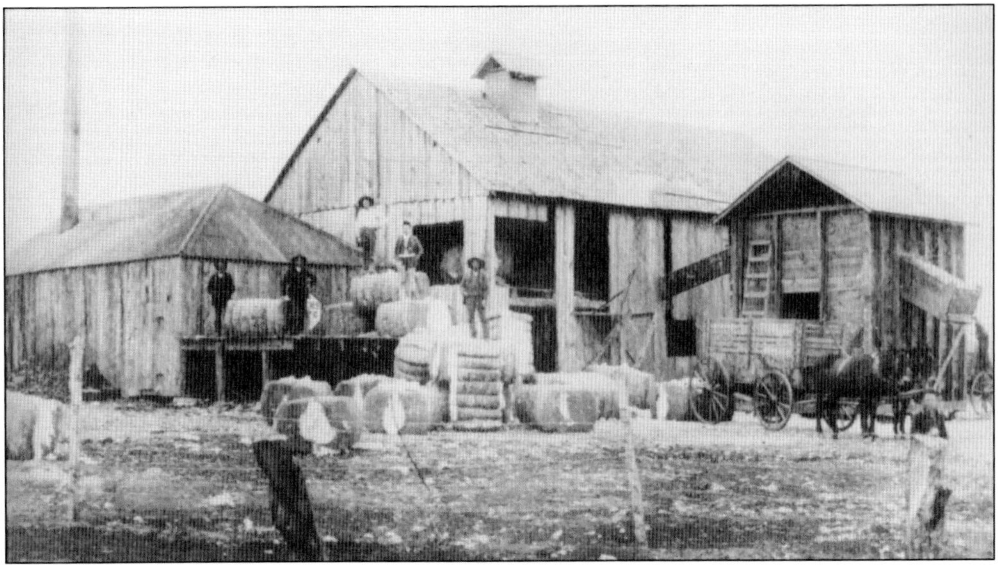

From the time of the earliest settler to the middle of the 20th century, agriculture was the major occupation for those living in the Royse City area. In 1900, there were 1,090 farms in Rockwall County, mostly growing cotton. At least 18 cotton gins were built throughout the county, including the Royse City cotton gin, pictured here around 1903.

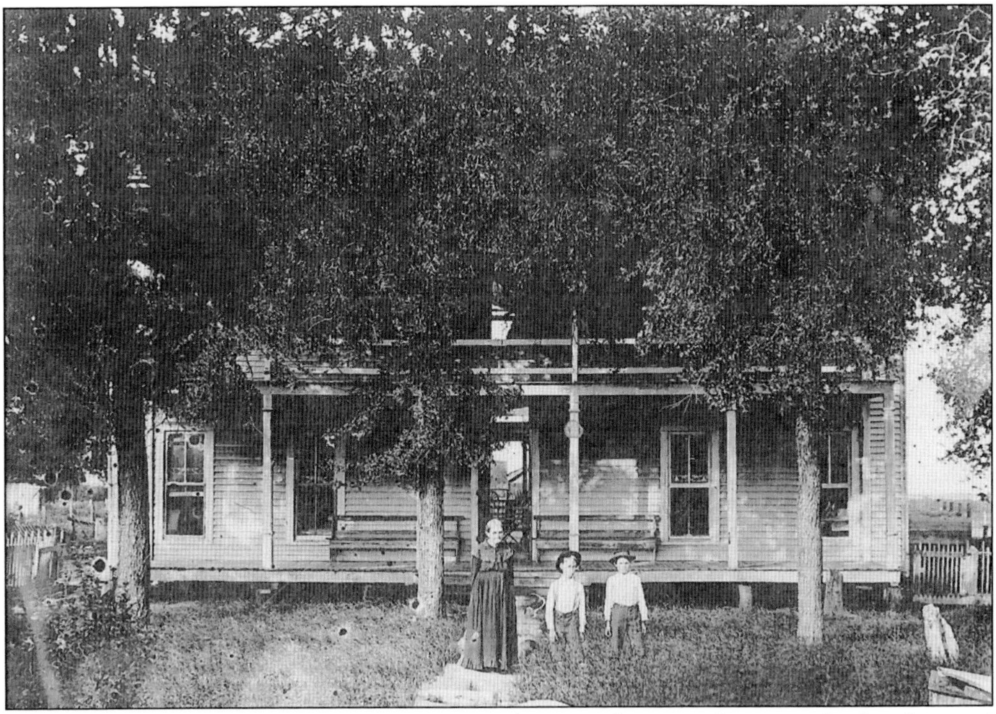

Most early settlers in the Royse City area were farmers who grew their own food and earned their livings from the land. Clapboard farmhouses dotted the blackland prairie, often reflecting a modified dogtrot architectural style, which included an open hallway down the middle of the home. The Russell family is pictured here around 1900.

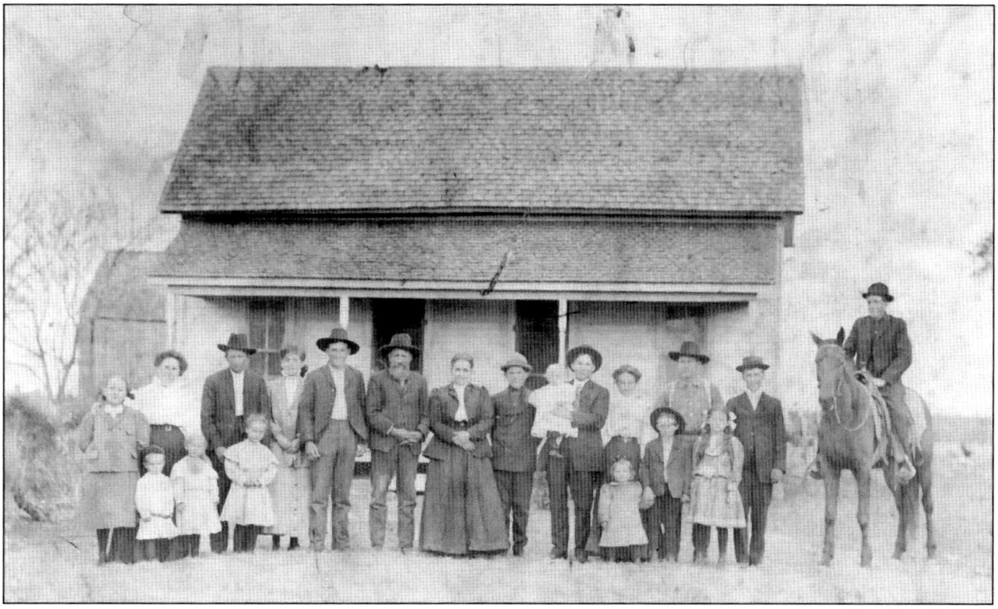

Many pioneer settlers came to Royse City for the fertile farmland and the town's proximity to the railroad. Francis Marion Cookston and his second wife, Sarah Adline Capps, moved from Tennessee to Texas with their family in the late 1800s; members of the Cookston family are pictured above. Brothers J.R. Terrell, J.W. Terrell, and W.A. Terrell—three of the children of Col. R.A. Terrell, namesake of the nearby town of Terrell—came to Royse City in 1880 and settled on adjoining farms southeast of town. Colonel Terrell's children and their spouses are pictured below at a family reunion held in Royse City around 1910. They are, from left to right, (first row) Mrs. A.H. Ables, J.O. Terrell, Mrs. W.B. Toone, W.A. Terrell, J.W. Terrell, James R. Terrell, Hon. John L. Terrell, Mrs. Joseph Huffmaster, and Mrs. J.W. Lively; (second row) A.H. Ables, Mrs. J.O. Terrell, Mrs. W.A. Terrell, Mrs. J.W. Terrell, Mrs. James R. Terrell, and Capt. Joseph Huffmaster.

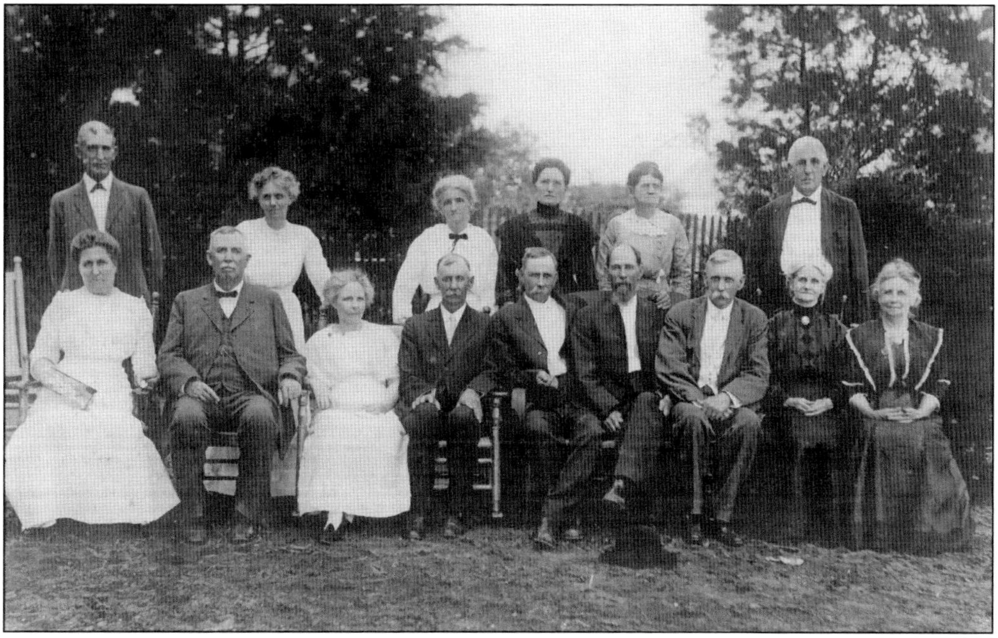

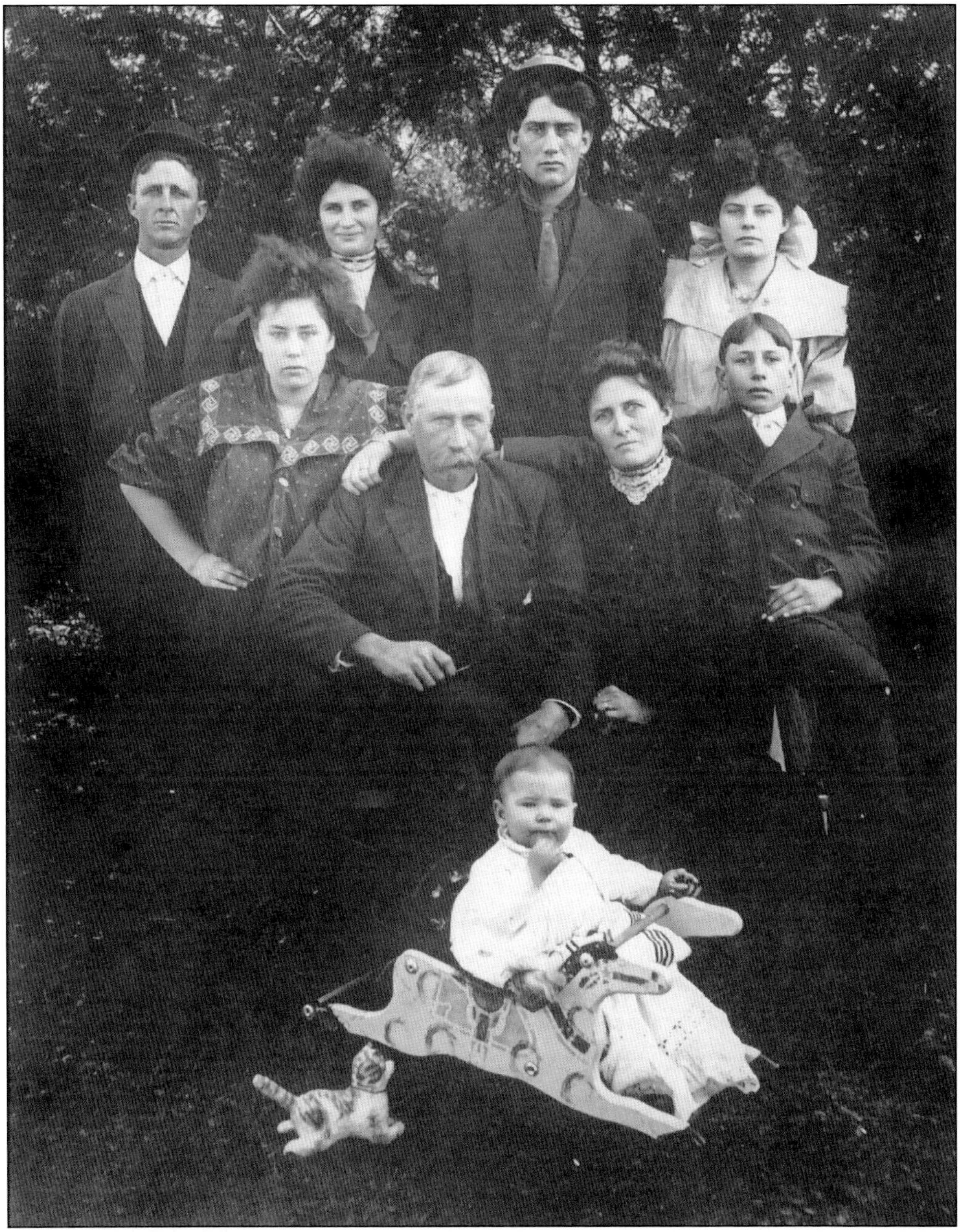

In the early 1900s, J.R. Terrell moved away, but his brothers J.W. and W.A. Terrell remained in Royse City. The Terrell brothers were involved in the community and were among the charter organizers of the First United Methodist Church of Royse City. Eventually, J.W. Terrell moved his family into town, built a Victorian home, and became a prosperous businessman, owning one of the first drugstores in Royse City. This c. 1906 Terrell family portrait includes, from left to right, (first row) Ernestine Miller, daughter of Tim and Edna Miller; (second row) Lot Terrell, J.W. Terrell, Florence Terrell, and Whit Terrell; (third row) Tim Miller, Edna Terrell Miller, Buddy Terrell, and Virginia "Dink" Terrell (soon after this photograph was taken, Virginia married prominent Royse City businessman Mike Cookston).

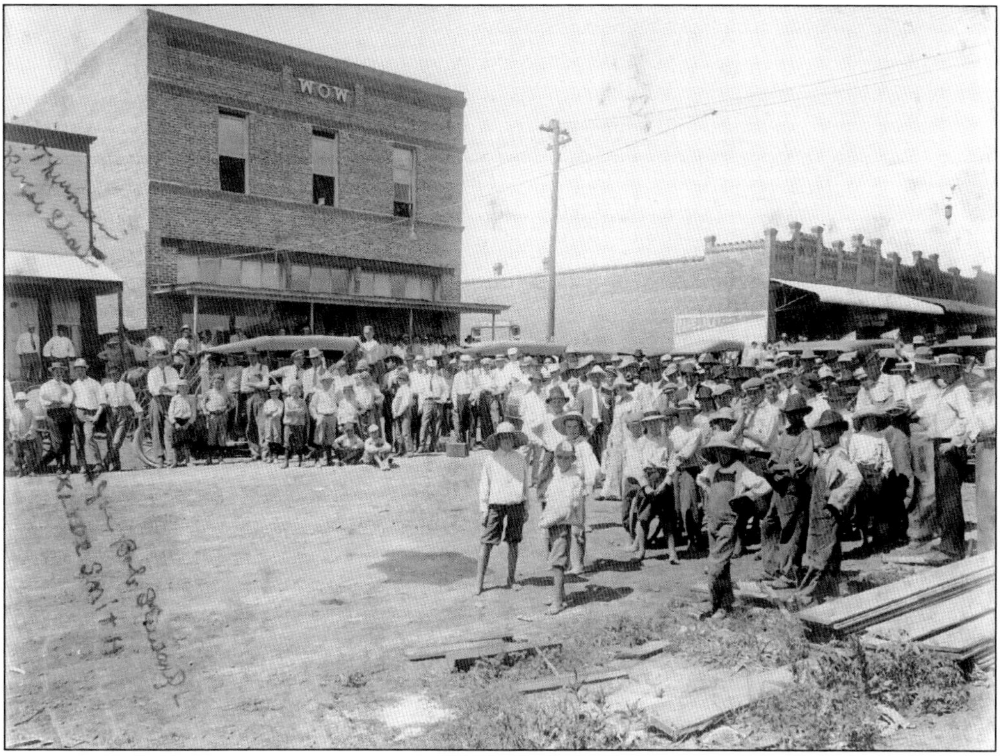

The clapboard buildings of the late 1800s had been mostly replaced by brick structures—including the prominent Woodmen of the World (WOW) building at left—by the time the c. 1910 photograph above was taken. WOW was founded in 1890 as a fraternal organization that offered life insurance benefits to its members. Members of the organization maintained local lodges and served as an active volunteer force within their communities, helping those in need. The Royse City chapter occupied this brick building on Main Street for many years; the building has been restored and now serves as the Royse City Police and Courts Building. Members of the Royse City WOW chapter are pictured below in front of the wooden WOW building, dating the image to sometime before the construction of the brick building pictured above.

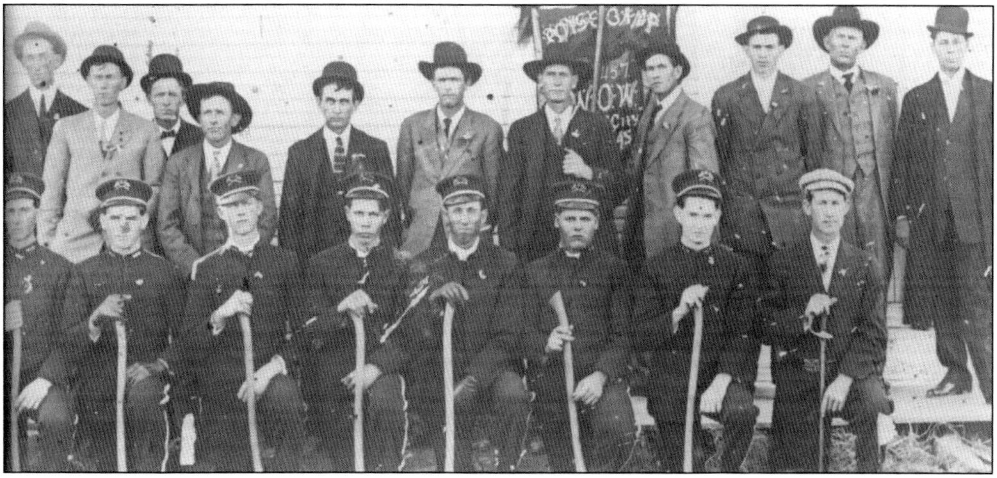

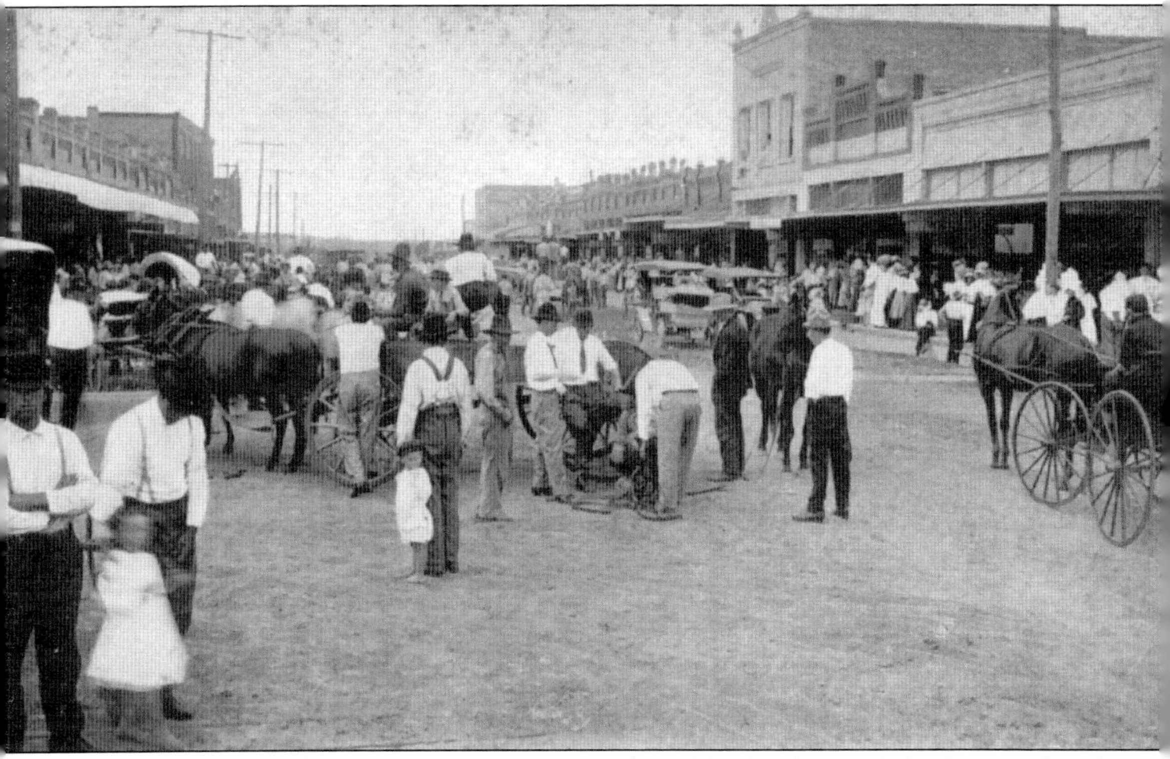

Prior to the arrival of the Missouri-Kansas-Texas (MKT) Railroad in 1886, the dusty roads and clapboard buildings that typified downtown Royse City would not have been frequented by the "fairer sex," necessity being the only reason for a female to visit the downtown area. However, as the clapboard buildings were replaced with brick ones and downtown became more respectable, Royse City's Main Street became a social gathering place, particularly on Saturdays. Merchants organized Trades Days and raffles to draw people into town. Around this same time, gasoline-powered automobiles became available for public purchase for the first time. The next decade would mark a nationwide shift in transportation that began in metropolitan areas but soon spread to small towns throughout America. This postcard from the early 1900s shows Main Street—filled with both men and women—as transportation modes were beginning to shift from the horse and buggy to the automobile.

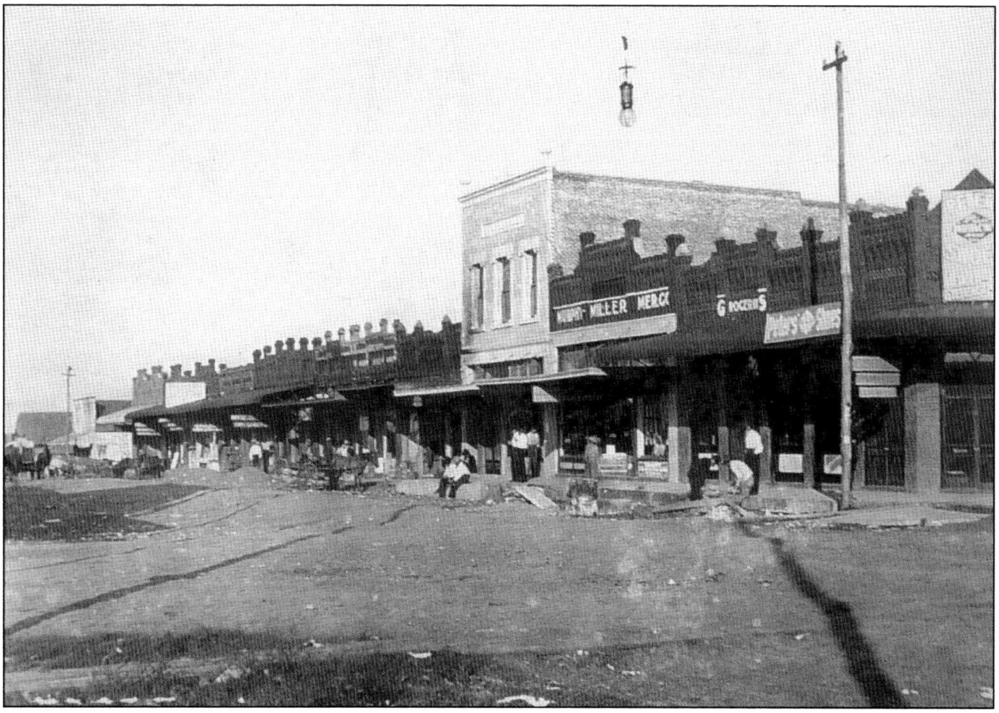

This c. 1900 view of the north side of Main Street shows an almost complete transformation from the clapboard buildings of the late 1800s. Electric poles and a single hanging streetlight—early evidence of the electrification of the town—testify to the city's growth and prosperity.

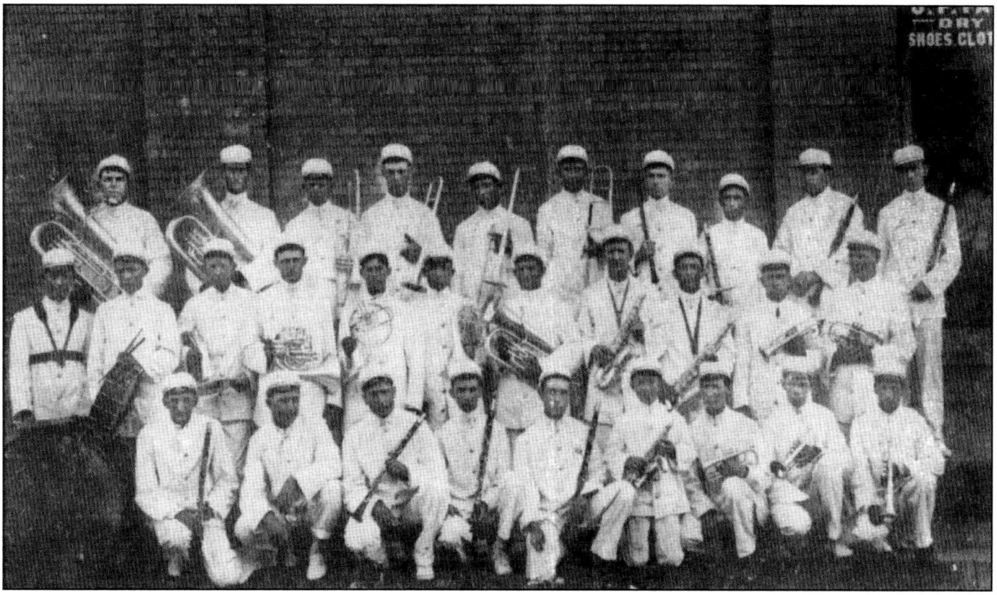

During the early 1900s, Royse City had many civic organizations. The 30-member Royse City Band is pictured here in 1917. The band, which was composed entirely of community members, played at special events and gatherings and even participated in regional competitions. The group rehearsed on the second floor of the J.P. Paschall Dry Goods Store, where they prepared for events such as the summer concert series at City Lake Park.

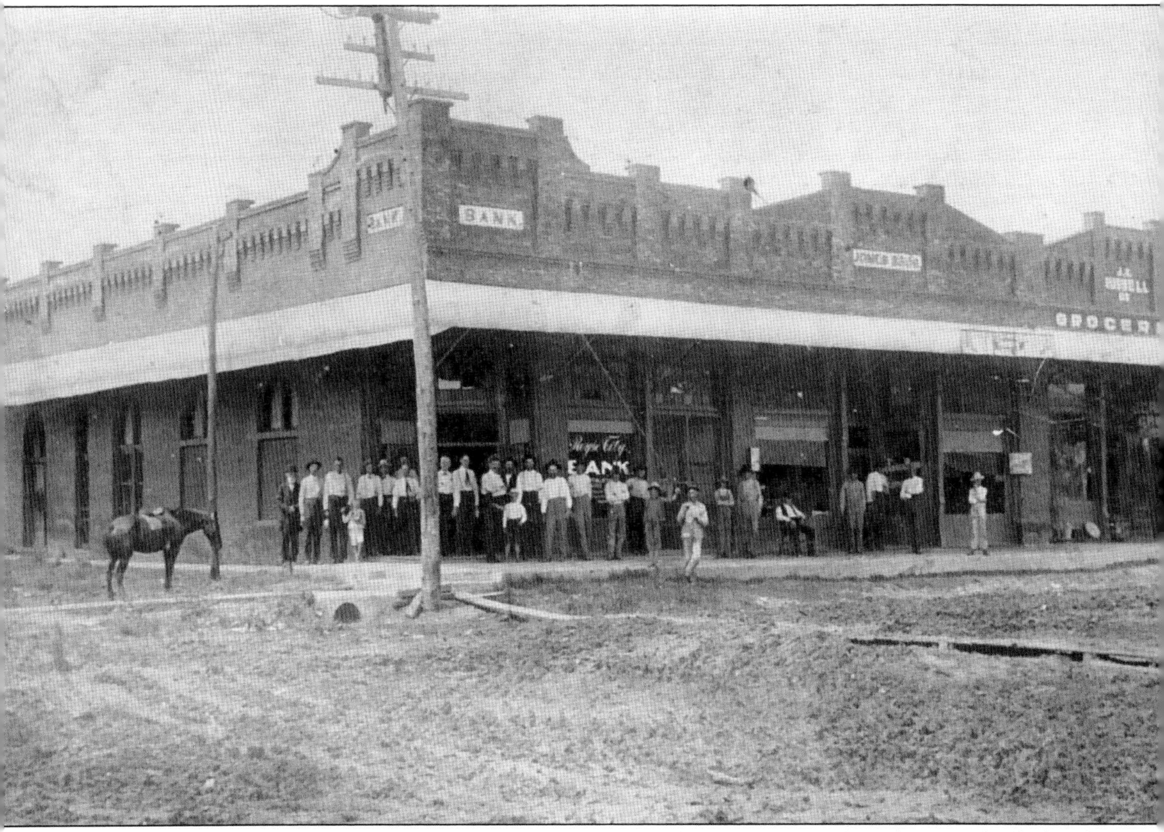

The Royse City Bank first opened to the public on October 11, 1897. Before the town had a bank, Royse City businessmen kept cash in safes at their stores during the day and took it home with them at night. The first president of the Royse City Bank was James Paulk, and the first cashier was his son, Edgar McDonald Paulk. The Paulk family—James; his wife, Betty; and their son Edgar—had come to Texas from Tennessee in the late 1800s, finally settling in Royse City, where they helped organize the first bank in town. The opening of the bank helped stimulate the local economy. James Paulk died in April 1917. Edgar continued working at the bank until 1924 and later pursued insurance and real estate. Edgar passed away in March 1940. The Royse City Bank eventually became the First State Bank, and, in 1933, Citizens State Bank—all were located in this building on the corner of Arch and Main Streets.

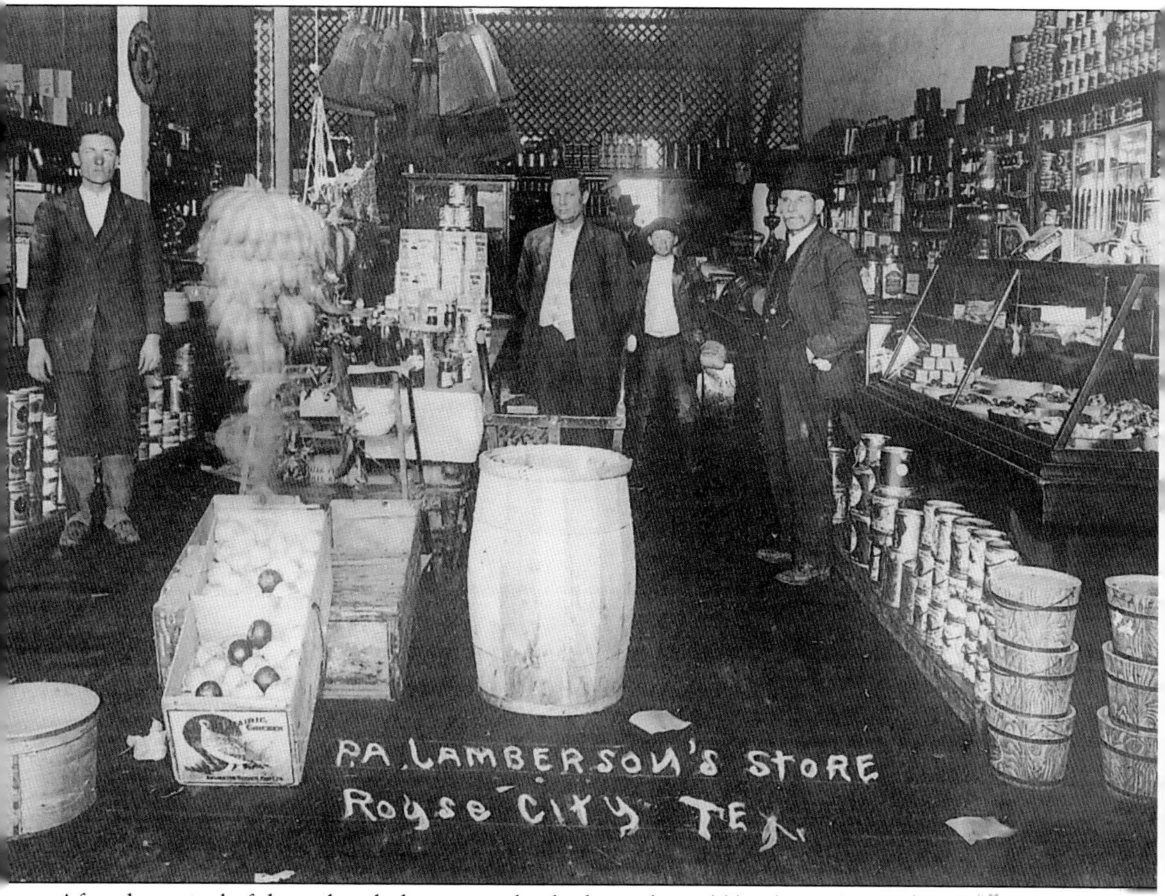

After the arrival of the railroad, the ease with which goods could be shipped in and out of Royse City caused expansion in the business district. Specialized stores sold general merchandise, hardware, furniture, and dry goods and sundries. Peter Lamberson's General Store, pictured in 1896, carried groceries and household goods like brooms and buckets. In addition to owning the store, Lamberson was involved in the community and was very active in the First Christian Church, where he served as an elder. He married a widow, Betty Vernon Walker, and they had one daughter, Bernice. In O.L. Steger's *History of Rockwall County*, the author describes Lamberson as "quite active in the civic, religious, political and educational affairs of Royse City . . . to think of Royse City, you could not but help thinking of his lovable, Christian and courteous character."

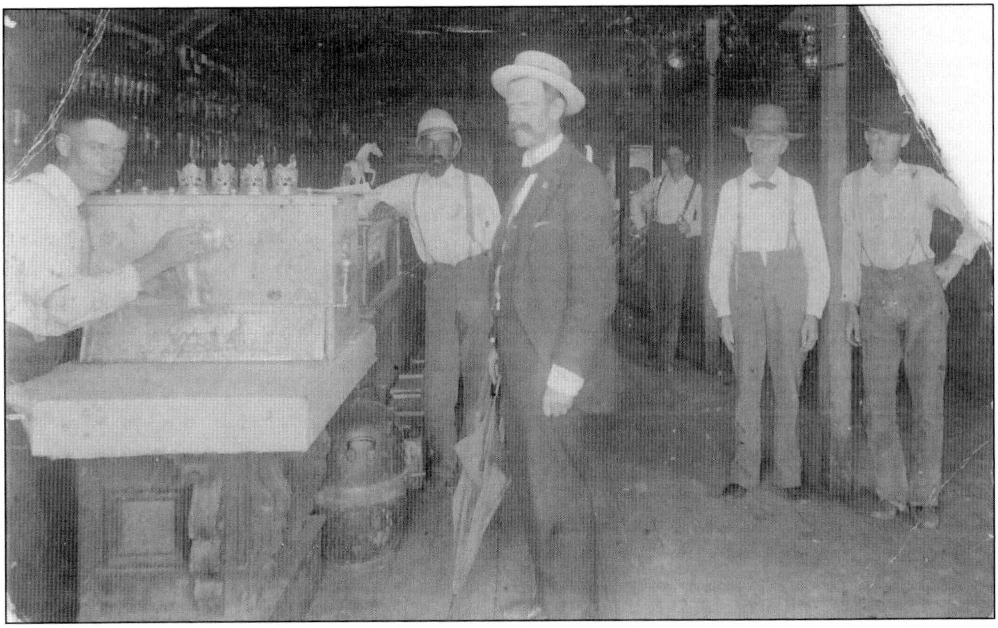

Early businesses in Royse City included dry goods stores, cafés, hotels, and even a saloon. Pictured is the interior of what is believed to have been Royse City's first and only real saloon. It was located at the corner of present-day Arch and Main Streets. The men are unidentified, but the surnames listed on the back of photograph are Charvie, Lovejoy, Terrell, Bass, and Loyd.

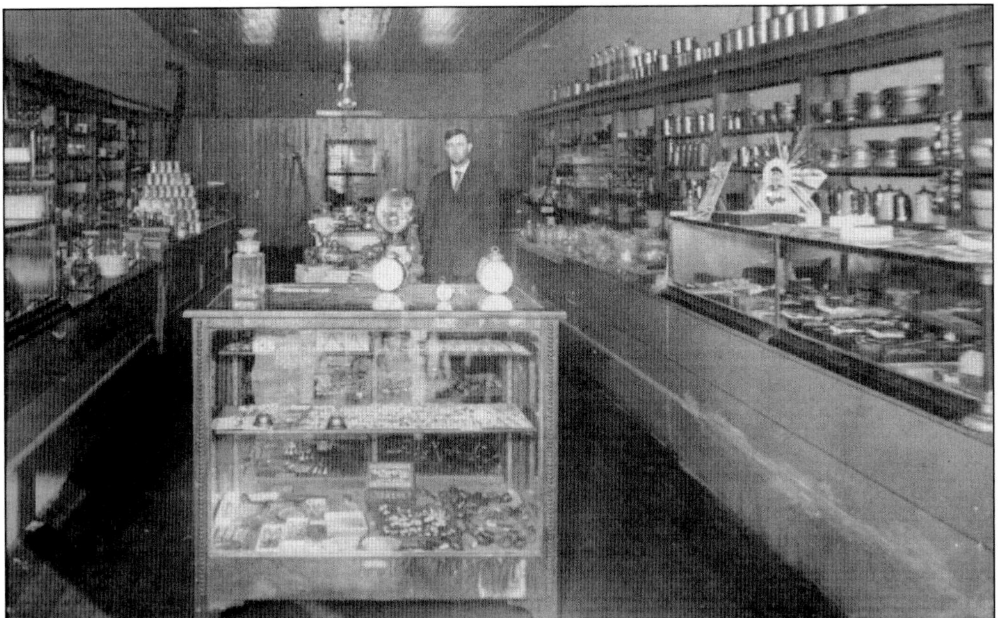

Vindex Stowers stands in his newly opened variety store in this 1908 photograph. In 1905, Stowers married Verna (Jack) Abernathy of Royse City. In 1908, the couple took up residence in Royse City and opened the store. According to the Stowers family history published in *Rockwall County History*, they completely sold out of goods the first Christmas they were in business. The store eventually expanded into dry goods, and Stowers operated the business until his death in 1944.

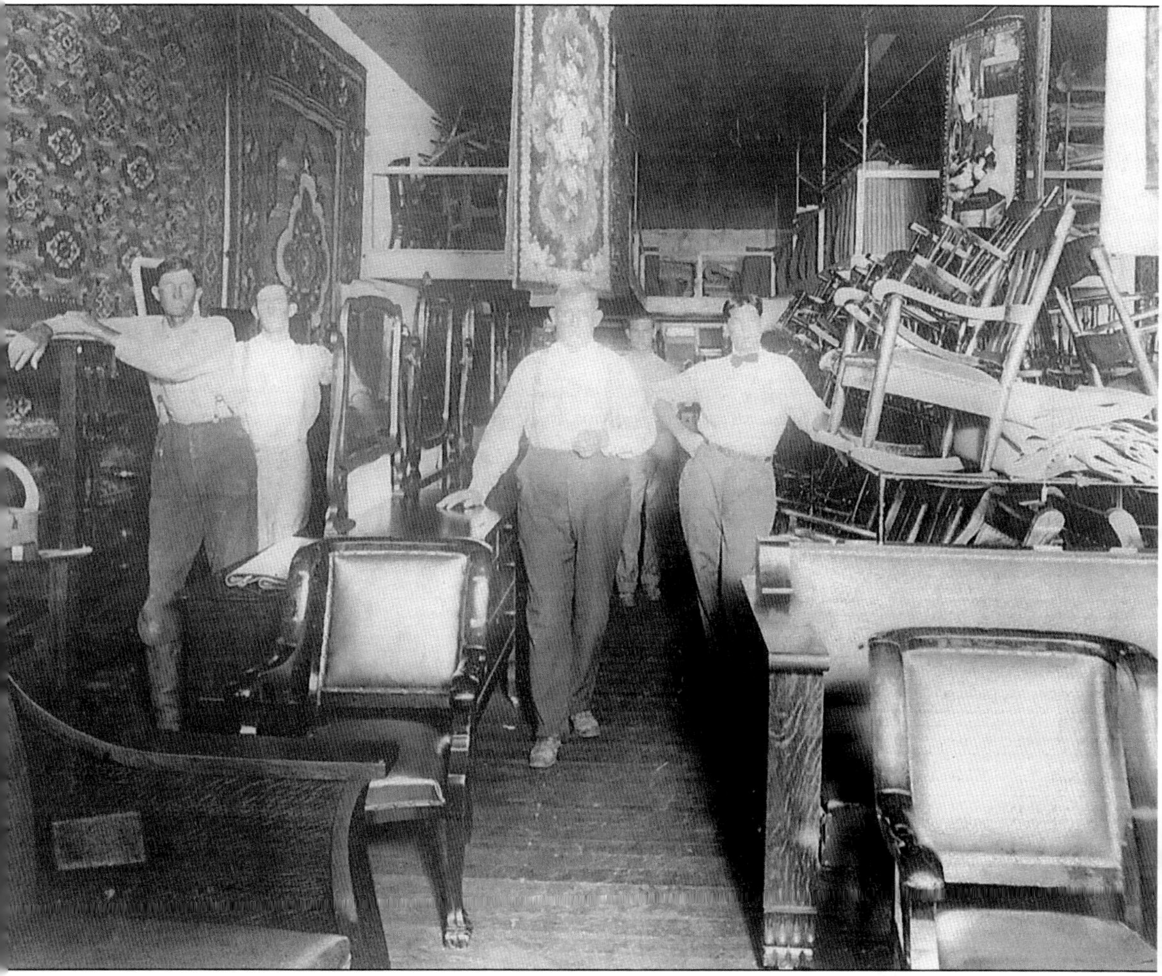

The early 1900s marked a shift from handcrafted to mass-produced furniture. The continued expansion of the railroad meant that furniture manufacturing companies could ship items more easily and cheaply to stores in smaller towns throughout the country. Mass-produced pieces cost less and were sometimes made out of flimsier material, such as wicker, but the savings were passed on to consumers, making mass-produced furniture more affordable for the average farmer than handmade items. As furniture sales increased, so did advertising budgets, and furniture stores advertised heavily in the early 1900s. In a 1927 advertisement that ran in a local paper, the Rhoton and Knight Furniture Store touted themselves as "The Leading Furniture Dealers of Royse City." The advertisement also promised that "every desire of your heart may be met in up-to-date quality furniture."

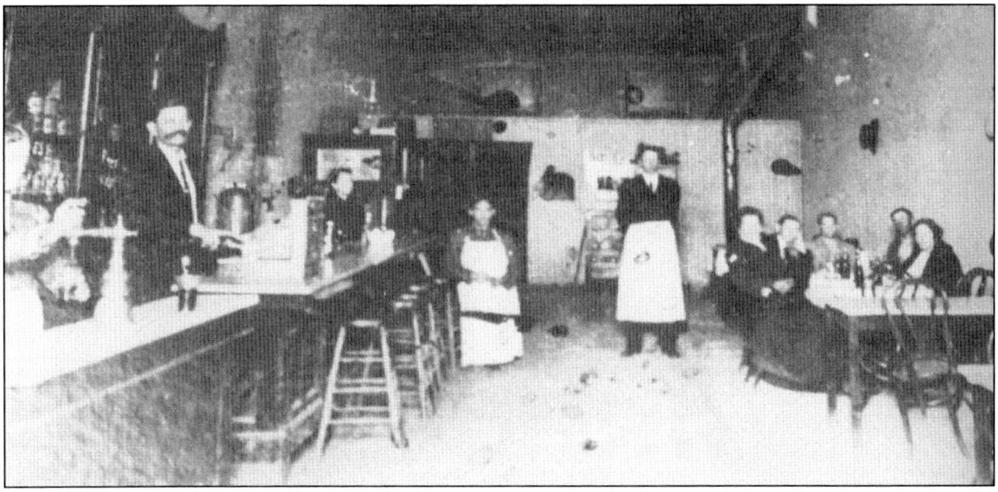

This c. 1900 photograph shows an early Royse City eatery, Fred Black's Café, which was located across the street from the lumberyard. Pictured here are, from left to right, Robert Douglas; Fred Black; Fred's wife, Duke; Shorty Tate; Henry Black; Mae Black; three unidentified men; and Sue Herndon.

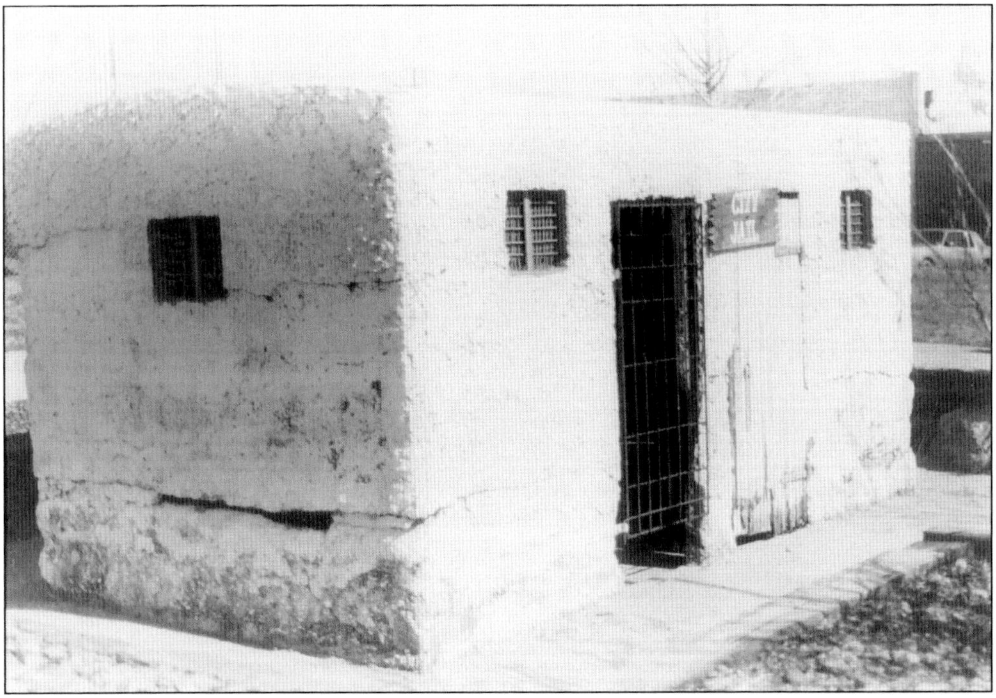

Although the county seat of Rockwall was only a short distance away, Royse City needed its own holding cell for lawbreakers—offenses could occur late at night, or the weather could be too treacherous for travel. To solve this problem, city officials transformed an old caboose into a temporary cell for prisoners. This structure still stands and is the centerpiece of downtown's Old City Jail Park.

Two

BUSINESS GROWTH IN "ROCKWALL COUNTY'S LARGEST TOWN"

Firsthand accounts of Royse City in the early 1900s describe a growing town busy with commerce, civic interest, and community pride. The population of Royse City even exceeded that of the nearby county seat of Rockwall, making it "Rockwall County's Largest Town" for a period of time.

In recollections gathered by the Rockwall County Historical Foundation, Royse City resident Lillian Hankins said:

> It is easy to recall the days when Royse City could boast of two banks, four grocery stores, two furniture stores, a hotel, WOW Hall, with an active lodge and an annual great oyster supper, doctors' and lawyers' buildings, several garages, and even Will Gardner's Coca-Cola Bottling Works, a huge picnic ground with a bandstand and a band. The Fourth of July was a real event in those days. Every building on Main Street was occupied. We had a movie theater, and I recall walking home on the plank sidewalks facing the north wind to our home on North Maple Street. There were no paved streets except the slab down the middle of Main Street. We would park the family car Saturday on Main at an early hour, so we could later sit and watch the walking traffic go by. On Sunday afternoon, it was an exciting pastime to walk the tracks or perhaps just go down to the depot and watch the train come in.

Similarly, in his book *History of Rockwall County*, O.L. Steger recounts having worked in Royse City sporadically in his youth, writing, "Again in the year 1908, I worked in Royse City for about six months . . . Royse City in that year was a 'wide-awake' town doing a lot of retail merchandising, cotton market, cotton seed oil milling and cotton ginning. There were no vacant business houses and no vacant residences."

Although multiple fires in the business district and the effects of the Depression certainly strained the town, Royse City was resilient and maintained a thriving business district for many decades.

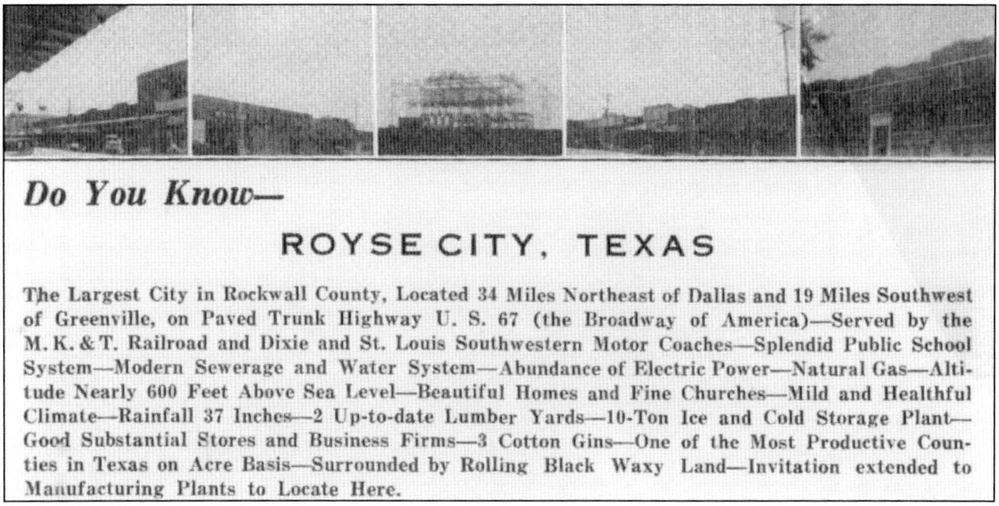

Do You Know—

ROYSE CITY, TEXAS

The Largest City in Rockwall County, Located 34 Miles Northeast of Dallas and 19 Miles Southwest of Greenville, on Paved Trunk Highway U. S. 67 (the Broadway of America)—Served by the M. K. & T. Railroad and Dixie and St. Louis Southwestern Motor Coaches—Splendid Public School System—Modern Sewerage and Water System—Abundance of Electric Power—Natural Gas—Altitude Nearly 600 Feet Above Sea Level—Beautiful Homes and Fine Churches—Mild and Healthful Climate—Rainfall 37 Inches—2 Up-to-date Lumber Yards—10-Ton Ice and Cold Storage Plant—Good Substantial Stores and Business Firms—3 Cotton Gins—One of the Most Productive Counties in Texas on Acre Basis—Surrounded by Rolling Black Waxy Land—Invitation extended to Manufacturing Plants to Locate Here.

By 1900, Royse City had a population of 1,245, making it the largest city in Rockwall County. This 1930s marketing postcard touts modern "Sewerage" [*sic*] and water systems, "Mild and Healthful Climate," an "Abundance of Electric Power," and "Up-to-date Lumber Yards" in an effort to lure new residents and manufacturing plants to the area.

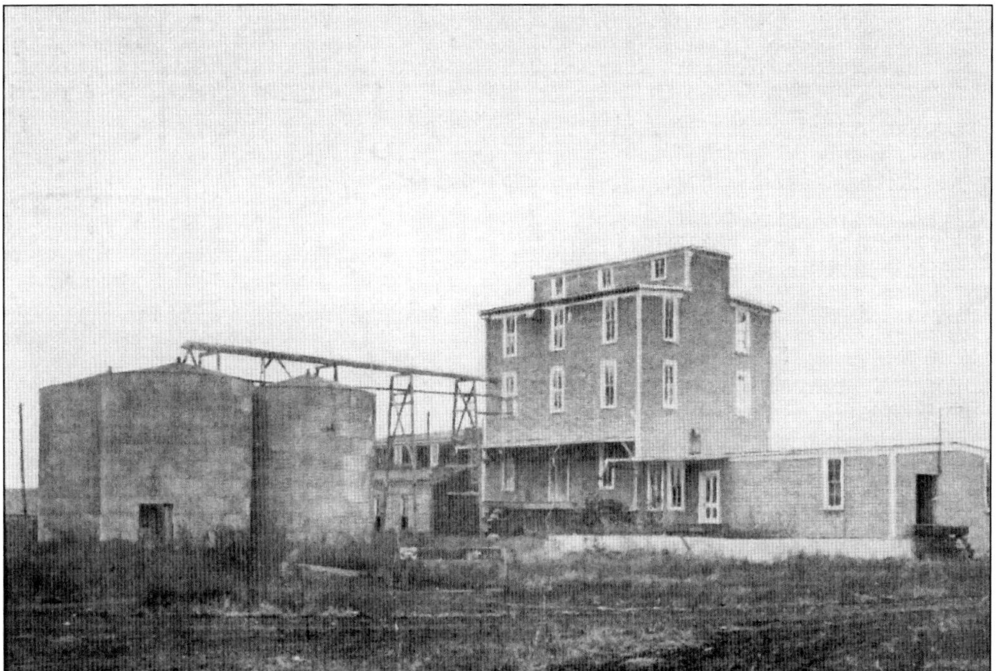

This vintage postcard features Royse City's flour mill, which was operated by Michael Byrd Wilson and his son Orange during World War I. Mills like this were primarily used to grind grain into flour for local farmers for sale or personal use. At the Royse City Flour Mill, the Wilsons made flour, cornmeal, and feed for livestock.

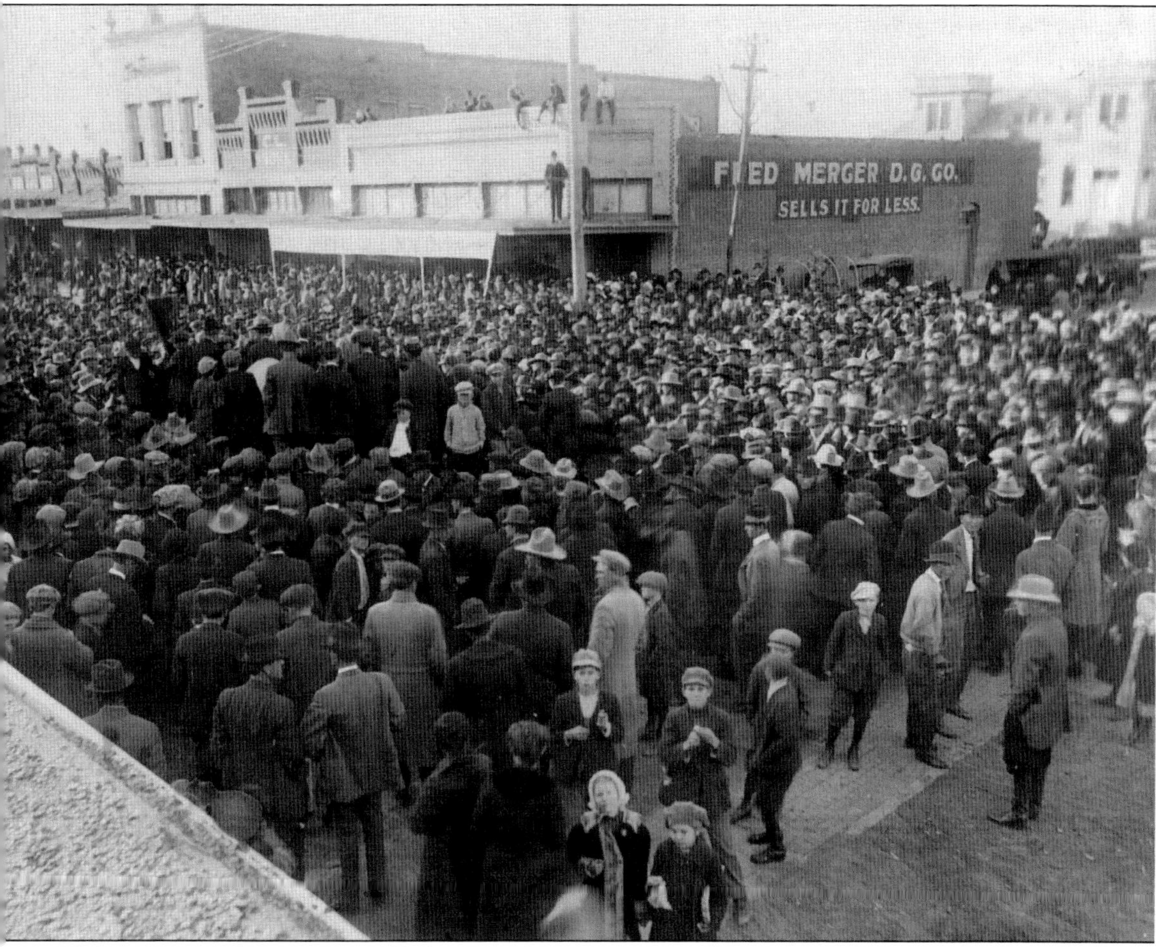

Although Saturdays were usually busy in the city anyway, the whole town is seemingly in attendance on this Saturday around 1912, as a lucky raffle ticket–holder would soon be the owner of a brand-new Ford automobile. Raffles and drawings—marketing devices used by merchants to drum up customers and encourage families to visit the business district—were commonplace in the early part of the 20th century. The Fred Mercer Dry Goods Company is pictured here. According to personal accounts, Mercer was well known as a "farmer's friend"—a merchant who would sell to farmers on credit and collect when crops were harvested in the fall. This was common practice for many stores at the time, but some merchants were more benevolent than others in their collection practices. If a farmer could not pay in full one year, Mercer would take their promissory note and carry it over until the next fall. Mercer also donated the land on the corner of Burton and Arch Streets that became home to the first brick structure that housed the First Christian Church.

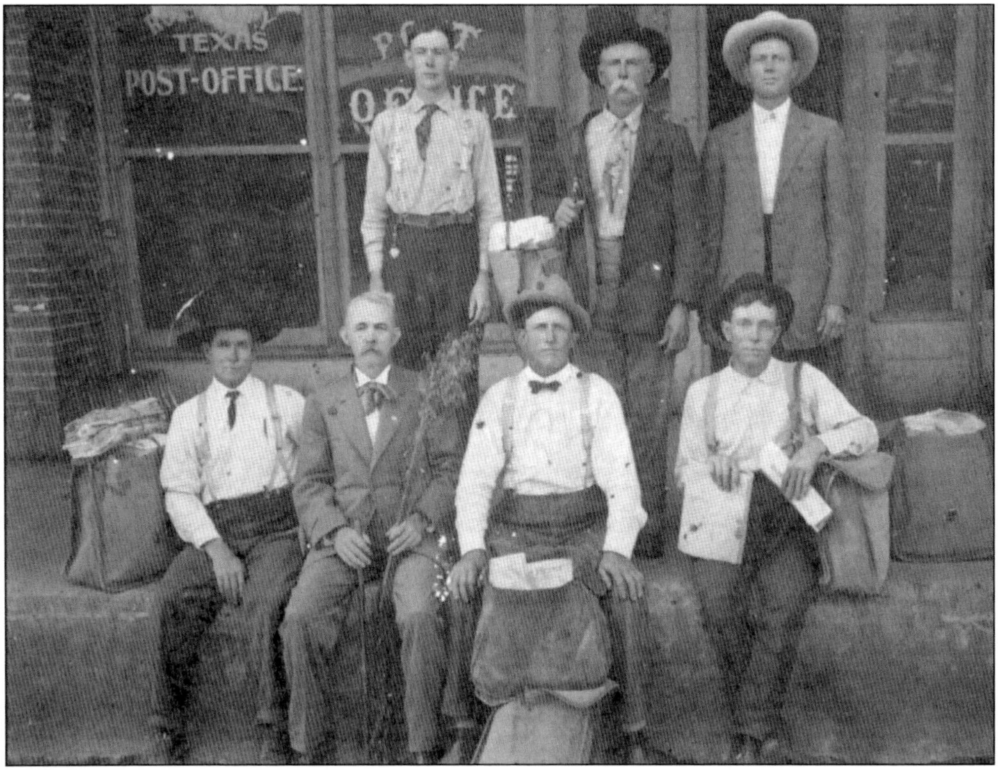

According to a story published in an early-1900s edition of the *Royse City News-Times*, the first post office to serve the area was a country office in Collin County. This office closed when the railroad was built through Royse City, and a permit was granted for a post office in town. K. Martin Peterson was the first postmaster. In the c. 1915 photograph above, the Royse City Post Office is visible along with, from left to right, (front row) Marvin Womack, J.F. Taylor, R.E. Blair, and Walter Bryant; (second row) ? Harrison, ? Clark, and Thomas Bailey. Bailey was a rural mail carrier; in 1922, he became postmaster of Royse City, a position he held for 15 years. His daughter Orpha (pictured below with her father) served beside him as assistant postmaster.

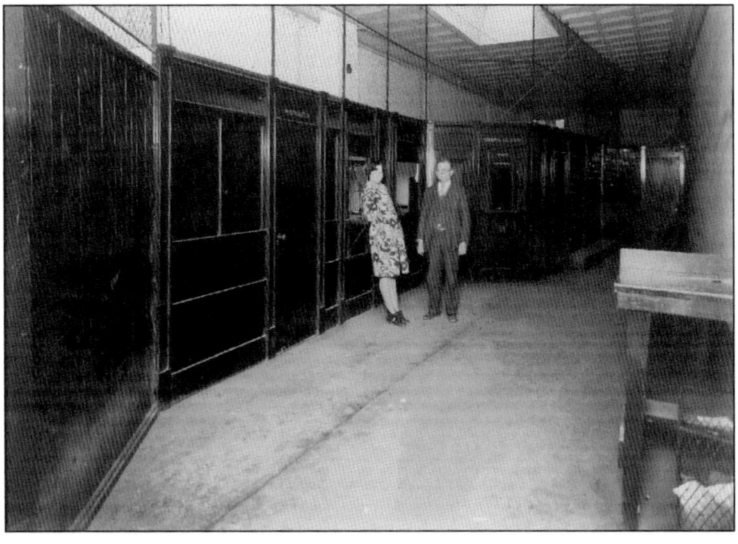

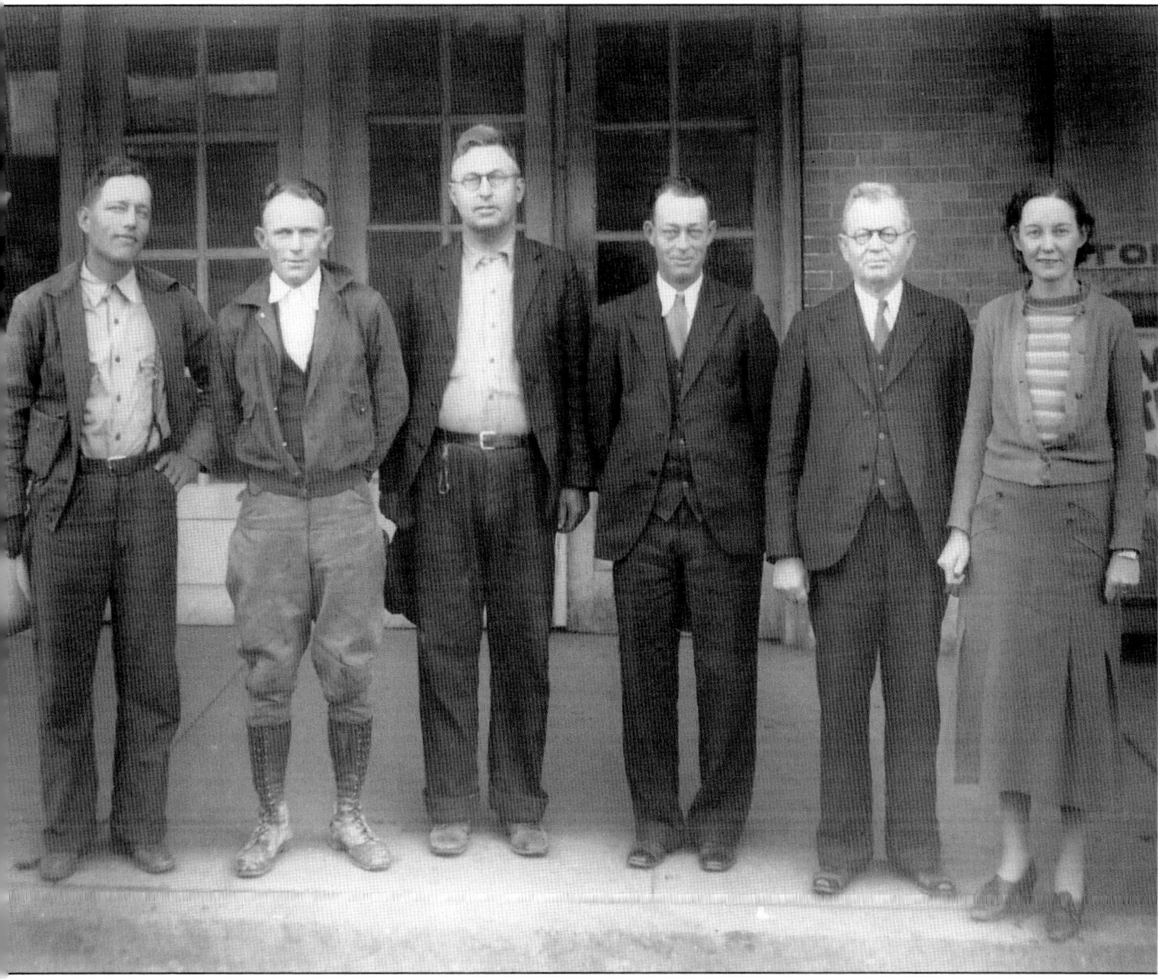

The first known post office building located in Royse City proper was a frame building that sat on the northeast corner of Main and Arch Streets. In 1899, the post office took up residence in a new brick building on the south side of Main Street and remained in that location until 1962. The US Postal Service established free city delivery in 1863, but rural free delivery (RFD) was not implemented until 1896. RFD reached Texas in 1899, with nearby Fate being one of the first rural routes in the state. Other Rockwall County post offices implemented the service in the first years of the 20th century, with rural delivery reaching Royse City in October 1901. At that time, a mere name and city were the only requirements for successful delivery. Royse City post office employees posed outside the office for this 1930s photograph; they are, from left to right, Homer Pierce, Roy Sisk, M.O. Flemmons, Tom Dowell, Tom Bailey, and Orpha Bailey.

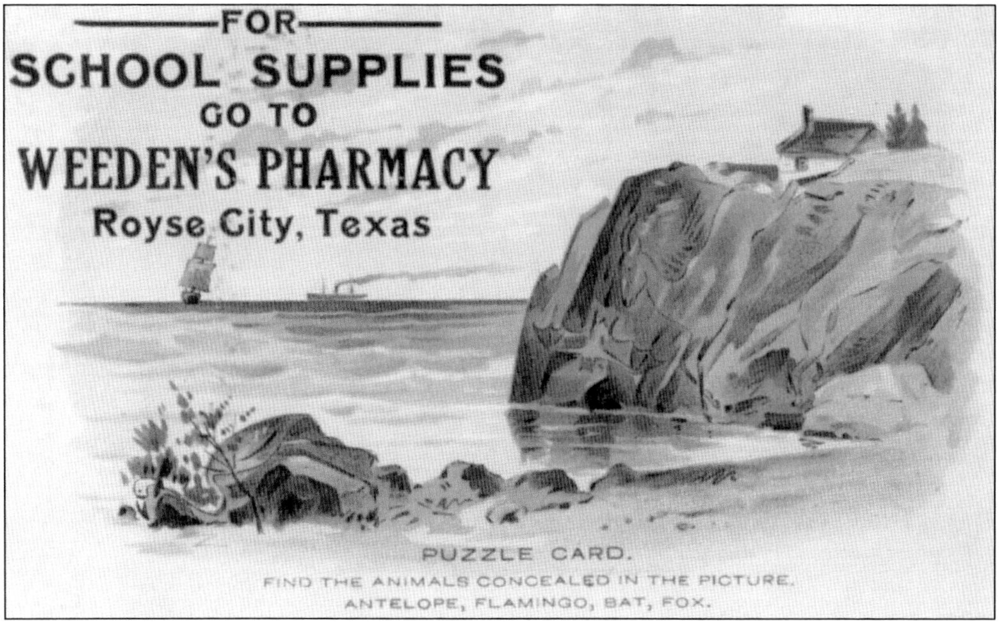

Advertising postcards were used to promote goods and services and were either mailed to prospective clients or handed out in-store with other purchases. The early-20th-century postcard above was distributed by Weeden's Pharmacy and was actually a puzzle. Puzzle postcards from this era commonly included hidden pictures (as shown) or rebuses in which words or sentences were represented by symbols. Sometimes, businesses used small giveaways to entice customers. Thermometers were extremely popular and were often distributed by large companies, such as Dr. Pepper or Coca-Cola. However, small-town stores were able to order these marketing items in lesser quantities for distribution in their own communities. A Burton Motor Company thermometer giveaway, featuring gold foil trim and a photograph unrelated to the area, is pictured below. Note the misspelling of Royse City.

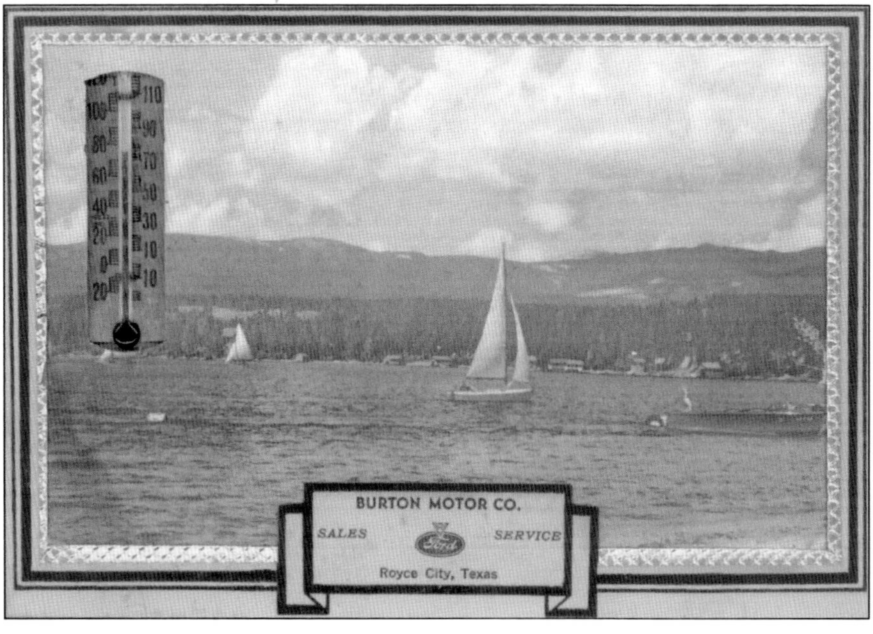

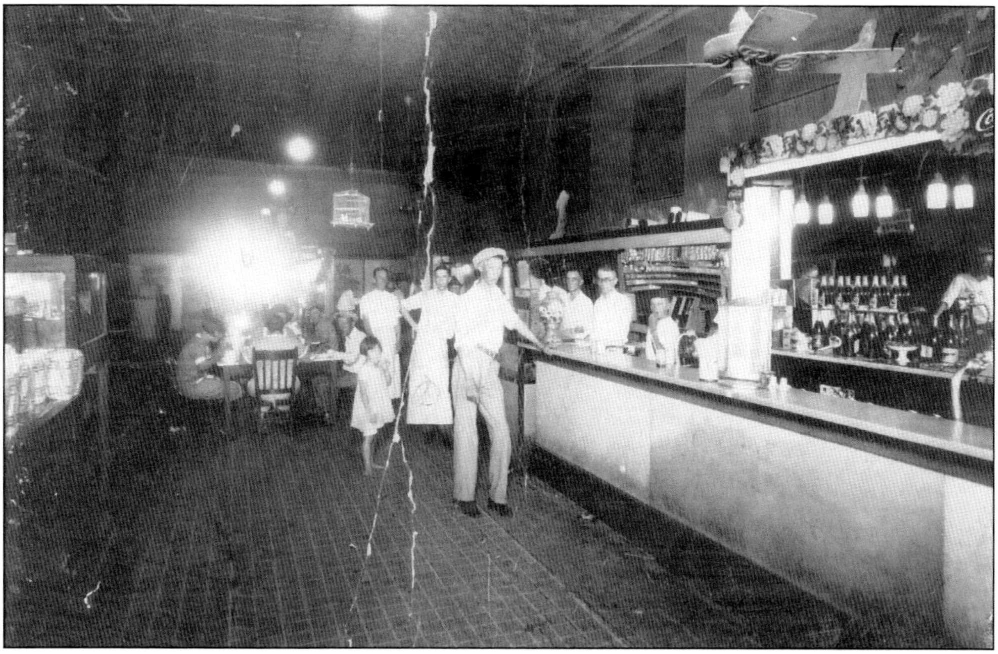

The Cookston family migrated from Tennessee to Texas in the late 19th century. Patriarch Francis Marion Cookston and his second wife, Sarah Adline Capps, had 10 children of their own and raised three from Cookston's first marriage. The family was prominent in the Royse City area and owned many businesses throughout the years. Francis and Sarah's son Mike Cookston owned and operated the Cookston Café (pictured above in 1905 and below around 1944), which adjoined the Cookston Hotel. The Cookston Café operated in downtown Royse City for more than five decades before it burned down in 1956.

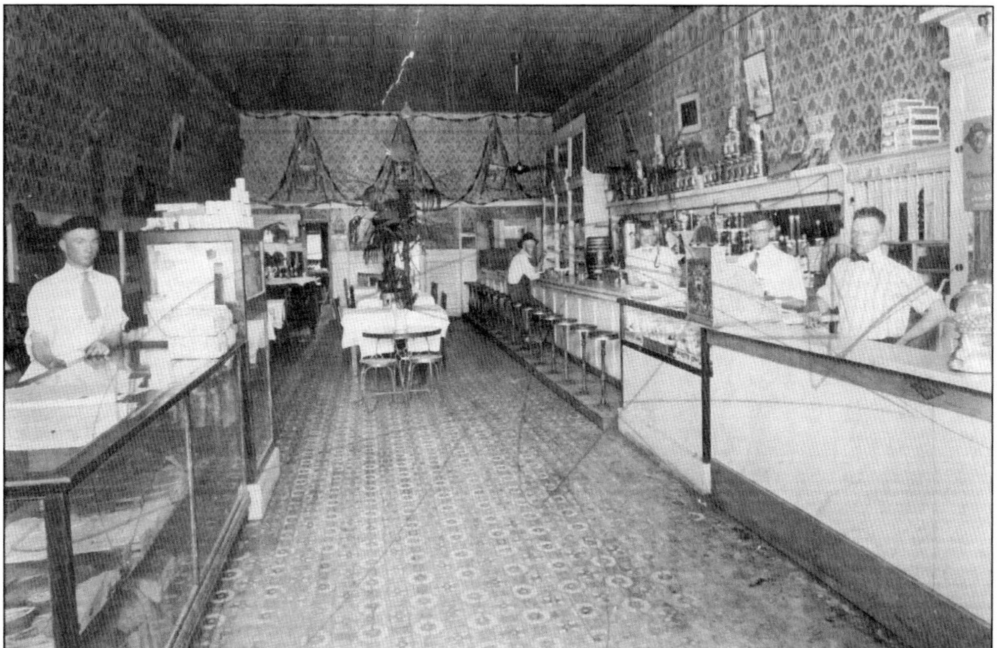

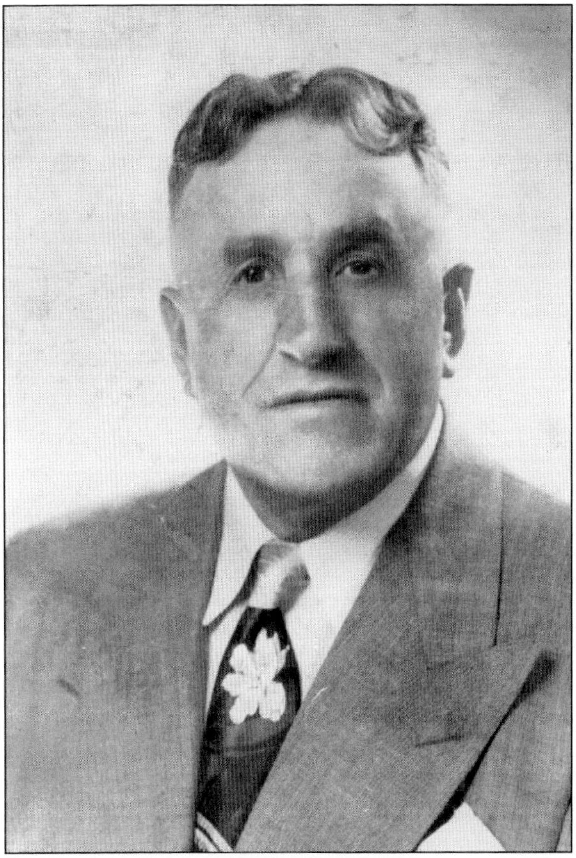

Roy Cookston, another son of Francis and Sarah Cookston, was also prominent in the community. Cookston was active in civic affairs, serving as mayor of Royse City from January 1943 until April 1951. He also served on the board of the North Texas Municipal Water District, was a member of the Royse City Masonic Lodge for more than 50 years, and served as a deacon and the Sunday school superintendent for the First Christian Church.

Mike Cookston, shown behind the counter of the Cookston Café, was well known for serving Woodsmen of the World's annual oyster supper for more than 50 years. The first oyster supper was served in 1904, and it remained the lodge's primary social event for five decades. During the Depression, Cookston served the meal at no charge.

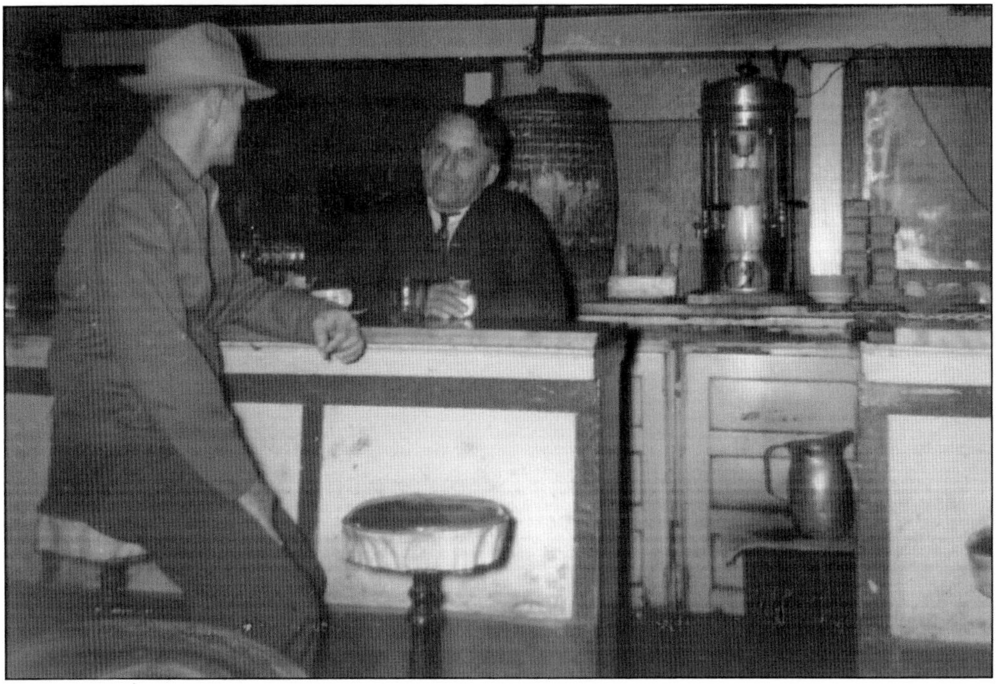

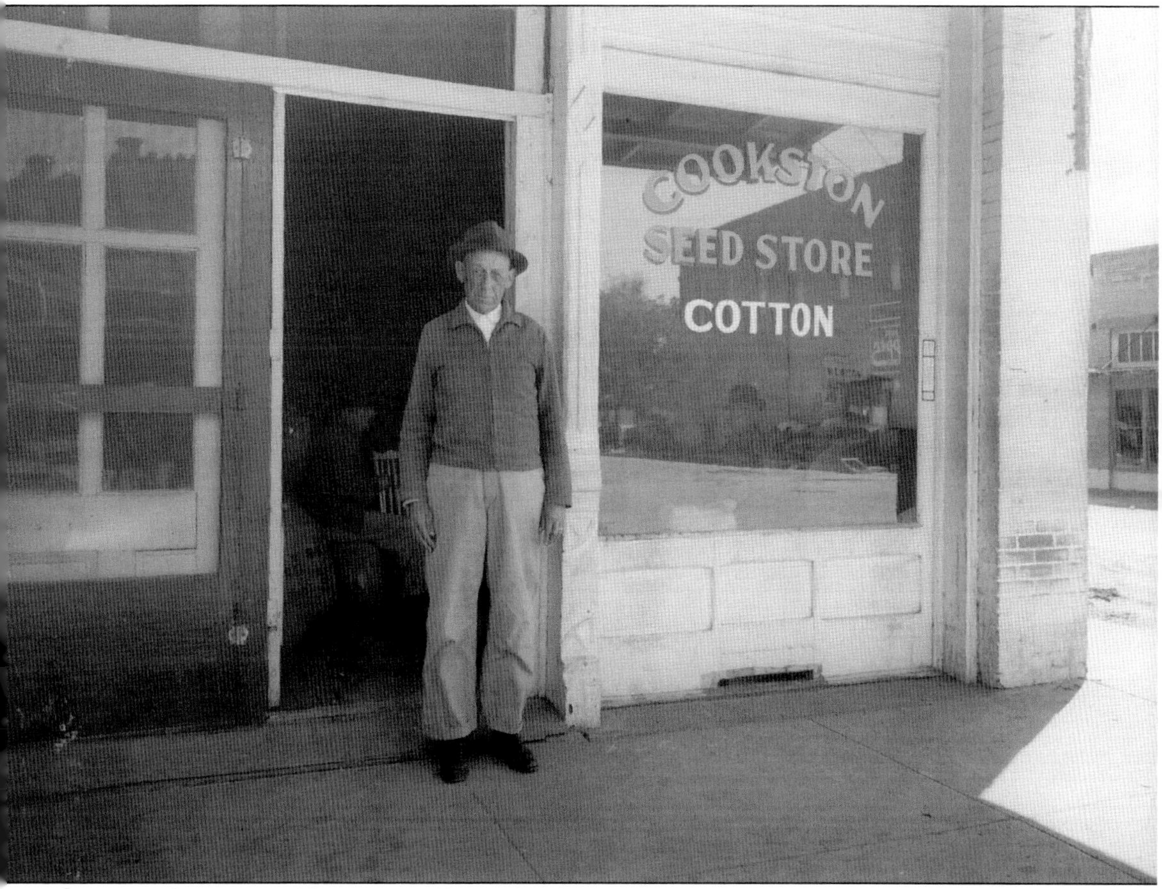

Cottonseed is separated from cotton lint in the ginning process and is considered a separate crop because of its distinct uses, including as livestock feed, oil, and fertilizer. According to the Texas State Historical Association, the processing of cottonseed was one of the earliest large-scale industries established in Texas. By 1900, it was the second-most-important industry in the state in value of product, eclipsed only by lumber. By the end of the 19th century, Texas had become the leading processor of cottonseed in the nation. During this time, cotton mills used manually powered mechanical pressure to squeeze the oil from the seed. This was very labor-intensive, and estimates indicate that, at best, this process recovered only half of the oil contained in the seed. Above, Bob Cross (a relative of the Cookston family) stands in front of the Cookston Seed Store, which was located on the southeast corner of Elm and Main Streets.

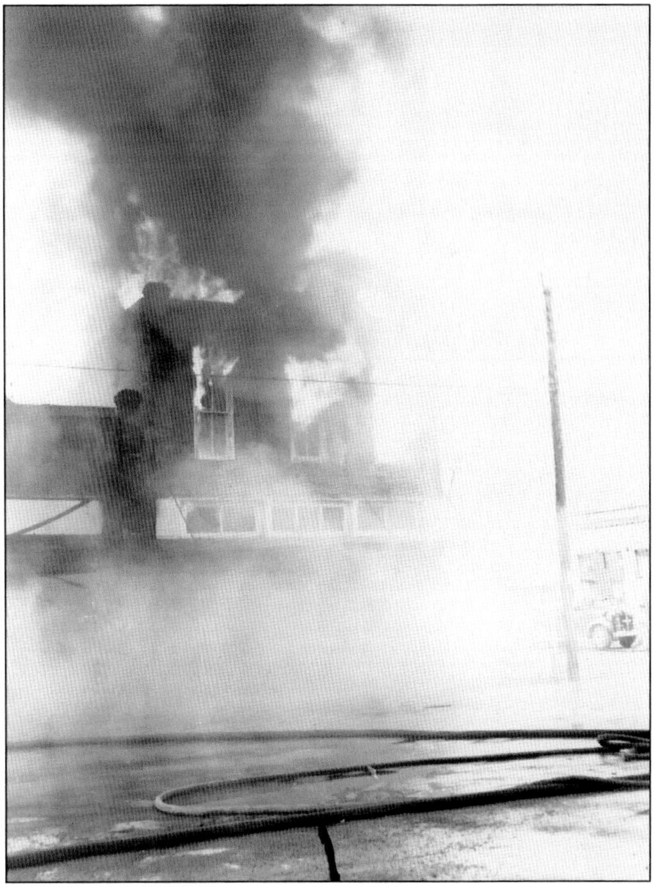

Royse City has endured several large fires that were devastating to the business district, including four during the decade between 1952 and 1962. In the c. 1960 image at left, fire engulfs what was then the two-story Cookston and Bass Seed Store (center) and the Cookston Body Shop (partially visible at left). The Burton Motor Company was established in 1921 by brothers Newt and Charlie Burton. Around 1929, the dealership moved to the downtown building pictured below, which had previously housed a Whippet car dealership. For more than 25 years, the Burton Motor Company sold Ford vehicles at this location. The photograph below shows the building after a 1957 fire. Other fires during this time destroyed the meat locker, ice-cream parlor, theater, and Cookston Hotel.

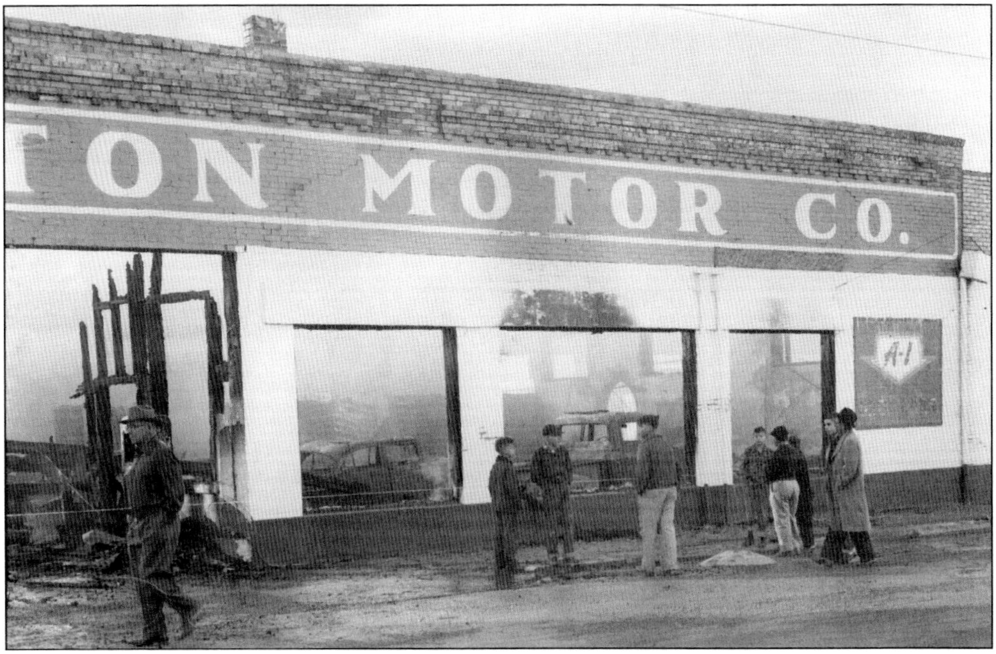

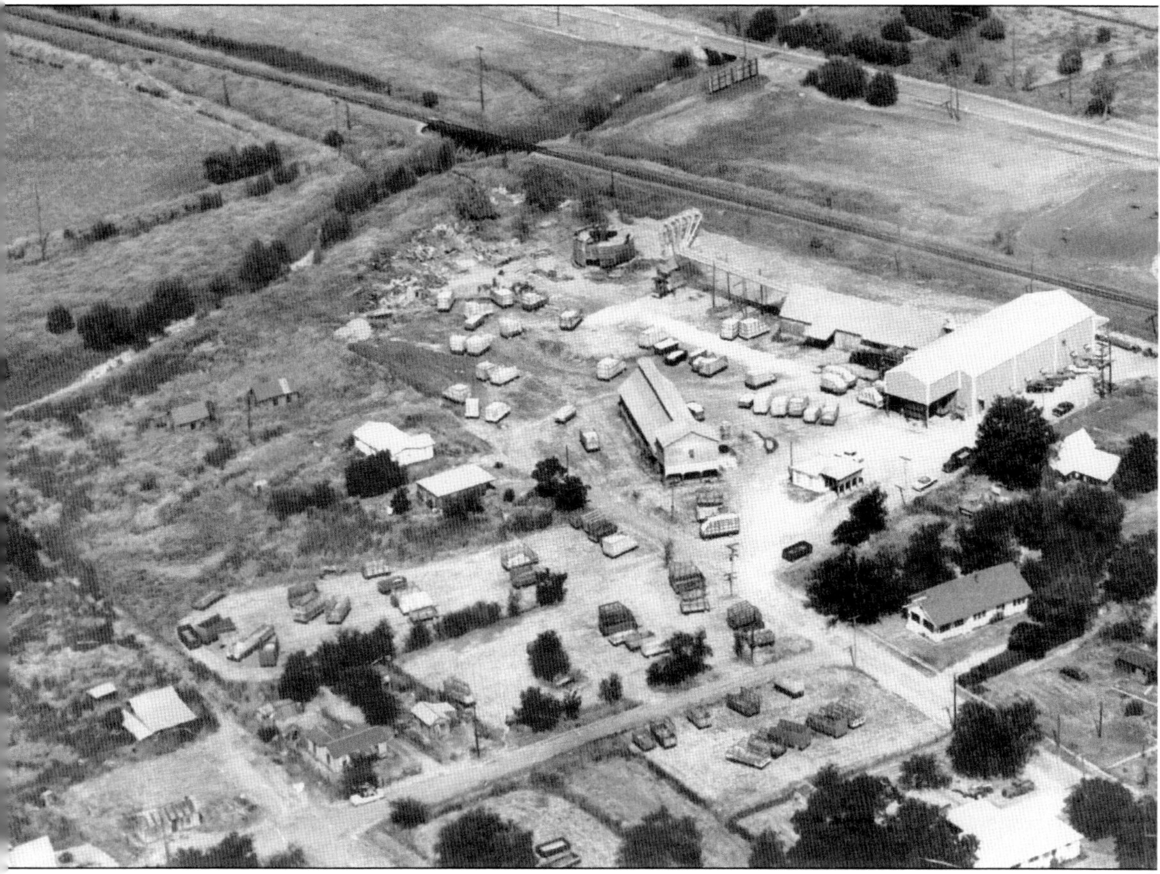

Throughout the last part of the 19th century and the first half of the 20th, cotton was the primary cash crop for Rockwall County. In 1900, there were approximately 1,000 farms in Rockwall County, with almost all of them growing cotton as the main crop. Through the years that cotton was king, Rockwall County had at least 18 cotton gins, several of which were in Royse City. Royse City once boasted three cotton gins that operated 24 hours per day for eight months of the year: the Cooperative Society Gin was established in 1930, the Cavitt Gin (pictured) was located west of South Houston Street near the railroad tracks, and the Farmers Gin was also located on Houston Street. The last cotton gin built in Royse City was located east of town and is still standing along present-day State Highway 66.

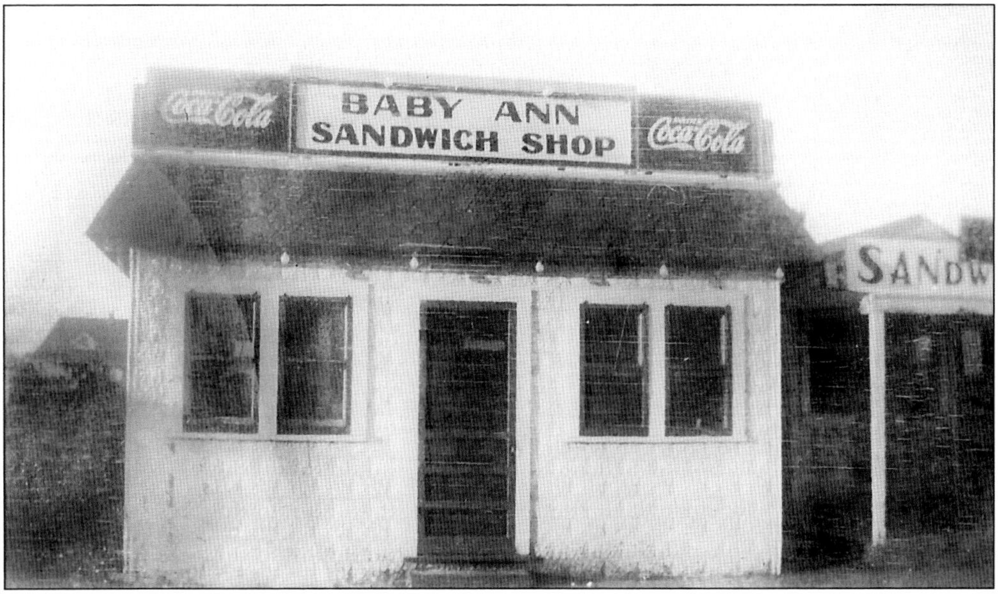

In the late 1930s and early 1940s, Laura Ruth (Shook) Rutherford owned and operated the Baby Ann Sandwich Shop (pictured above) just off Royse City's Main Street. In the 1937 photograph below, Laura Ruth holds her daughter Elizabeth Ann, for whom the sandwich shop was named; the other woman in the picture is unidentified. The Baby Ann Sandwich Shop offered a basic menu and cold Coca-Cola, as shown on their signage. Small, independently owned sandwich shops and grocery stores were the mainstay of many small towns when main thoroughfares went directly through the downtown areas. Interstates that bypassed central business districts, along with the development of chain restaurants and supermarkets, caused the widespread demise of mom-and-pop stores in the 1960s and 1970s.

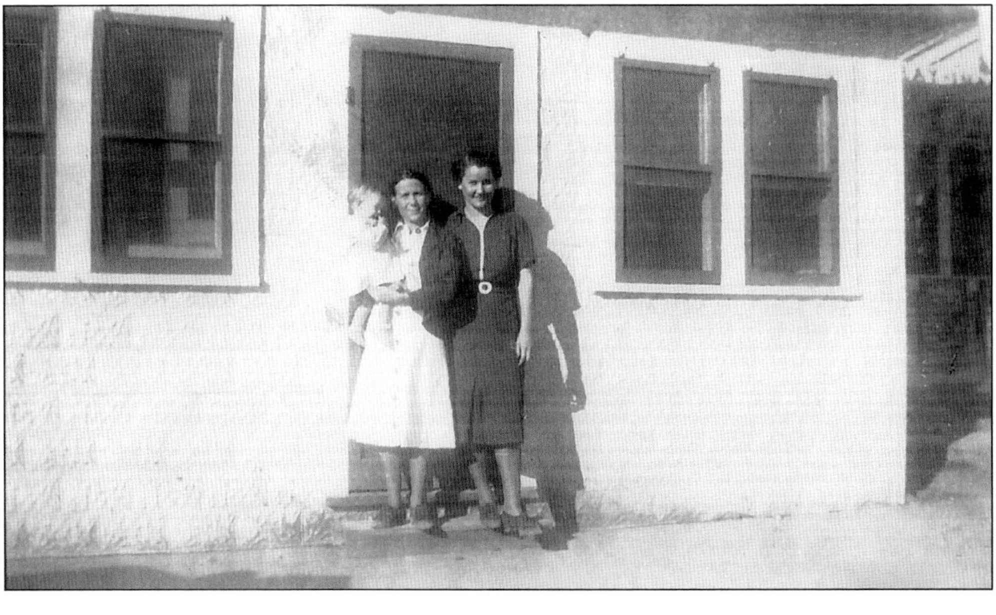

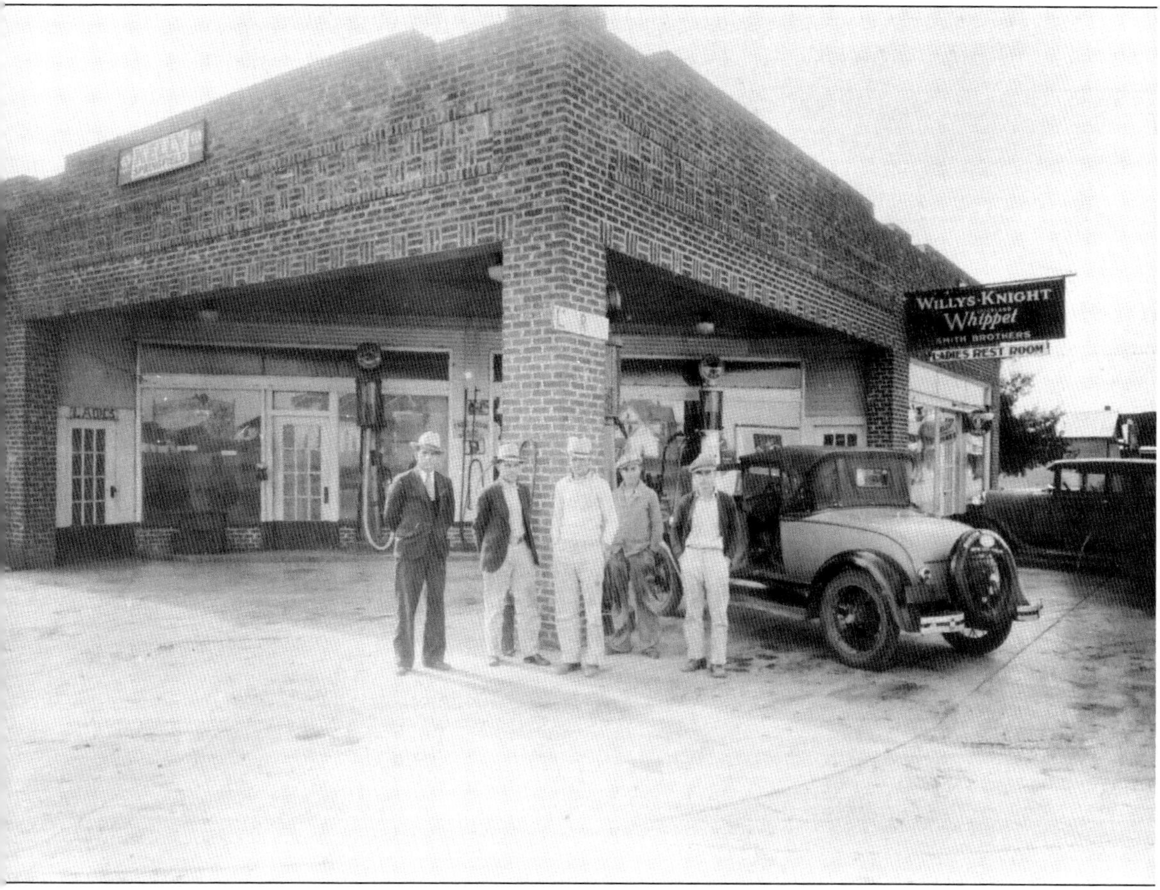

The Smith family owned and operated the Smith Brothers service garage and car dealership on the corner of Main and Elm Streets. They specialized in products from the Willys-Overland Motor Company. From 1912 to 1918, Willys-Overland was the second-largest producer of automobiles in the United States (after the Ford Motor Company). In 1913, the company added the Willys-Knight nameplate, and in 1926, the Whippet. Starting in the 1920s, the company began to experience severe financial problems. After the Depression, the brand faltered, with production of the Whippet ending in 1931 followed by the Willys-Knight in 1933. Although Willys-Overland remained active in the car industry—even participating in Jeep production during World War II—the company would never regain the popularity it enjoyed during the early 1900s. Signage on the Smith Brothers' building noted Kelly Tires and a "Ladies Rest Room."

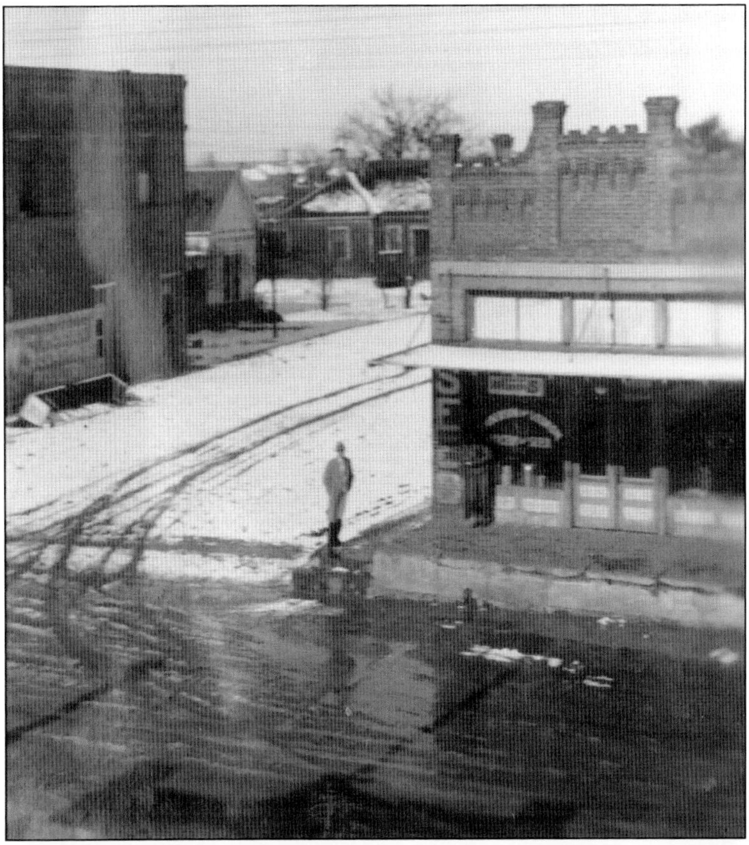

At left, a Royse City street corner is pictured in the snow around 1930. The building at right displays elements of Neoclassical Revival architecture, which was prominent in commercial and public buildings from 1900 to 1940. In downtown areas, this style often featured symmetrical facades and squared off rooflines with decorative features. As small-town businesses transformed from clapboard buildings to brick, this style of architecture became prevalent, as it signified prosperity and stability.

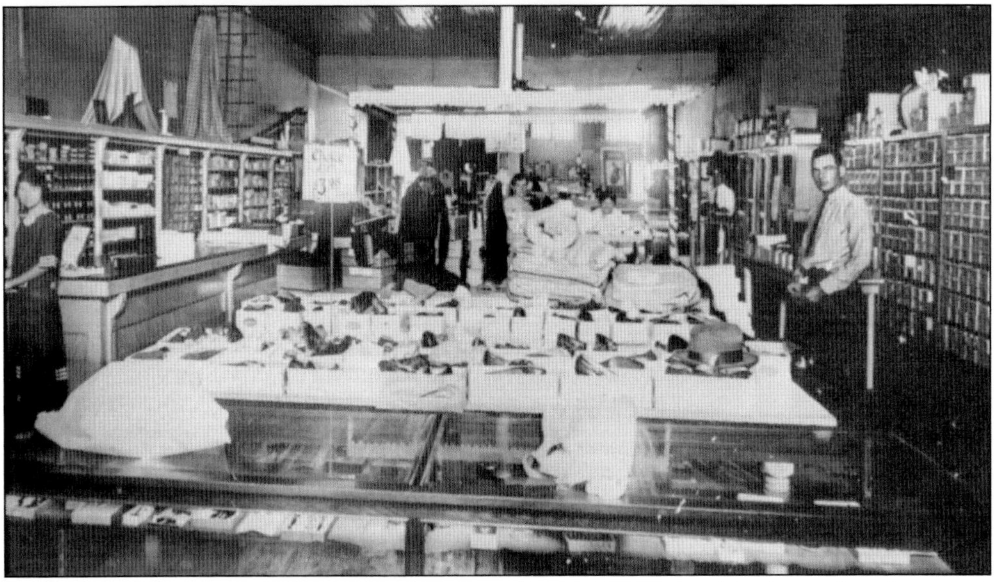

The C.L. Bridgman Store, located in downtown Royse City, carried both men's and women's fashions, including shoes, hats, and accessories. Styles available in small-town clothing stores throughout the country reflected a generalized version of the fashion trends featured in magazines and advertisements and on movie screens.

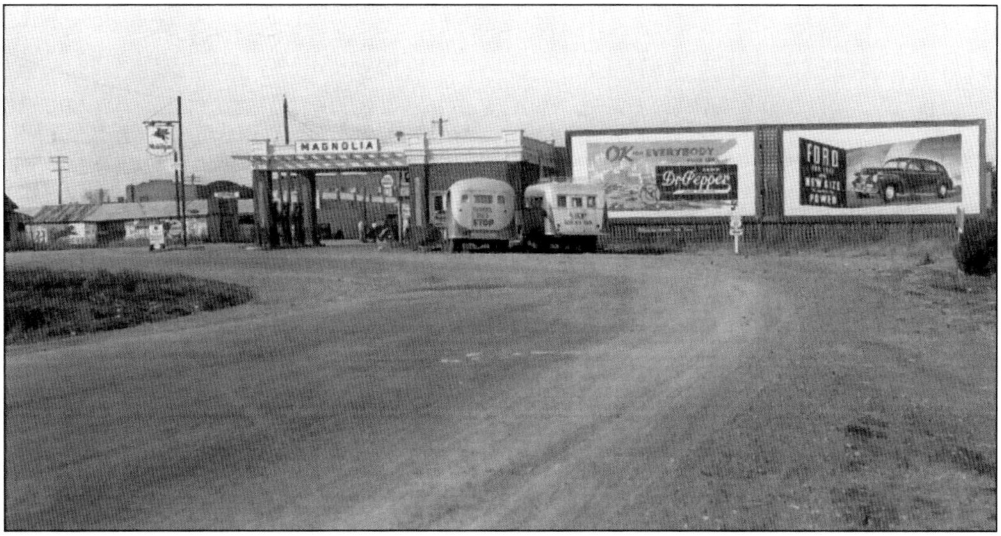

The Bankhead Highway, also known as US Highway 67, became Main Street on its way through downtown Royse City. As part of the National Auto Trail system, routes such as the Bankhead were marked with colored bands on telephone poles. Gas stations, eateries, and other small-town shops thrived along the Bankhead in its heyday. The Magnolia Gas Station (pictured) was on the side of the Bankhead as it led into Royse City from the east.

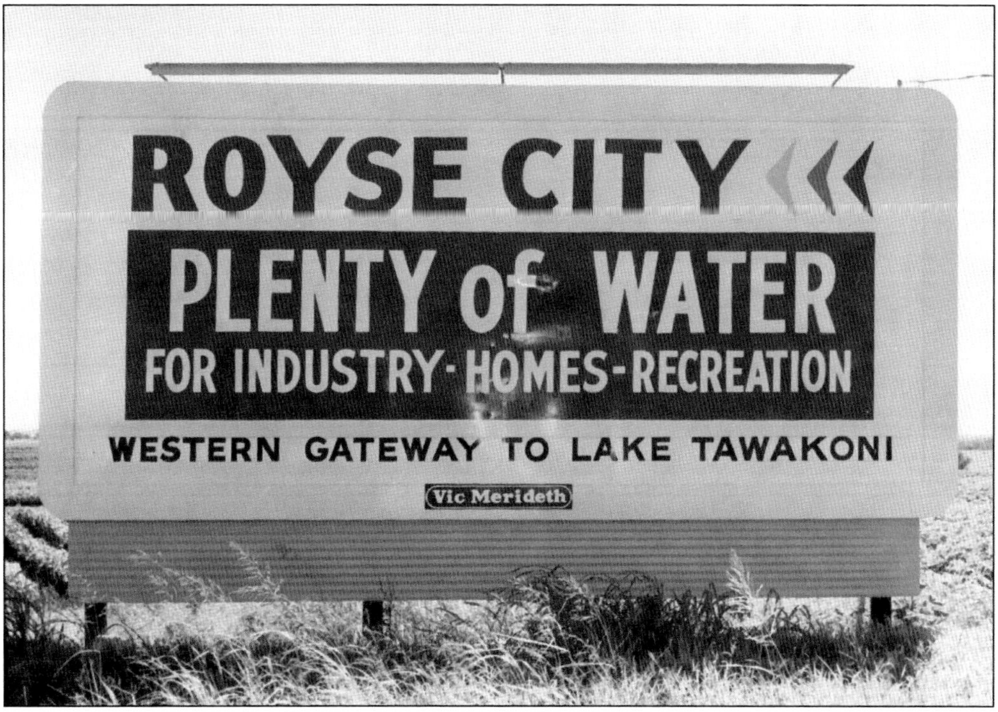

In the 1950s, the city of Dallas was suffering from a drought so severe that it eventually led to the construction of Lake Ray Hubbard. Surrounding communities, such as Royse City, touted their access to water as a way to lure potential residents and new businesses. In 1950, the population of Royse City was 1,190, with 55 businesses, and community leaders were actively promoting the area.

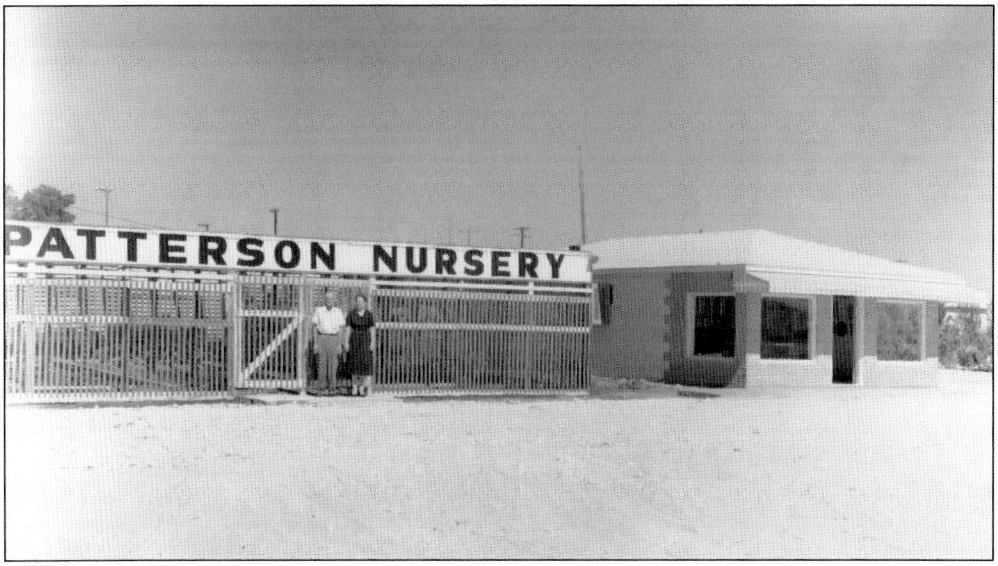

When Interstate 30 was built south of town, the Patterson family opened a nursery, which offered grass and all types of plants to Rockwall County residents, on the north service road. The Pattersons lived in a redbrick home near the nursery.

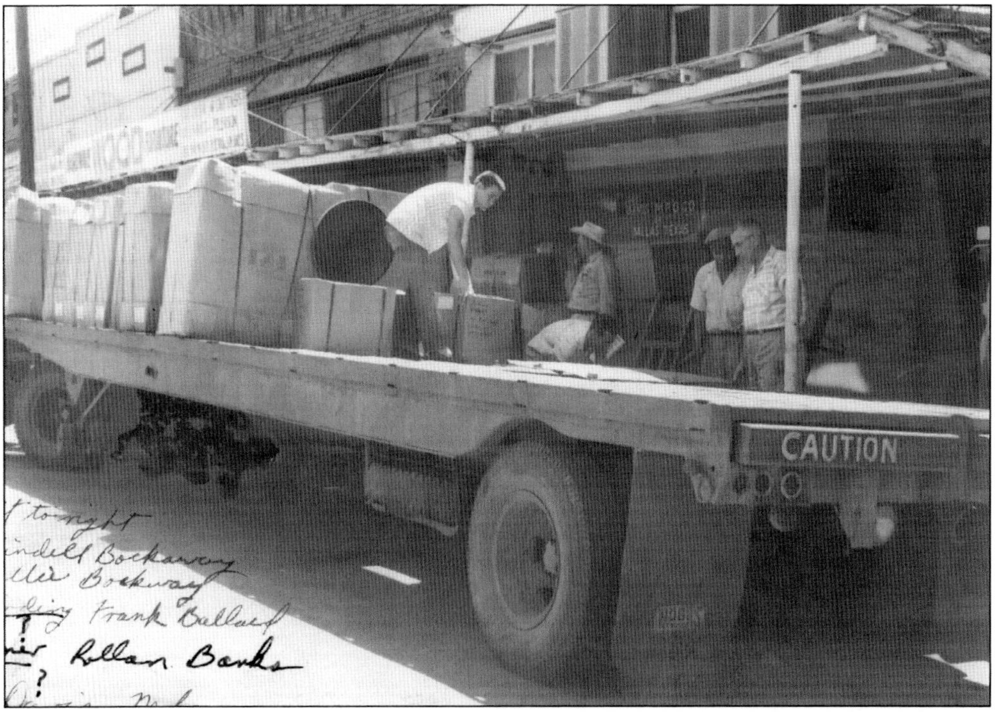

Davis Manufacturing Company was a sewing factory located on the south side of downtown's Main Street. Both Royse City and nearby Rockwall had sewing factories in the 1940s and 1950s. The mostly female staff constructed mass-produced clothing, which was then shipped to retailers. Pictured in front of the sewing factory are, from left to right, Windell Brockway, Billie Brockway (bending down), unidentified, Frank Ballard, unidentified, and Rollan Banks (the owner of Davis Manufacturing, cut off at the right side of the photograph).

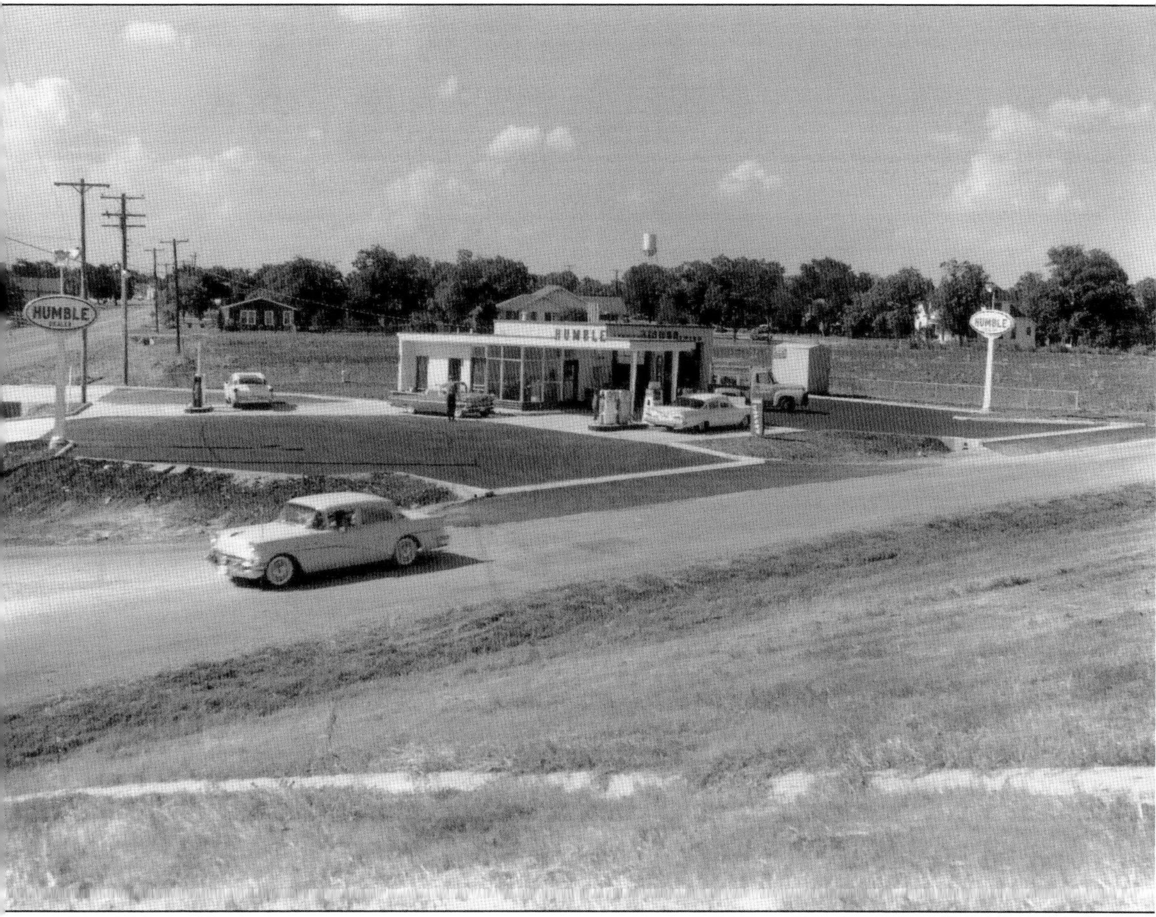

The Humble Oil Company was founded in the city of Humble, Texas, in 1911. Throughout the next five decades, Humble gas stations could be found throughout Texas and the United States. In 1962, the last of the Texas stations was rebranded as Enco. Fuller's Humble Station, pictured in 1959, was located on the north side of the interstate and was the first commercial business built on the new highway. The new Interstate 30 route through Royse City would parallel US 67 (the Bankhead Highway), which went directly through downtown. The interstate system, which expanded drastically during the 1960s and 1970s and bypassed downtown business districts, resulted in great economic hardship for many small towns throughout the country, including Royse City. Travelers who had once frequented the downtown gas stations and small cafés often opted for newer businesses along the interstate.

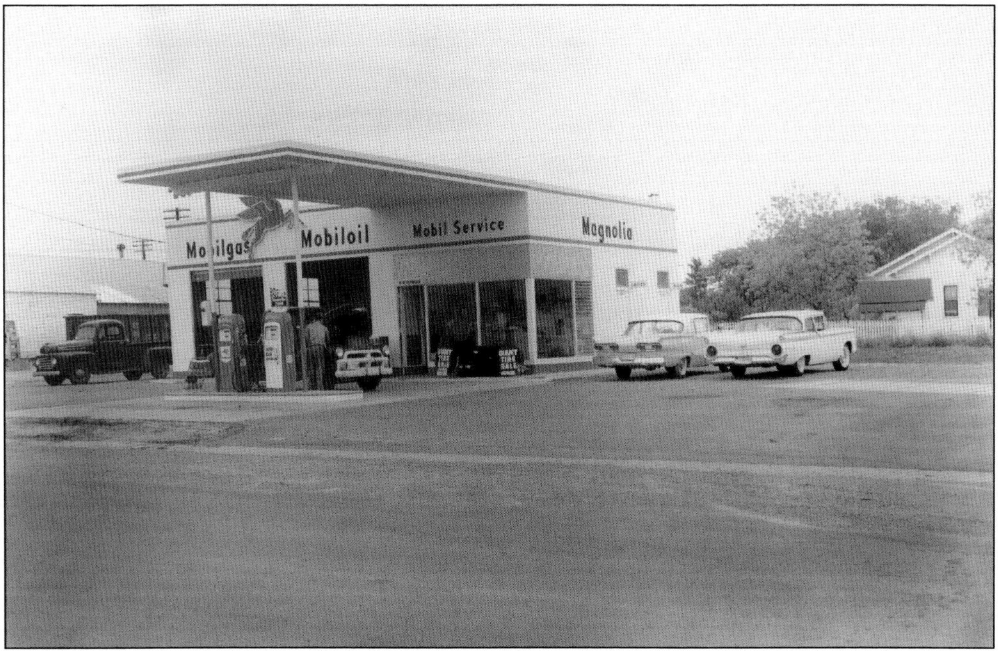

In 1920, the name Mobiloil was registered as a trademark by the Standard Oil Company of New York. In the 1930s, Mobilgas began an affiliation with the Magnolia Petroleum Company, and the Pegasus was often associated with stations bearing the Magnolia and Mobilgas labels. The Royse City Mobil station is pictured in the 1950s.

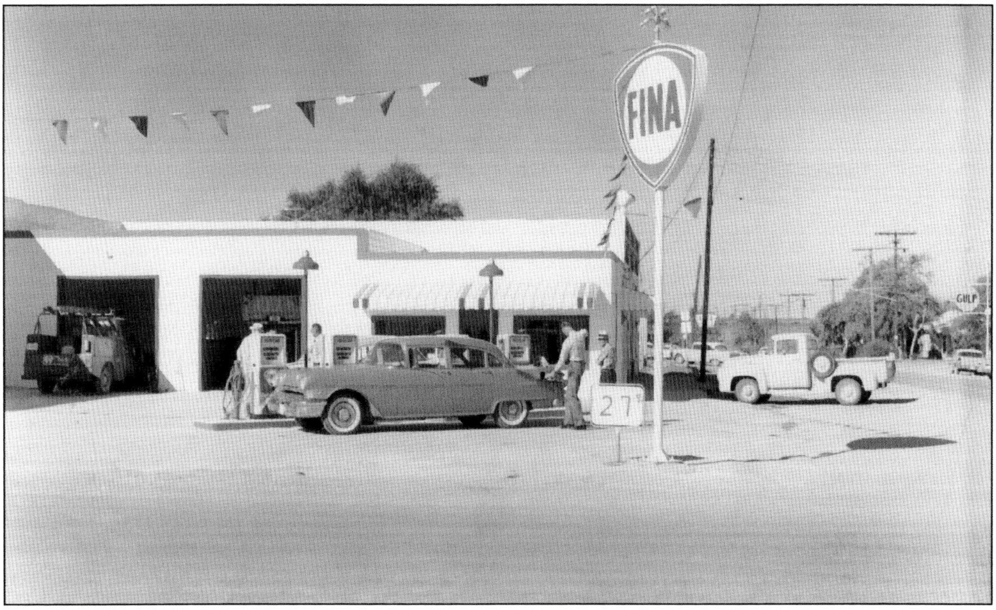

Although the alternate I-30 route was becoming increasingly popular, downtown Royse City still enjoyed a steady flow of traffic in the early 1960s, as evidenced by the number of gas stations operating in the downtown area at that time. The Fina Station opened in 1961. The Arco and Gulf stations are also visible in the background. Note the price of gas: 27.9¢ per gallon.

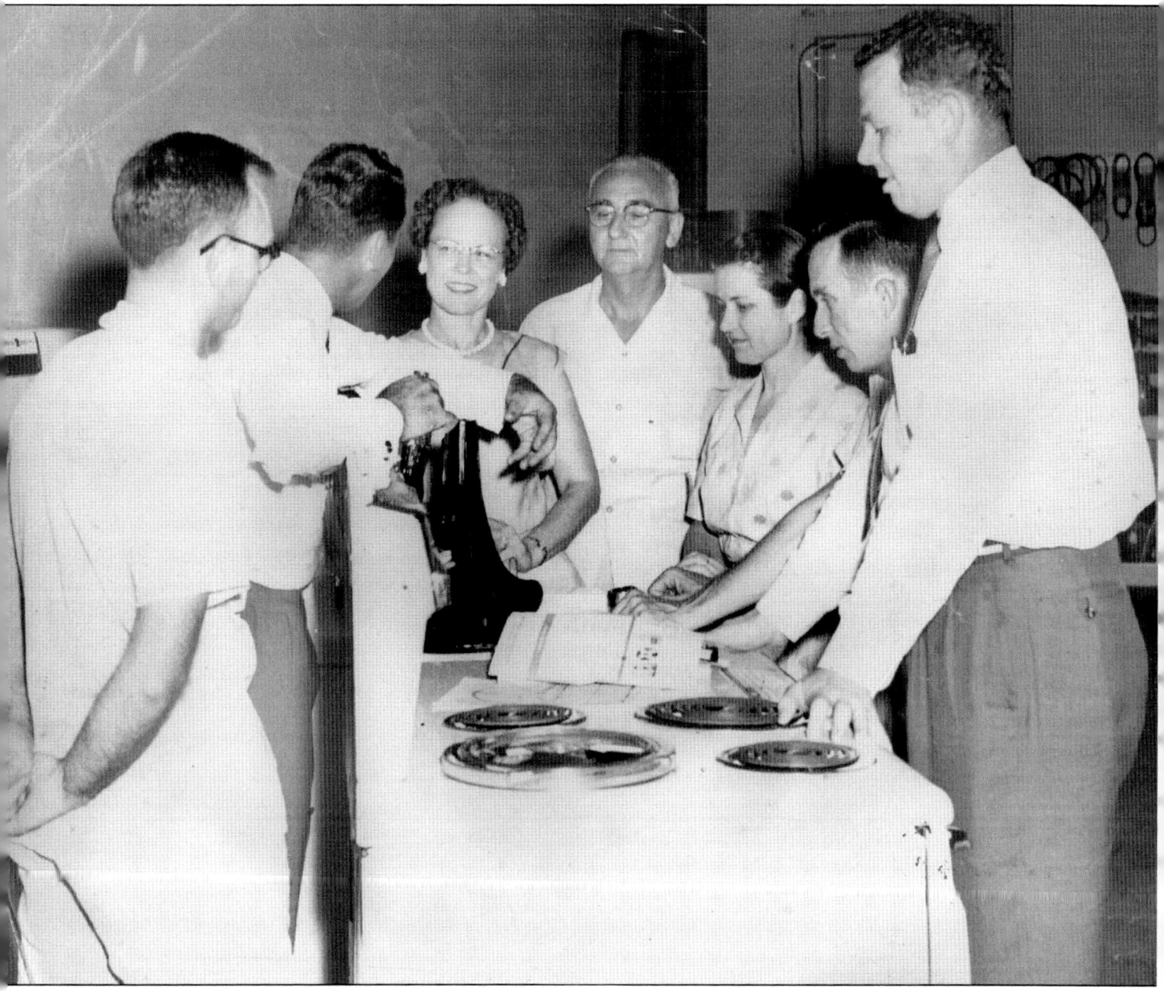

In this image, Mr. and Mrs. Fred Hathaway (center) are showing off the first electric stove to arrive at their store, the Hathaway Appliance Company, located at 413 Main Street. Although the first electric stove was showcased at the Chicago World's Fair in 1893, it took almost 50 years for it to become a common appliance in rural areas of the United States. Electric stove manufacturers—primarily General Electric (GE)— heavily advertised the appliance in women's magazines and other publications. An entire advertising campaign urged husbands to buy the stoves for their wives as a gift with a tagline that read, "Here's what mother really wants . . . a gift that keeps on giving." In 1959, a GE campaign advertised their new electric stove model for $149 and used images of women talking on the phone or doing other tasks with the tagline, "No pot watching." In truth, items such as electric stoves, refrigerators, and irons were welcome additions to kitchens.

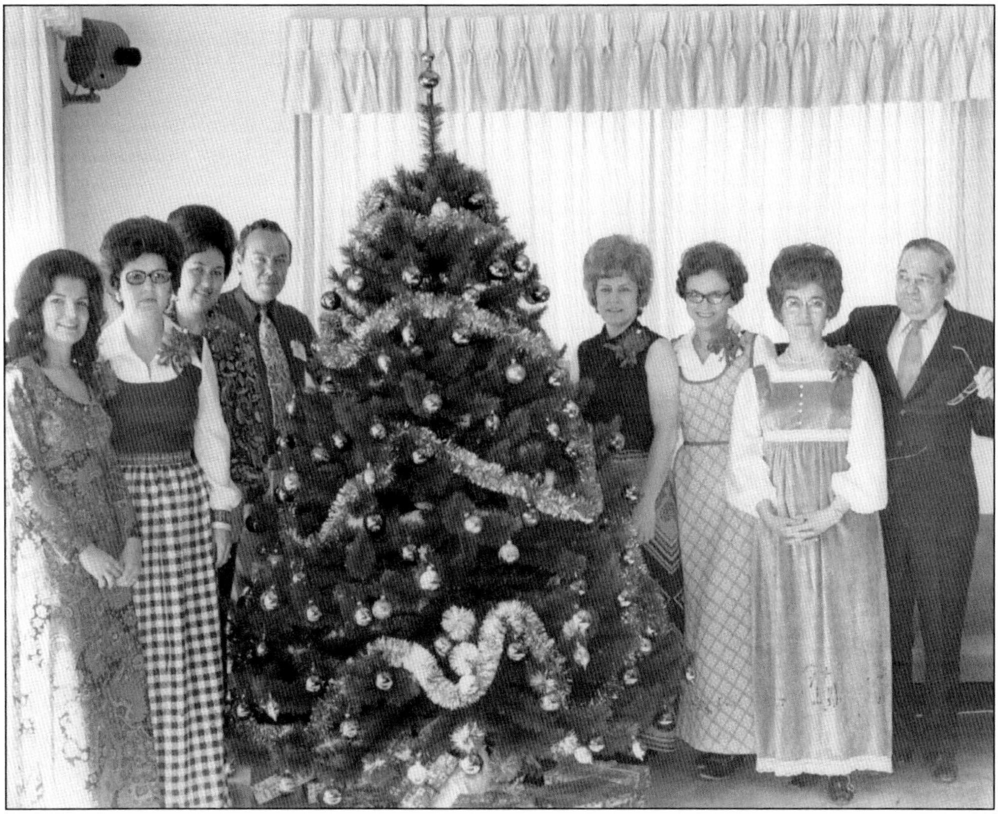

Citizens State Bank was established on August 3, 1933, and, for many decades, was located at the corner of Main and Arch Streets in downtown Royse City in a location previously occupied by the Royse City Bank and the First State Bank. The first president was J.D. Dowell. Joe Van Cleave was appointed the second president of the bank, a position he held until 1974. Citizens State was a cornerstone of Royse City commerce for approximately 50 years. It was acquired by Benchmark Bank in the mid-1990s. Above, Citizens State Bank employees pose with the lobby Christmas tree in the 1970s. C.B. Irwin, vice president of the bank, is pictured below.

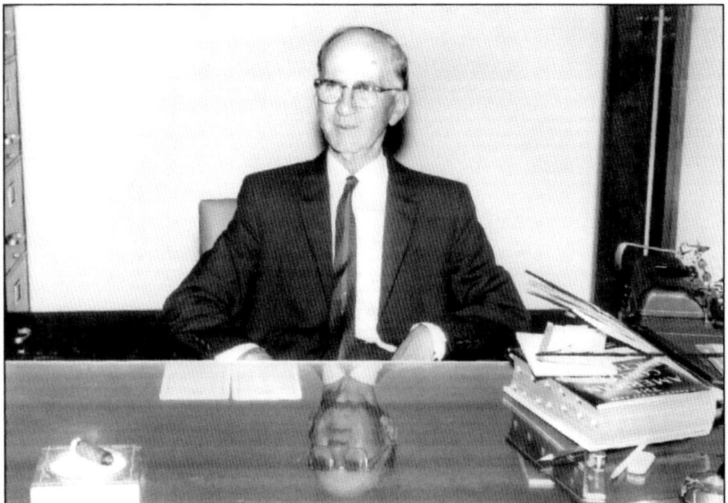

Three

Farm and Family Life

Although there were merchants, doctors, and lawyers who lived the "city life," the majority of Royse City's early citizenry was made up of farmers. Farm life was labor-intensive and dependent on outside factors such as soil and weather. Crops such as cotton were grown and sold for income, but farmers were also growing food for their own families and raising livestock. The late 1800s and early 1900s marked, for the most part, a time of self sufficiency.

Families tended to be large because children were assets to the farm and could help with chores. From the time they could walk, children were engaged in farm activities. Cotton production actually dictated the start of school—if the cotton crop came in early, classes would not begin until it had been harvested. If the cotton crop was ready for harvesting in the fall, schools would have a "split term" in which students would start school, stop for several weeks to pick cotton, and then resume their studies. Education was important, but cotton provided the livelihood for the family.

Washing, baking, milking, and other household chores kept families busy, but some did find time for social activities outside the home—mainly in conjunction with church or civic duties. The Depression, as well as the move to industrialized jobs during and after World War II, had a profound effect on farm culture. The amount of farms operating in Rockwall County decreased significantly during this time, as people found other ways to make a living.

During the 1940s and 1950s, electrical appliances, processed foods, and better transportation all made life less labor-intensive, and families found time for endeavors such as Boy Scouts, Girls Scouts, and Little League.

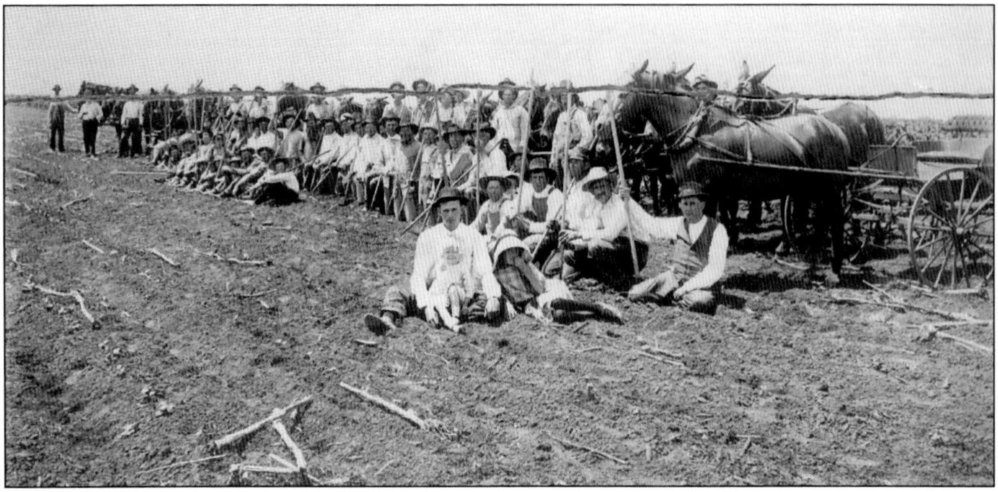

For the majority of the year—the warm months—farmers were engaged in plowing, planting, and harvesting. This was not a sole endeavor but rather a community effort. Farmers in one area would help each other plow and plant, often moving from one farm to the next until all the fields were prepared. The farmers' wives also worked together on quilting, canning, or making soap or candles.

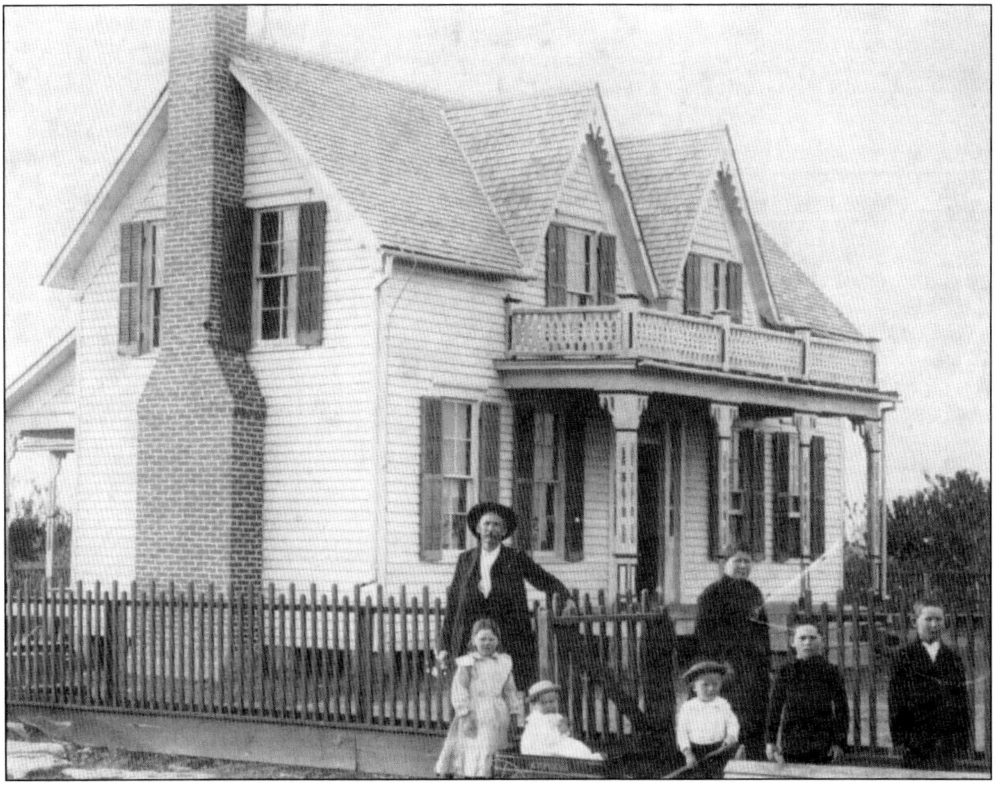

Sam and Susan McMurry and their children lived in the small community of Spunky Ridge, just two miles south of Royse City. McMurry was a farmer who also owned three buildings in downtown Royse City, which served as the civic and social center of their lives. Sam and Susan McMurry are pictured at their Spunky Ridge home with five of their ten children.

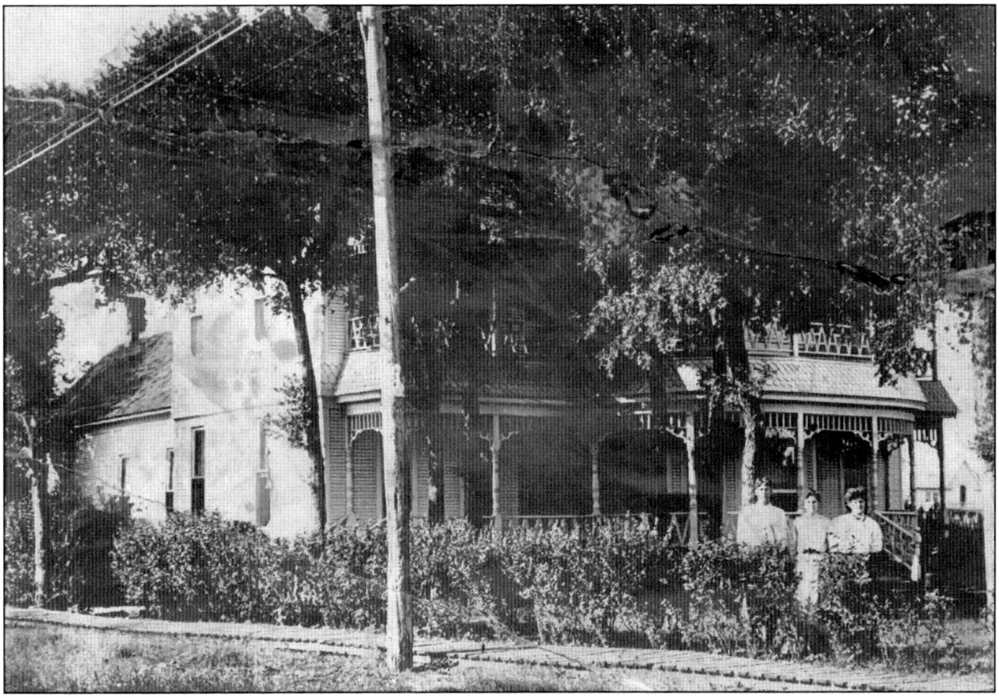

The J.W. Terrell house was located at 200 Arch Street. J.W. Terrell was the son of Col. R.A. Terrell, a pioneer settler for whom the nearby town of Terrell is named. After living on a farm for several years, the Terrell family moved to Royse City and built a home in the late 1800s. Pictured above in front of the home are Florence Terrell (center) and two of her children, Buddy Terrell (left) and Dink Terrell Cookston. At right are the Terrell children—Buddy (left), Edna (center), Lot (the baby), and Dink.

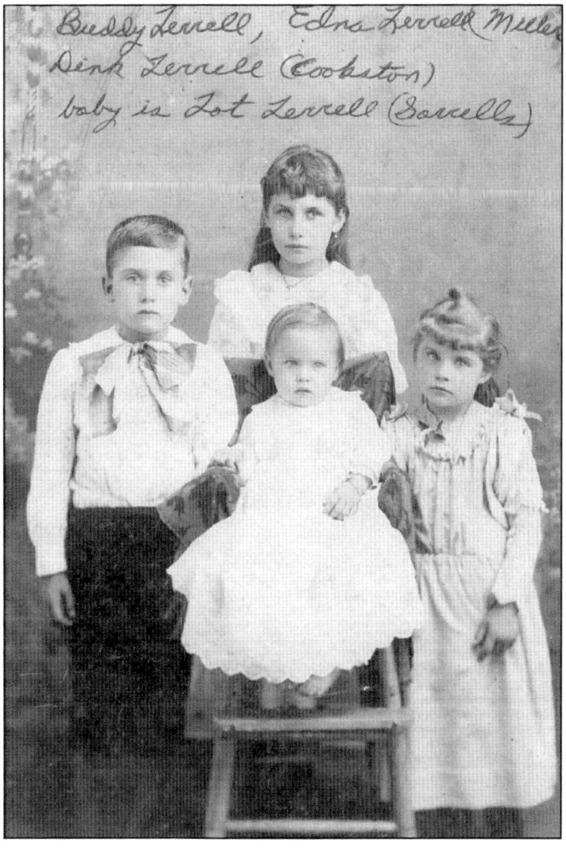

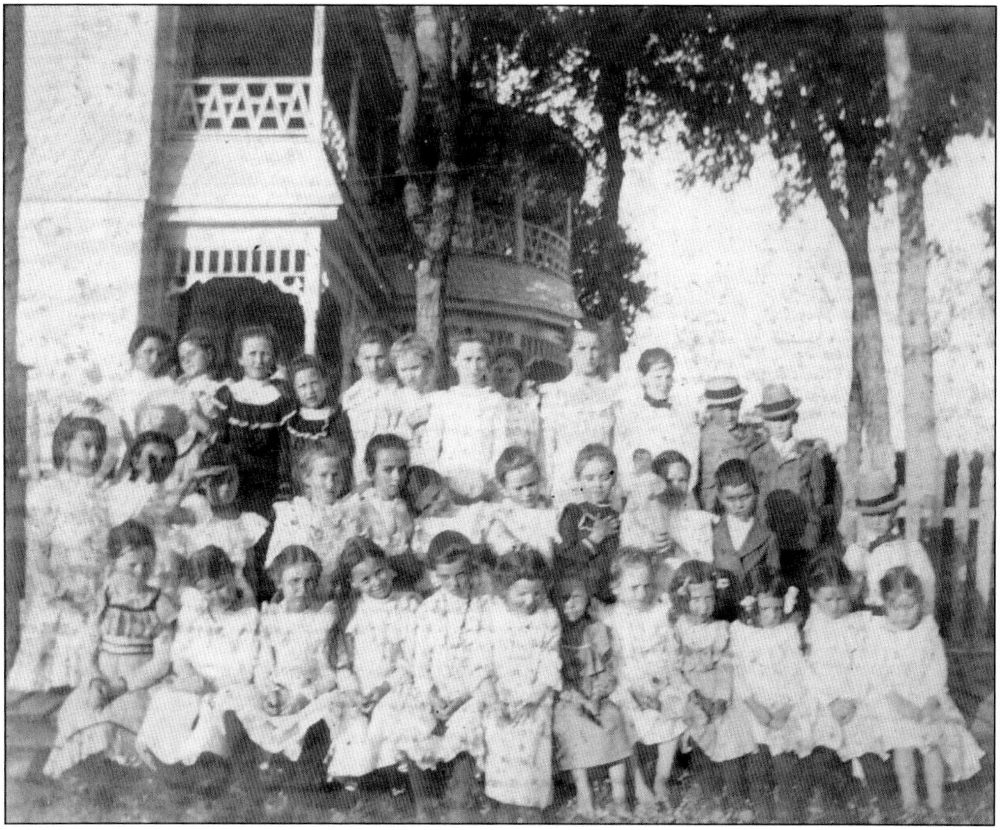

When J.W. Terrell moved from his farm into the town of Royse City, he built a home that became the center of family gatherings and social activities. He was a successful businessman who owned one of the first drugstores in town, and his prosperity allowed him to provide a comfortable life for his wife and children. The home was built in a Queen Anne (Victorian) style with a sweeping porch and ornamental spindles and brackets. This style symbolized refinement and was fitting for one of the town's leading citizens. Above, a group of children pose outside the Terrell home. Below is a social gathering inside the Terrell home.

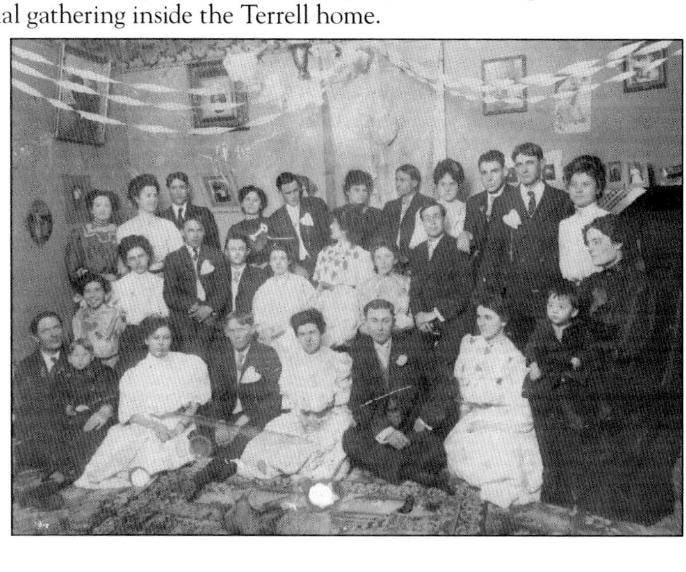

The finer homes of Royse City often provided backdrops for social activities and group portraits, as shown in this late 1800s photograph. During the Victorian era, almost all social activities—civic societies, social clubs, and even Sunday school classes—were segregated by sex.

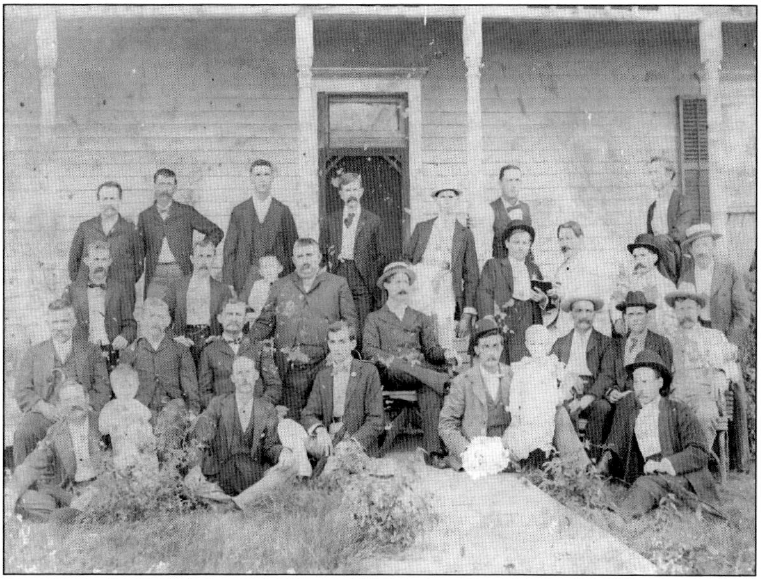

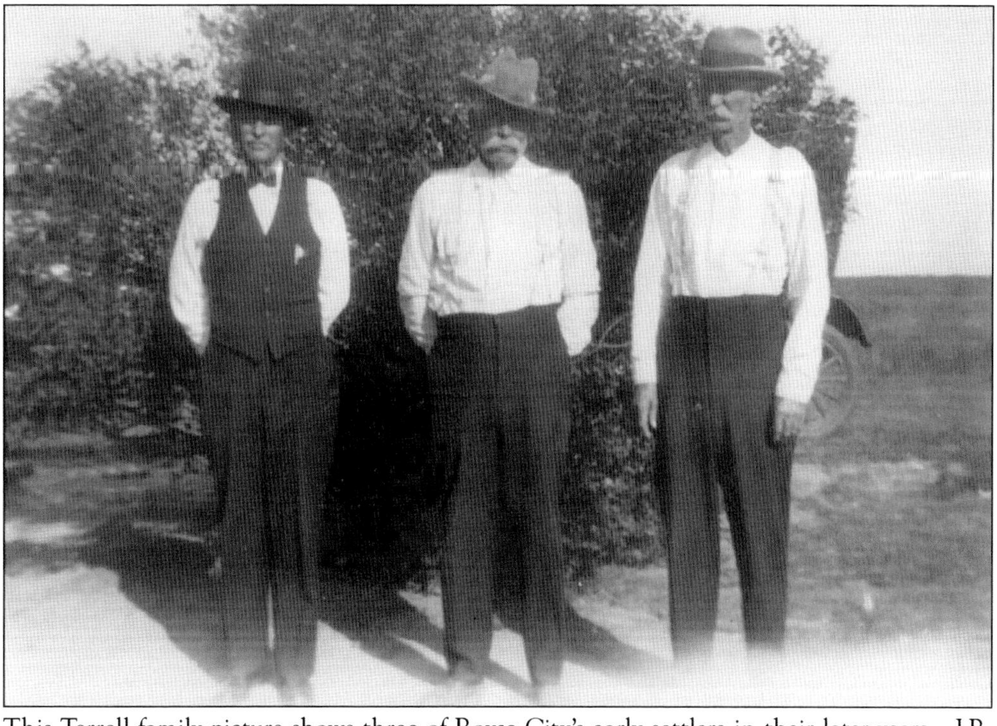

This Terrell family picture shows three of Royse City's early settlers in their later years—J.R. Terrell (left), J.W. Terrell (center), and W.A. Terrell. After moving to the Royse City area in 1880, both J.W. and W.A. made it a lifelong home for their families. Around 1900, J.R. moved west, eventually settling in Lorenzo, Texas.

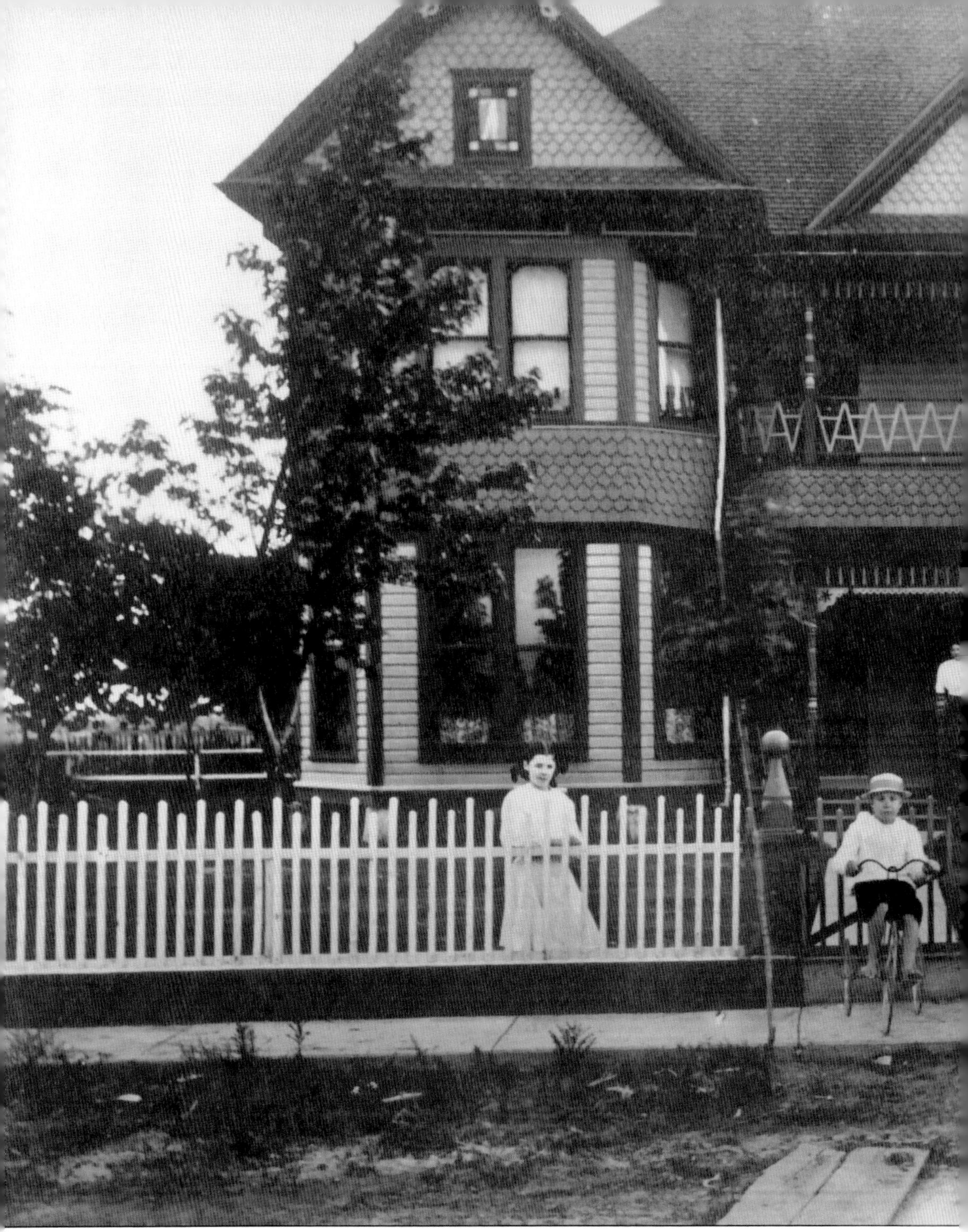

Meredith Ephraim Reinhardt and Mary Sue Marvin were married in Royse City on October 25, 1895. They had three children. Pictured here are Mary Belle (left, born in 1898), Marvin (center, born in 1902), and Mike (born in 1903). In 1905, the Reinhardts moved to a stately Victorian mansion on what is now Old Greenville Road in Royse City. Although farming was the family's primary occupation, both parents made education, religion, civic service, and neighborly

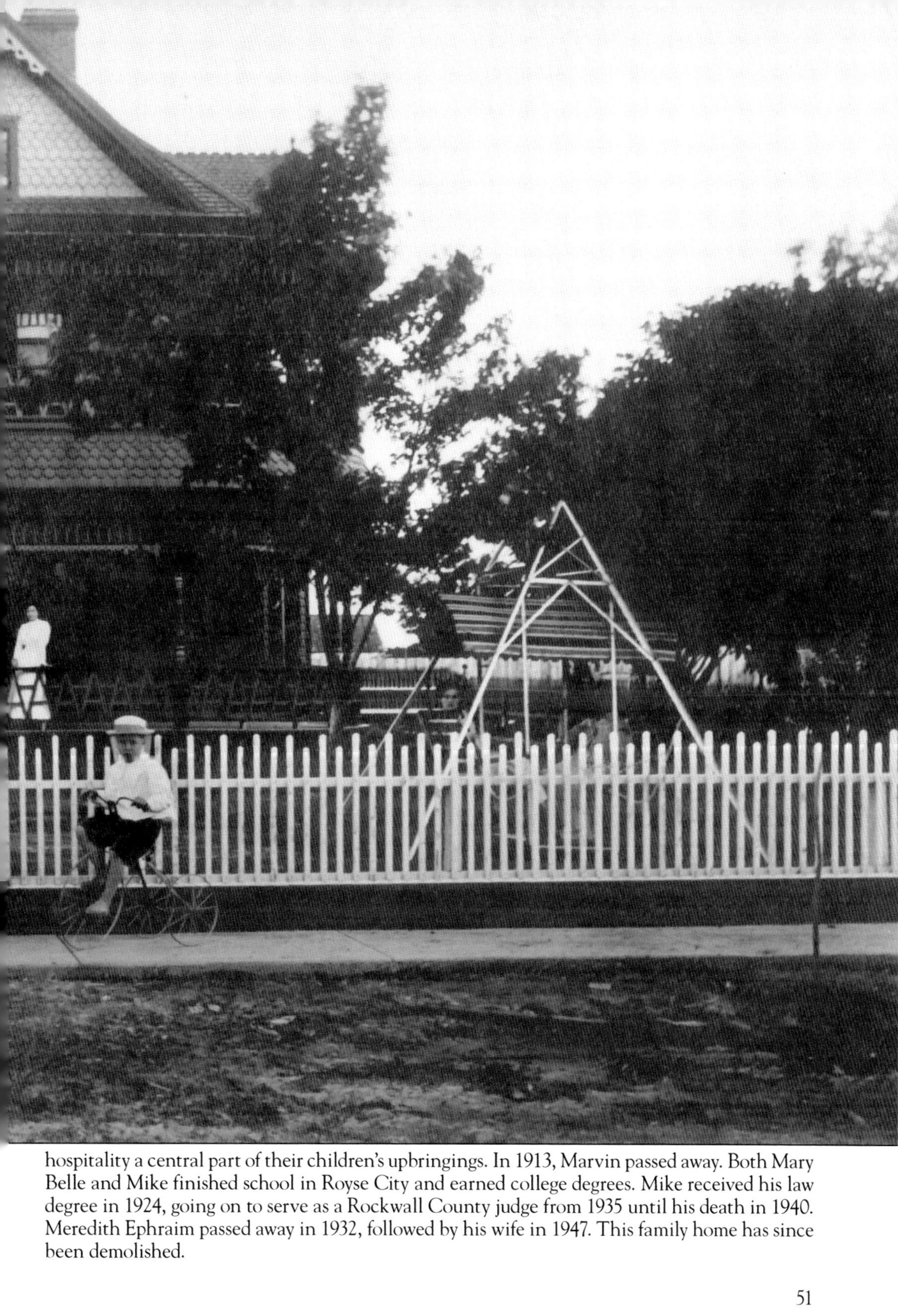

hospitality a central part of their children's upbringings. In 1913, Marvin passed away. Both Mary Belle and Mike finished school in Royse City and earned college degrees. Mike received his law degree in 1924, going on to serve as a Rockwall County judge from 1935 until his death in 1940. Meredith Ephraim passed away in 1932, followed by his wife in 1947. This family home has since been demolished.

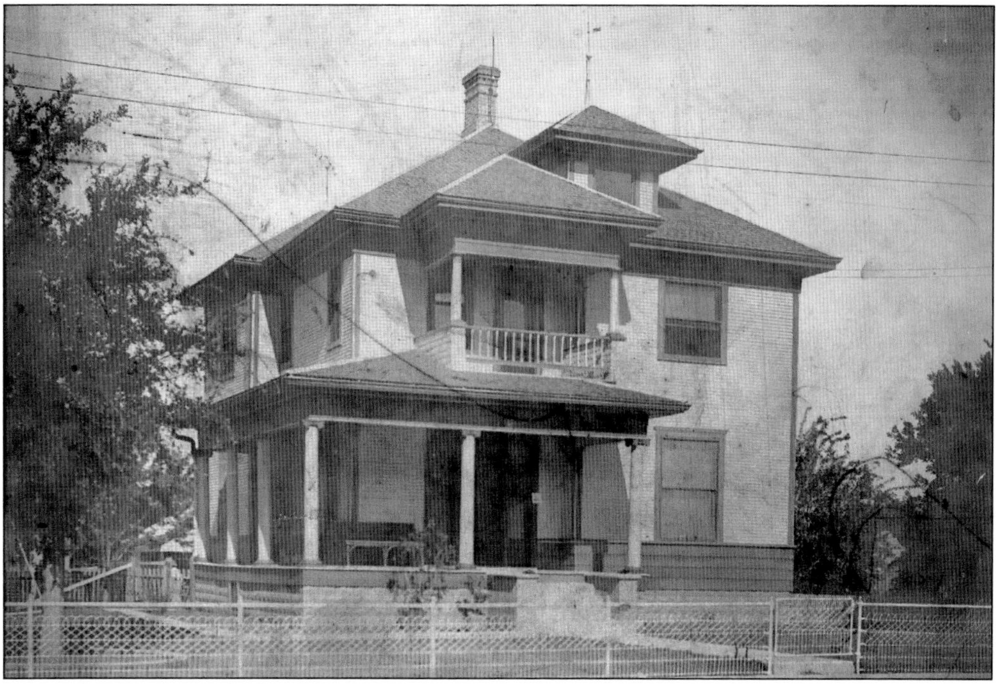

The Miller house was built in the late 1800s on the west side of Arch Street, just north of the First Christian Church. The structure served as a family home for many years, but was eventually sold to the First Baptist Church of Royse City; their building was located just north of the property. This lot was subsequently sold to the city and is now the location of city hall.

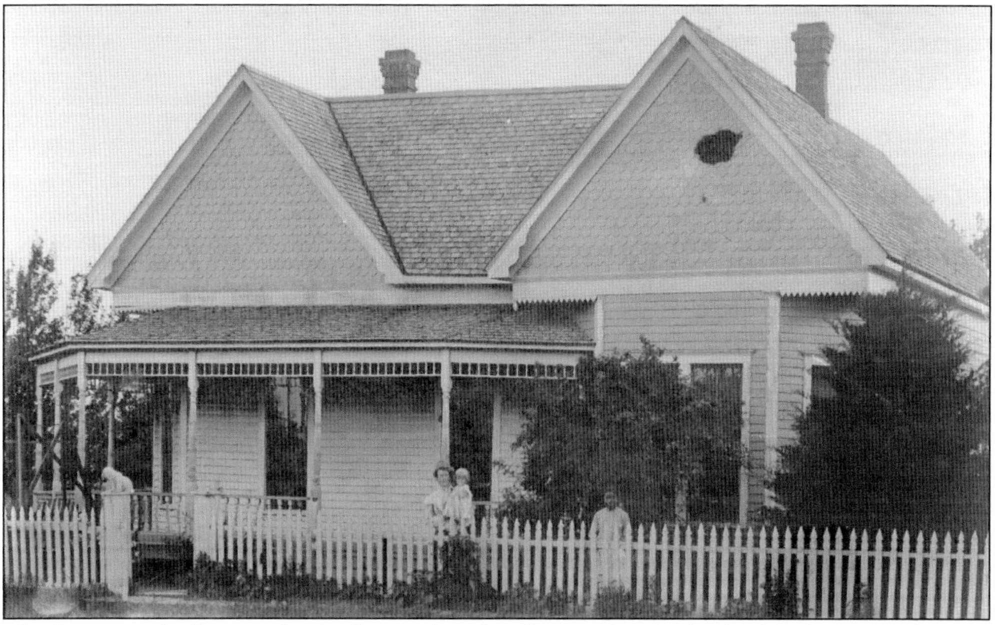

This home was built around 1900 for Frank and Nellie Smith. The back of the house was located across from the schoolyard on Lamar Street, and the front faced east on Theda Street. In the 1940s, Frank Smith had a small building at the back, facing Lamar Street, where he sold hamburgers, hot dogs, cold drinks, and candy to schoolchildren.

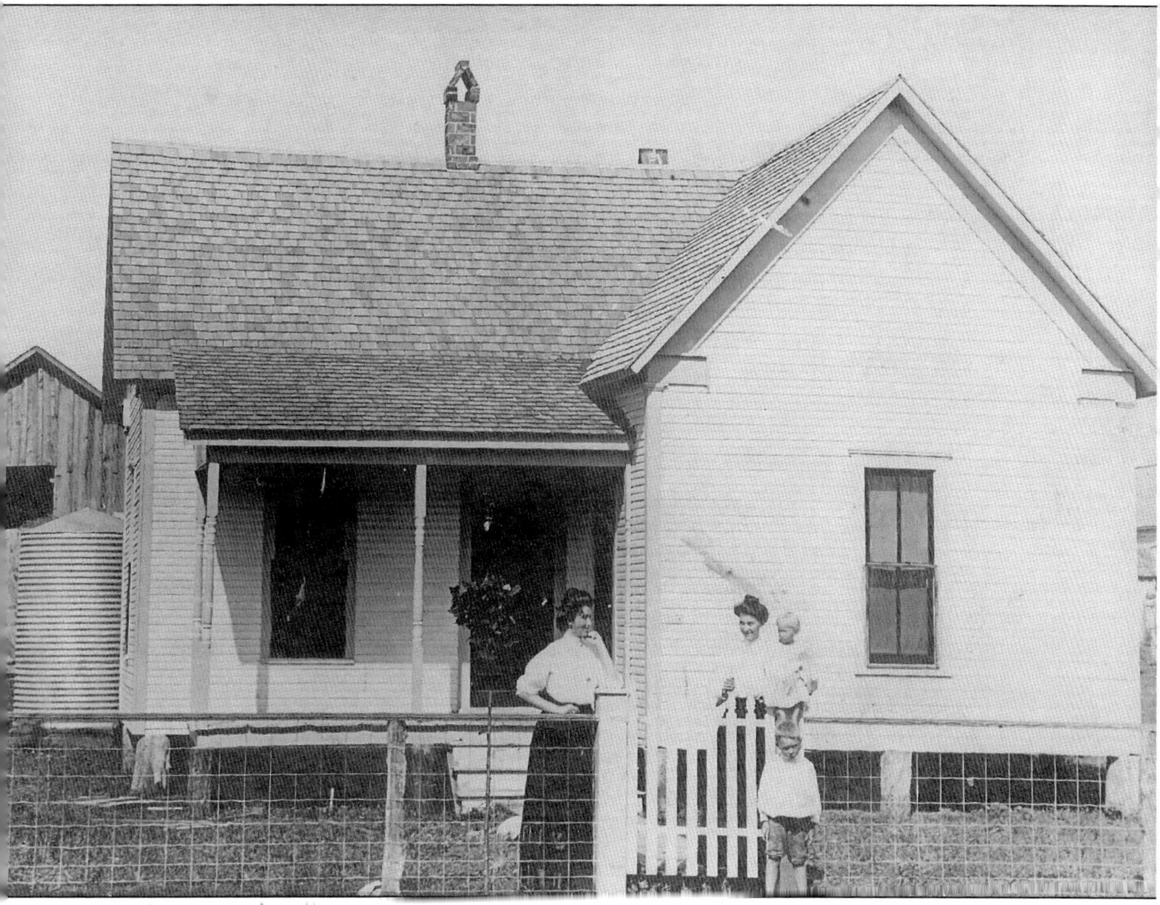

Tom Bailey married Nellie Parkerson in 1901 and took up residence in Royse City in 1905. He initially tried the mercantile business, but became a rural mail carrier after two years. In 1922, he became postmaster of Royse City and served for 15 years. In 1936, he was elected city secretary and served in the position until his death. Tom and Nellie Bailey had four children—Thomas Burke, Hazel Nell, Orpha Mae, and Opal Juanita. The family was active in the First Christian Church. Tom was also a member of the Masonic Lodge, and both he and Nellie were members of the Order of the Eastern Star. The Bailey home, which sat on Houston Street in Royse City, is pictured here. This typical Victorian farmhouse, with its gabled roof and spindled columns, is representative of the most common architectural style for rural homes built around 1900.

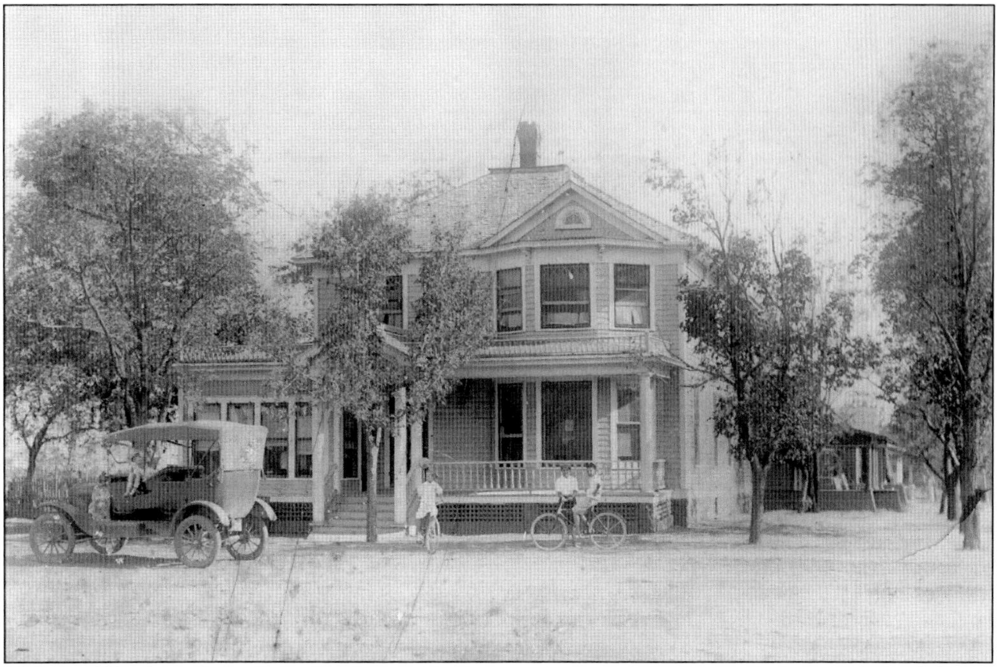

This is a prime example of the upscale houses built around Royse City in the early 1900s. Successful merchants and businessmen constructed homes close to town in architectural styles that reflected their prosperity and prominence. The name of the family that lived in this home is not known.

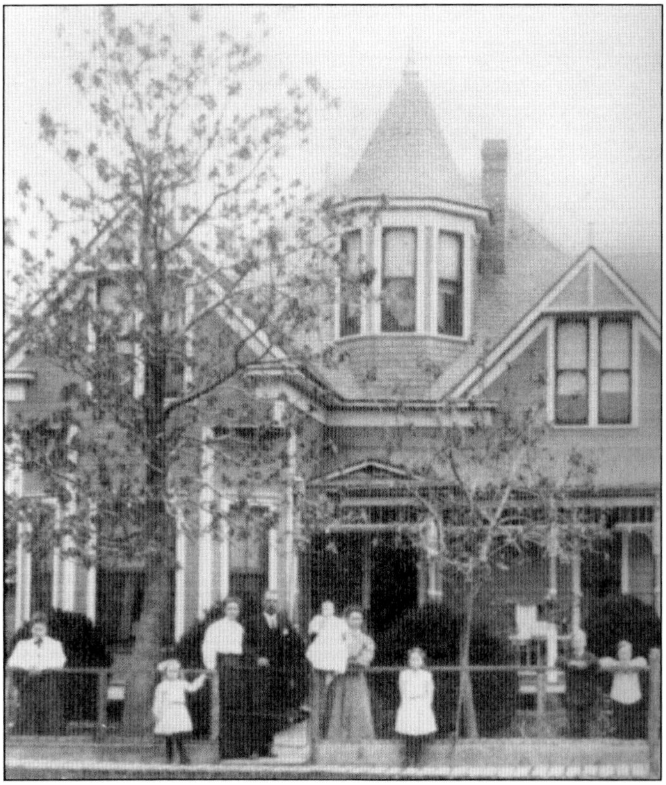

The home of Bettie and Augustus "Gus" Caesar Pedigo was located on the corner of Howard Street. The Pedigos had a large, extended family. Pictured here are, from left to right, Grace Hensley, Nell Dowell, Bettie Pedigo, Gus Pedigo, Fannie Dowell (holding her son Joe Frank Dowell), Beth Dowell, Walter Hensley, and Tom Dowell. Gus was an editor, schoolteacher, music teacher, and a choir director at the First Christian Church.

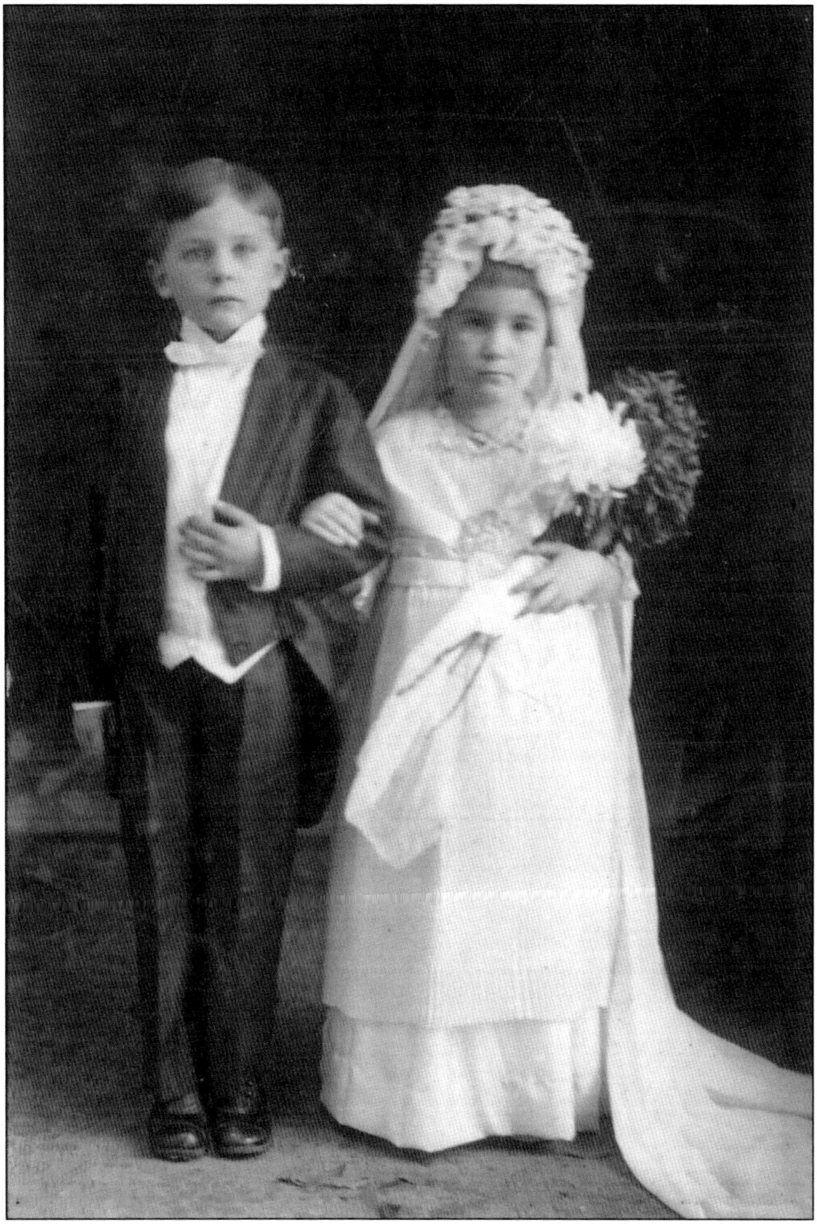

Inspired by the wedding of P.T. Barnum circus star Charles Stratton (who used the stage name General Tom Thumb) and Lavinia Warren, Tom Thumb wedding plays were a popular pastime for many decades. For most of his life, Stratton was only 25 inches tall. Barnum taught Stratton to sing, dance, and perform and made him an international star. When Stratton met Warren, who was also small in stature, the couple professed that it was love at first sight. The couple married in a lavish ceremony in New York City in 1863. The wedding was highly publicized (a pencil drawing of the couple at their wedding appeared on the cover of *Harper's Weekly* magazine) and captured the imagination of the nation. Soon after, Tom Thumb weddings—reenactments of the famous ceremony with children portraying the main participants—became a popular trend. This c. 1912 photograph captured Sonny Cookston and Margaret Earl (Morts) Russell in a Tom Thumb wedding.

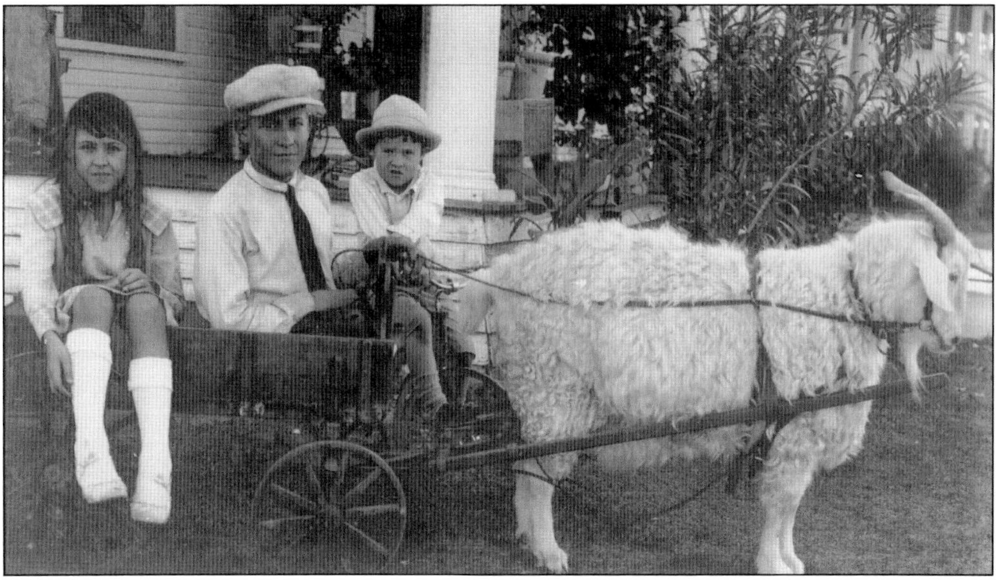

Before the advent of go-karts or mechanized children's vehicles, the goat cart was a popular and fun method of transportation. Goats were harnessed to pull small wooden wagons or carts in which children would ride, and goat cart races were popular in some communities. Pictured here in their goat cart are siblings Ima Ruth (left), Dock (center), and Billy Joe Ellis.

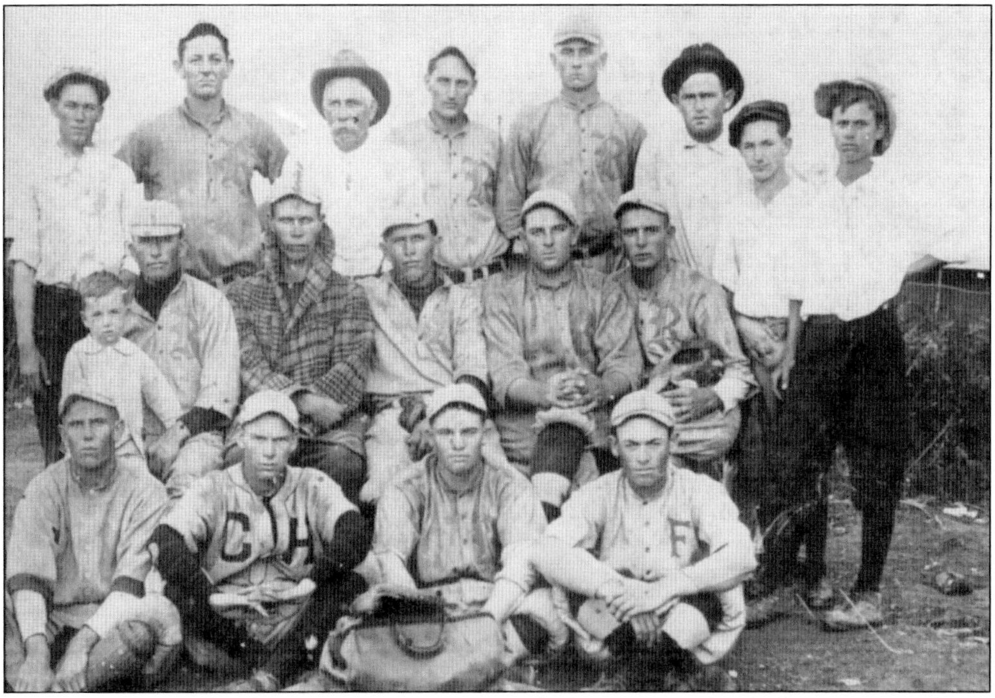

In the late 1800s and early 1900s, many Texas towns had community baseball teams. In Rockwall County and the surrounding area, these teams inspired intense rivalry. If a team had enough financial support, they would wear matching uniforms, but many players wore the uniforms they had donned in their high school days. This c. 1914 photograph features the Royse City baseball team.

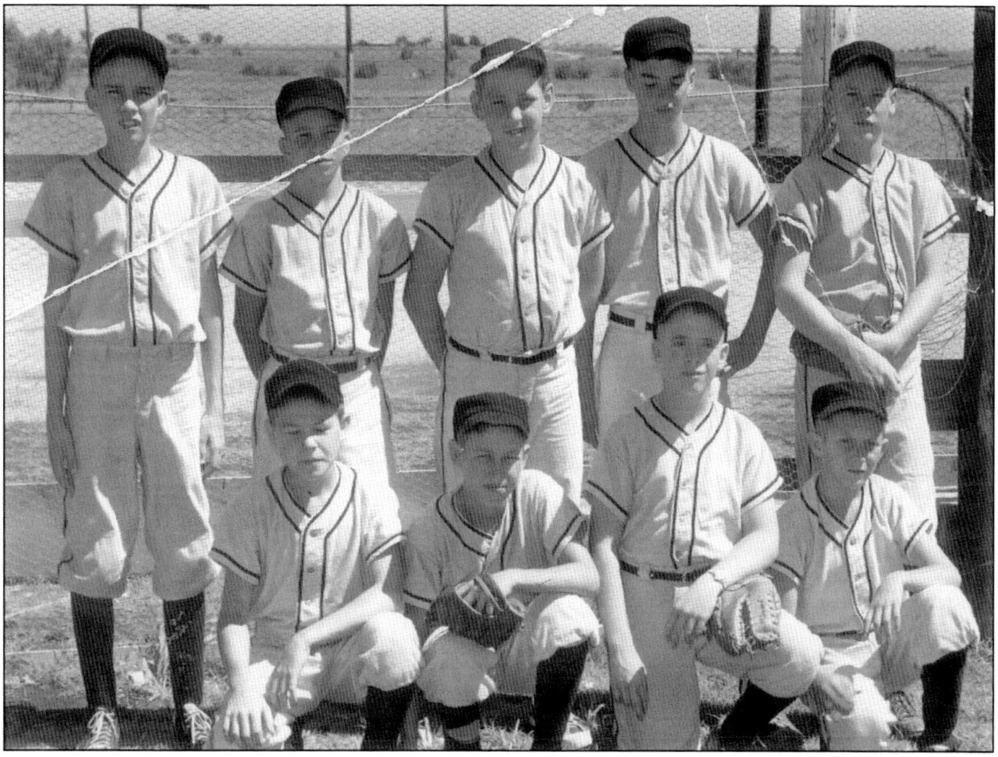

Dr. H.B. Peters brought Little League baseball to Royse City in 1954. At the time, Peters had only been practicing in the area for a year; however, as the team physician for the high school football program, he noticed that Royse City had an elementary-school program for football but not for baseball. The very first Little League game was played in Pennsylvania in 1939. The success of that league spread, and by the mid-1950s, Little League baseball was a nationwide sensation. Peters began recruiting community sponsors and coaches for a Royse City Little League program, and before long, both Royse City and Caddo Mills had enough teams to form an official Little League. Two early Little League teams are pictured here.

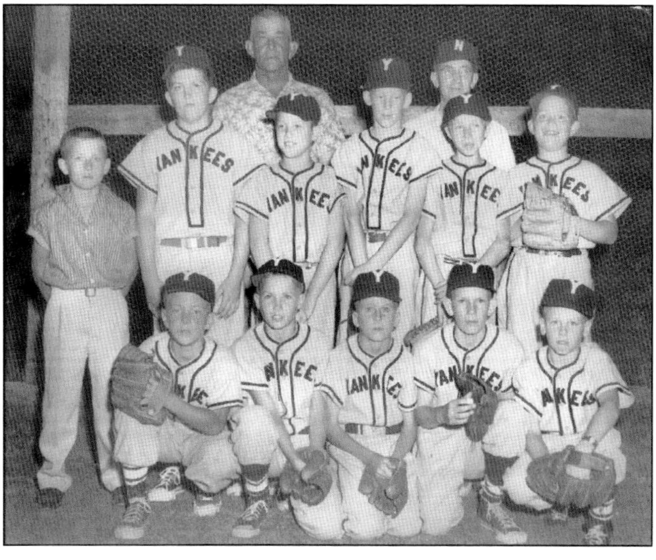

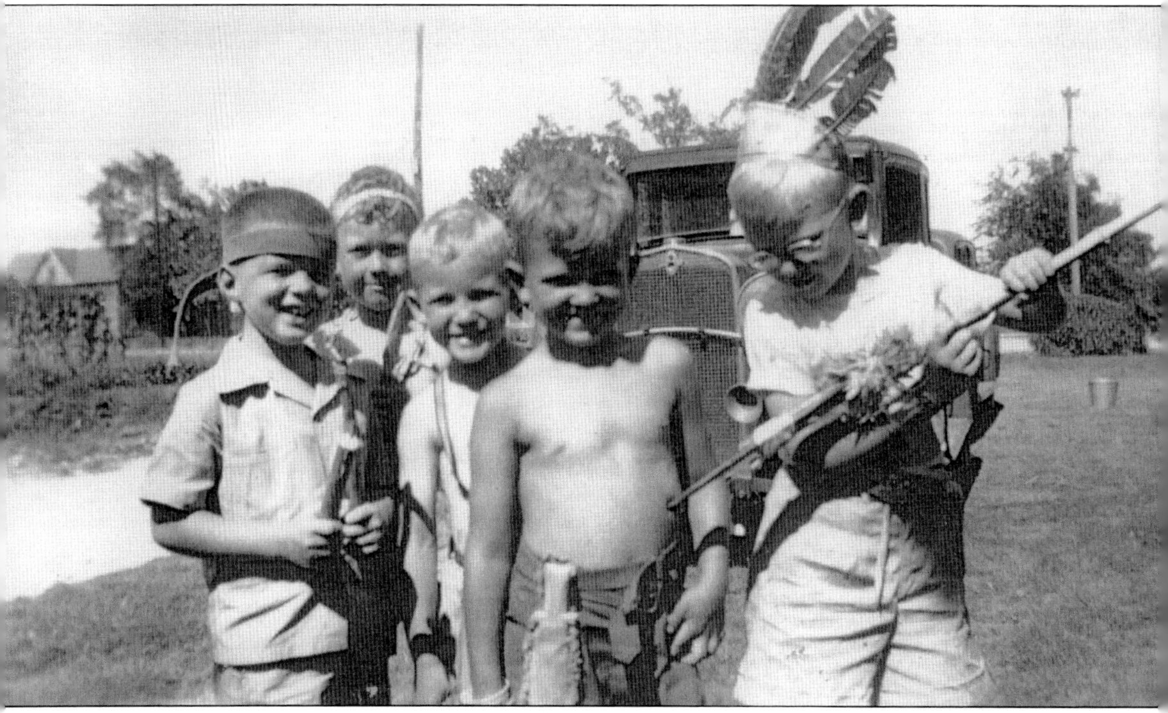

In addition to participating in organized activities, the boys of Royse City spent ample time enjoying their rural upbringings. Pictured around 1946 are, from left to right, Joe Mack Turentine, Thomas Earl Gilleland, Danny Davison, Bobby Crowell, and Joel Davison, who appear to be playing cowboys and Indians. During this postwar time, popular culture was filled with Western influences. Gene Autry, Roy Rogers, Randolph Scott, and John Wayne were on the big screen, and the Lone Ranger debuted on radio in 1933 and ran through 1954. As television became popular, Westerns such as *Maverick* and *Rawhide* took to the airwaves. Toy companies heavily marketed Western-style gear during the 1940s and 1950s; Rogers, Autry, the Lone Ranger, and the Red Ryder all advertised toy gun and holster sets for their young fans.

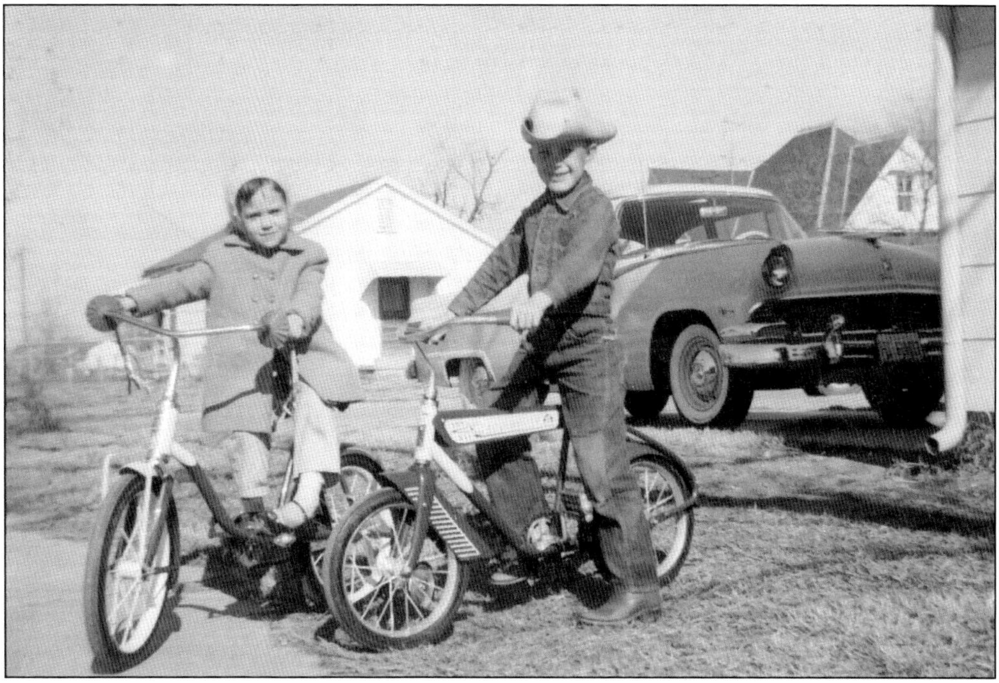

In the 1940s and 1950s, bicycles became a must-have mode of transportation for children. After the invention and rise in popularity of the automobile, bicycle manufacturers were challenged with finding a new market; since bicycles had previously been made for adults (who were now driving cars), the manufacturers decided it was time to cater to children. Major department stores such as Sears, Roebuck & Co. and Montgomery Ward began making children's bicycles after World War I, and soon Schwinn, Murray, and Huffy were creating bikes for kids, too. Becky and Billy Betts are pictured above on their bicycles.

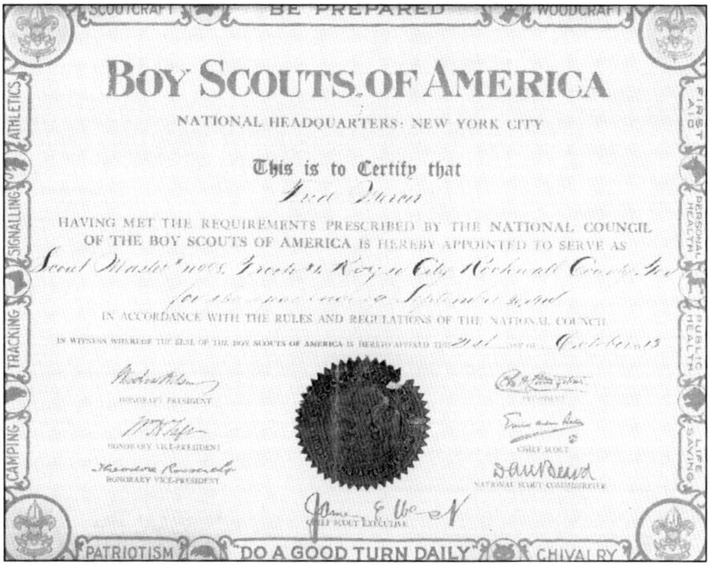

SCOUTCRAFT BE PREPARED WOODCRAFT

BOY SCOUTS OF AMERICA

NATIONAL HEADQUARTERS: NEW YORK CITY

This is to Certify that

HAVING MET THE REQUIREMENTS PRESCRIBED BY THE NATIONAL COUNCIL OF THE BOY SCOUTS OF AMERICA IS HEREBY APPOINTED TO SERVE AS

IN ACCORDANCE WITH THE RULES AND REGULATIONS OF THE NATIONAL COUNCIL

PATRIOTISM DO A GOOD TURN DAILY CHIVALRY

In the early 1900s, organizations began to form that would provide leadership and guidance to America's youth. The Boy Scouts of America was established in 1910, and by 1913, Royse City had organized a Boy Scout troop. The original charter, pictured at right, designates Troop No. 1, Royse City, Rockwall County. The troop was chartered by the First United Methodist Church and operates as Troop No. 312 today.

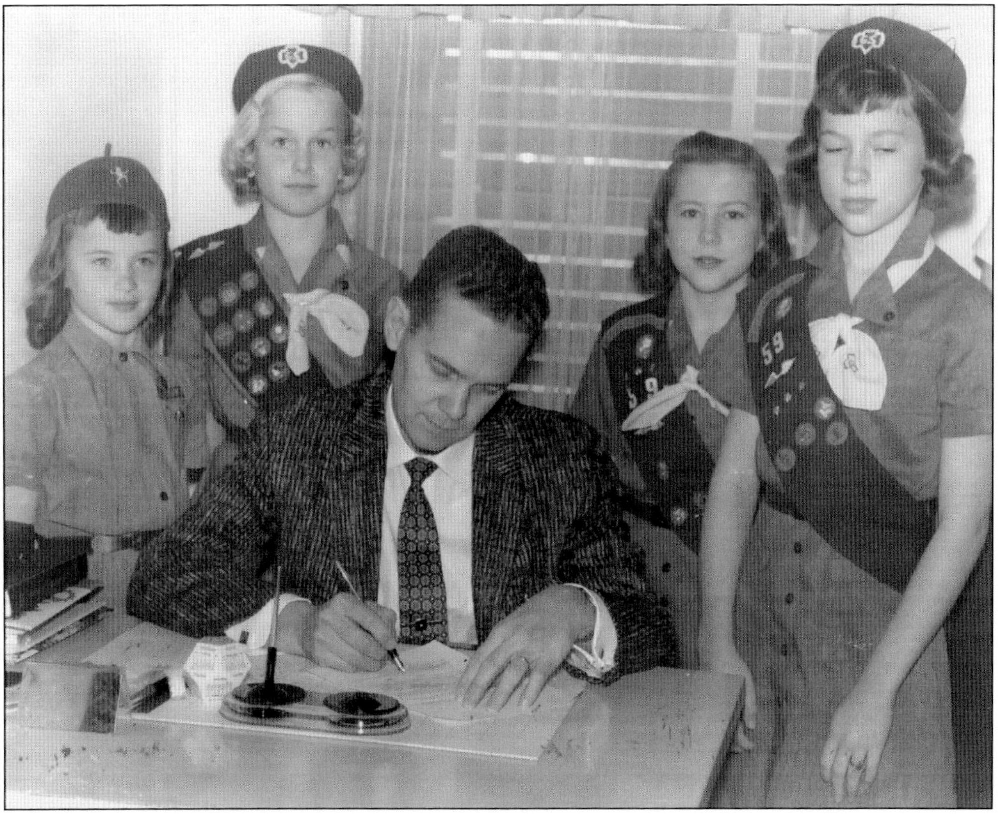

For the young ladies of Royse City, Girl Scouts offered an opportunity for learning and adventure. Pictured above are, from left to right, Vara Crowell, Sarah Crowell, Virginia Cross, and Barbara Sledge, who look on as Girl Scout Week is declared in Royse City on March 6, 1959. For decades, Girl Scout Week has been celebrated annually during the week of March 12, the day the first Girl Scout troop was founded by Juliette Gordon Low in 1912. Pictured below are, from left to right, Dick Pickens, unidentified, Girl Scout leader Emily Crowell, superintendent of schools Rudd B. Hughes, Dewitt Van Cleave, Robert Strain, and Girl Scout leader Vivian Hicks.

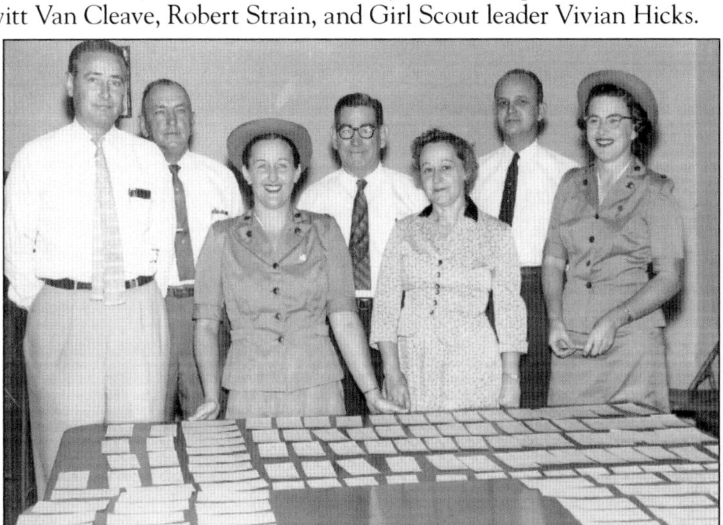

In 1907, a group of 14 Royse City women organized a literary club. One of their first orders of business was to assess 5¢ per member in order to purchase a secretary's book. The rules stipulate that each member is responsible for the book in her care; that books must not be loaned; and that bookmarks must be used so that no page corners are turned down. For several years, the Book Lovers Club produced cookbooks as a fundraiser. Pictured at right is a cookbook belonging to Emma Pennington. Below, two interior pages from the 1952 Royse City telephone book show advertisements for Citizens State Bank (telephone 6) and James Motor Company (telephone 15), as well as a listing for the Federal Bureau of Investigation that instructs residents to call "information."

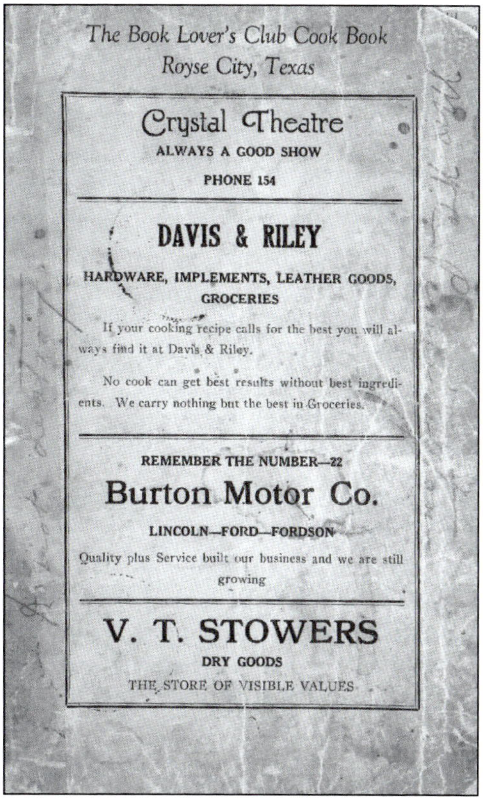
The Book Lover's Club Cook Book
Royse City, Texas

Crystal Theatre
ALWAYS A GOOD SHOW
PHONE 154

DAVIS & RILEY
HARDWARE, IMPLEMENTS, LEATHER GOODS, GROCERIES
If your cooking recipe calls for the best you will always find it at Davis & Riley.
No cook can get best results without best ingredients. We carry nothing but the best in Groceries.

REMEMBER THE NUMBER—22
Burton Motor Co.
LINCOLN—FORD—FORDSON
Quality plus Service built our business and we are still growing

V. T. STOWERS
DRY GOODS
THE STORE OF VISIBLE VALUES

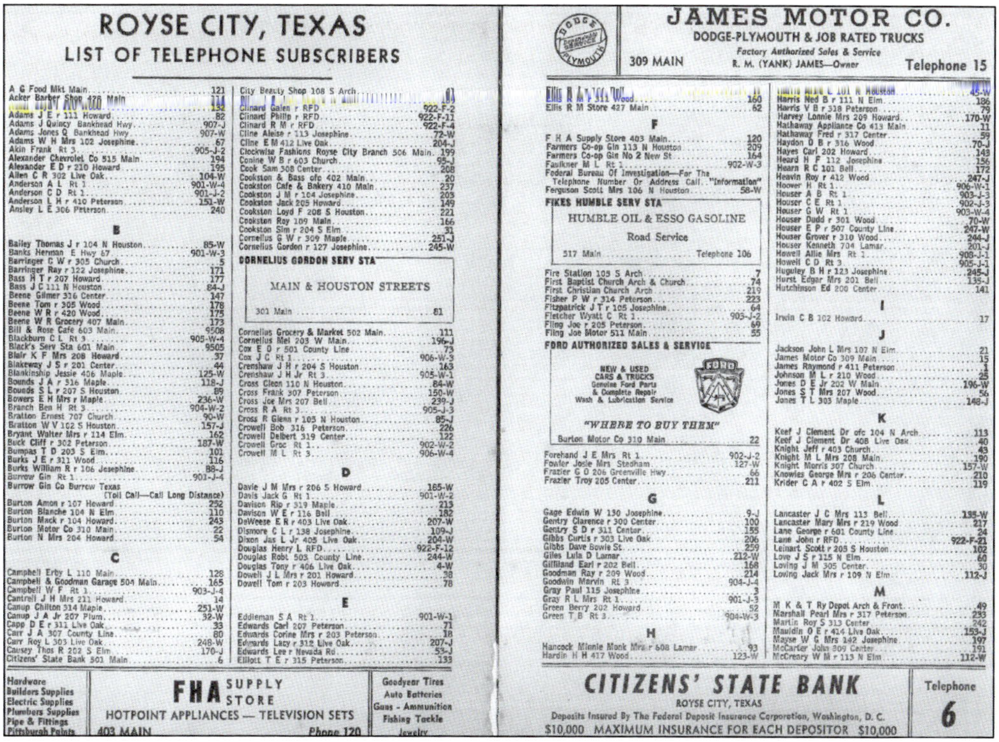
ROYSE CITY, TEXAS
LIST OF TELEPHONE SUBSCRIBERS

CORNELIUS GORDON SERV STA
MAIN & HOUSTON STREETS
301 Main 81

Hardware
Builders Supplies
Electric Supplies
Plumbers Supplies
Pipe & Fittings
Pittsburgh Paints

FHA SUPPLY STORE
HOTPOINT APPLIANCES — TELEVISION SETS
403 MAIN Phone 120

Goodyear Tires
Auto Batteries
Guns - Ammunition
Fishing Tackle
Jewelry

JAMES MOTOR CO.
DODGE-PLYMOUTH & JOB RATED TRUCKS
Factory Authorized Sales & Service
309 MAIN R. M. (YANK) JAMES—Owner Telephone 15

Federal Bureau Of Investigation—For The Telephone Number Or Address Call "Information"

FIKES HUMBLE SERV STA
HUMBLE OIL & ESSO GASOLINE
Road Service
517 Main Telephone 106

FORD AUTHORIZED SALES & SERVICE
NEW & USED CARS & TRUCKS
Genuine Ford Parts
& Complete Repair
Wash & Lubrication Service
"WHERE TO BUY THEM"
Burton Motor Co 310 Main 22

CITIZENS' STATE BANK
ROYSE CITY, TEXAS
Deposits Insured By The Federal Deposit Insurance Corporation, Washington, D. C.
$10,000 MAXIMUM INSURANCE FOR EACH DEPOSITOR $10,000
Telephone 6

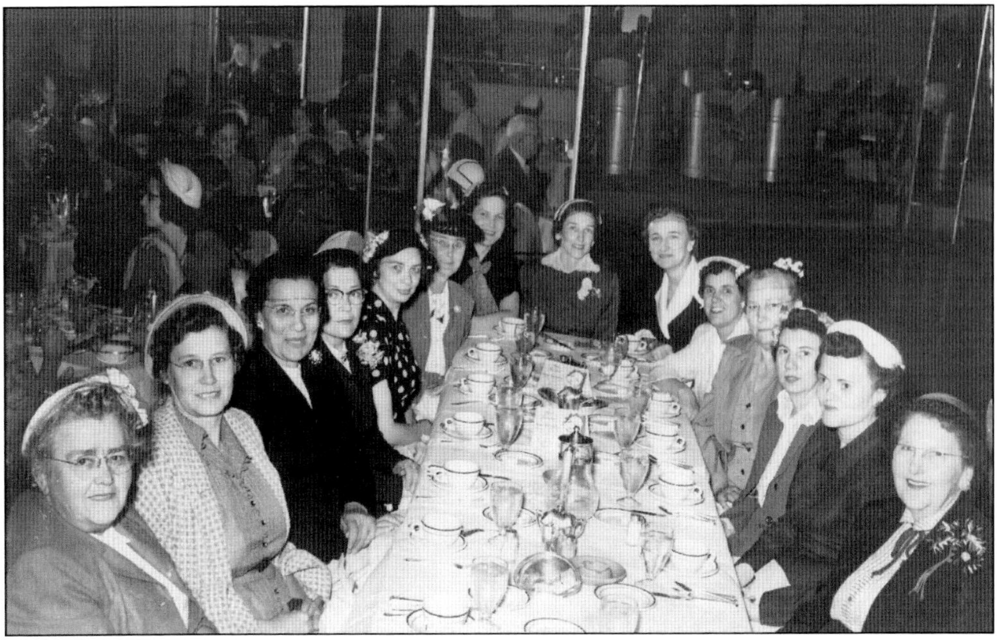

A trip to Dallas for a nice lunch was a special occasion for organized clubs and groups of friends during the 1940s and 1950s, just as it can be today. Pictured above are, from left to right, Minnie Houser, Ann Cornelius, Vi Shaw, Mable Nowlain, Mrs. W.W. Wright, Oleta O'Neal, Mary Davis, Louise Anderson, Willie Clark, Rosa Coleman, Edith Houser, Laura Belle Forehand, Mae Anderson, and Ruth Ellis. Pictured below are, from left to right, Billie Ryan, Gladys James, unidentified, Hazel Lancaster, Cora Price, unidentified, Lucy James, unidentified, Ruby Adams, Kat Jones, and Lula Fitzpatrick.

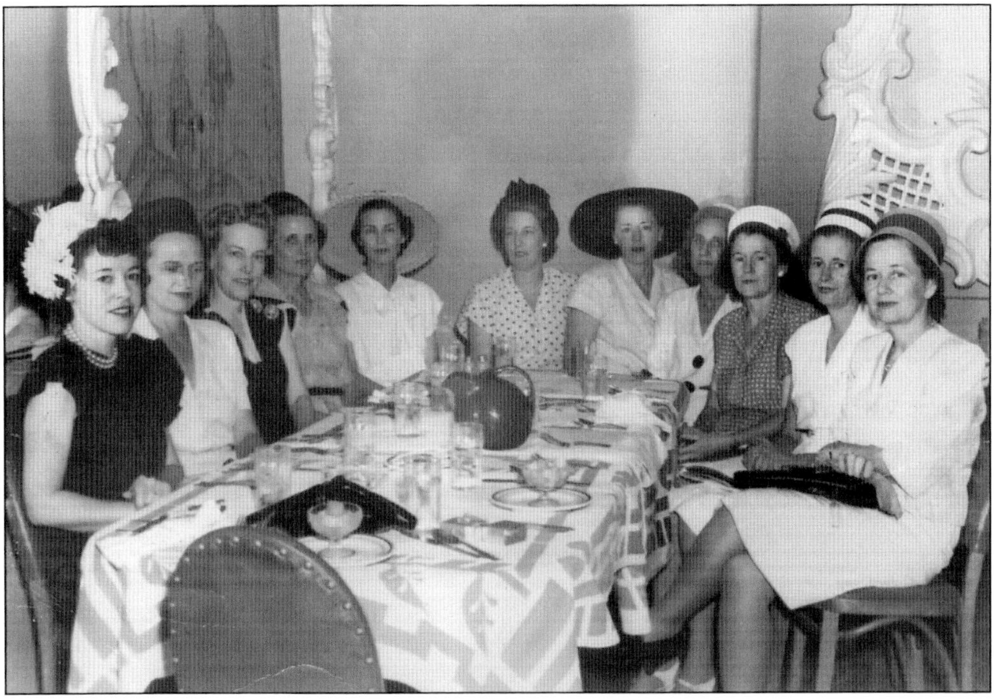

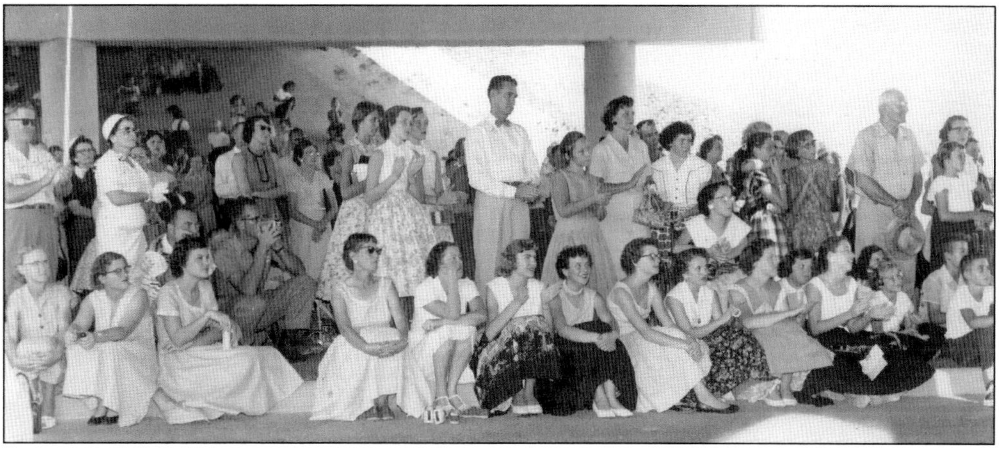

By the late 1950s, the expanding interstate system was swiftly becoming the main thoroughfare in cities across the United States. Many small-town residents throughout the country celebrated new construction milestones. Here, a Royse City crowd gathers for the dedication of the new interstate overpass. Such advances increased the ease of transportation, but caused significant economic decline for downtown areas that were now off the central route.

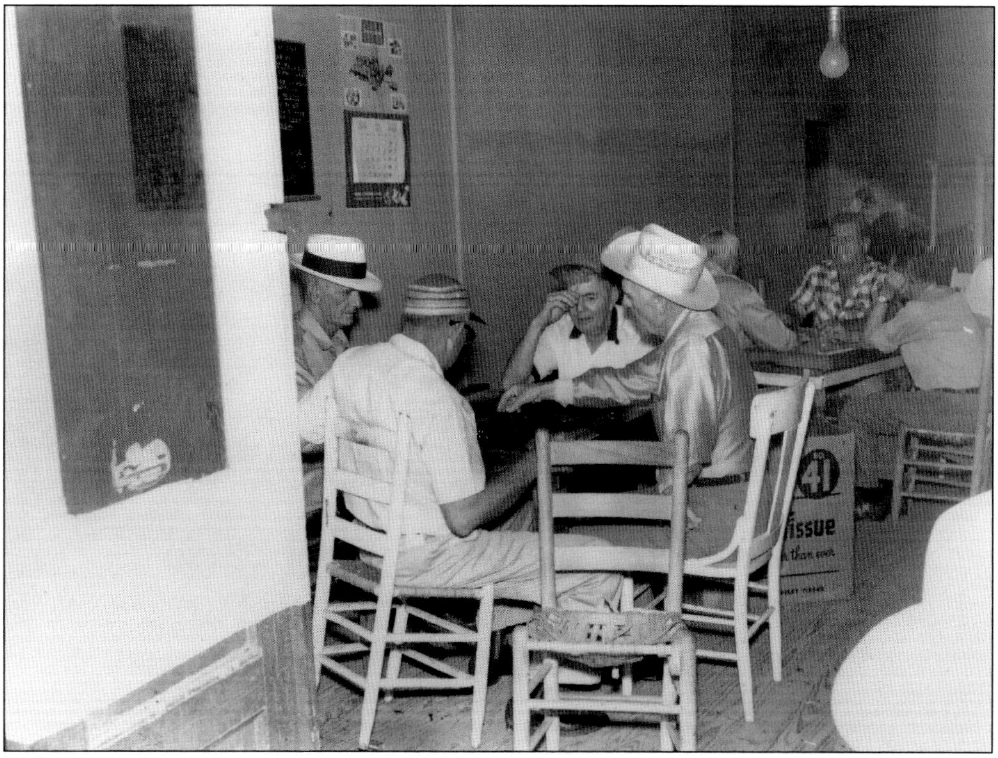

Although many table games provided entertainment, dominoes seemed to be the most prominent during the 1940s and 1950s. A corner of a store or a café would often be the setting for an impromptu game, but many small towns had set-ups that were more elaborate, with entire buildings—called domino halls—dedicated to the game. A Royse City domino hall is pictured above in the 1950s.

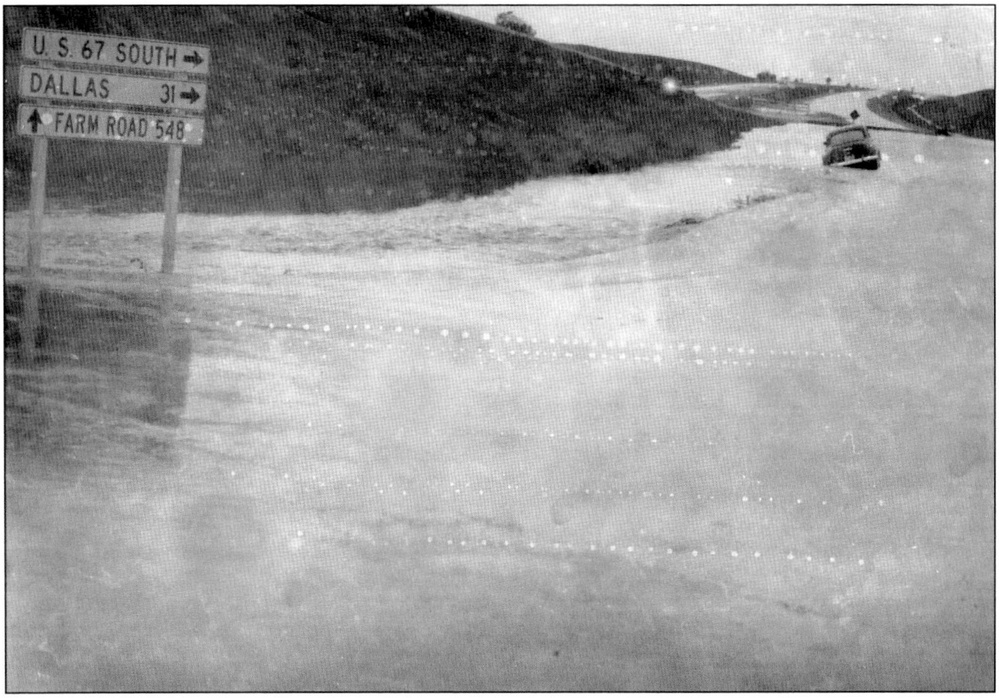

Although the Dallas area had suffered a severe drought from 1950 to 1957, flooding was the problem in May 1958. The rain was so extensive that residents could not get out of Royse City by either US Highway 67 or by the newly completed interstate. The Royse City High School senior banquet—which had been scheduled at an out-of-town venue—had to be canceled due to the impassable roadways.

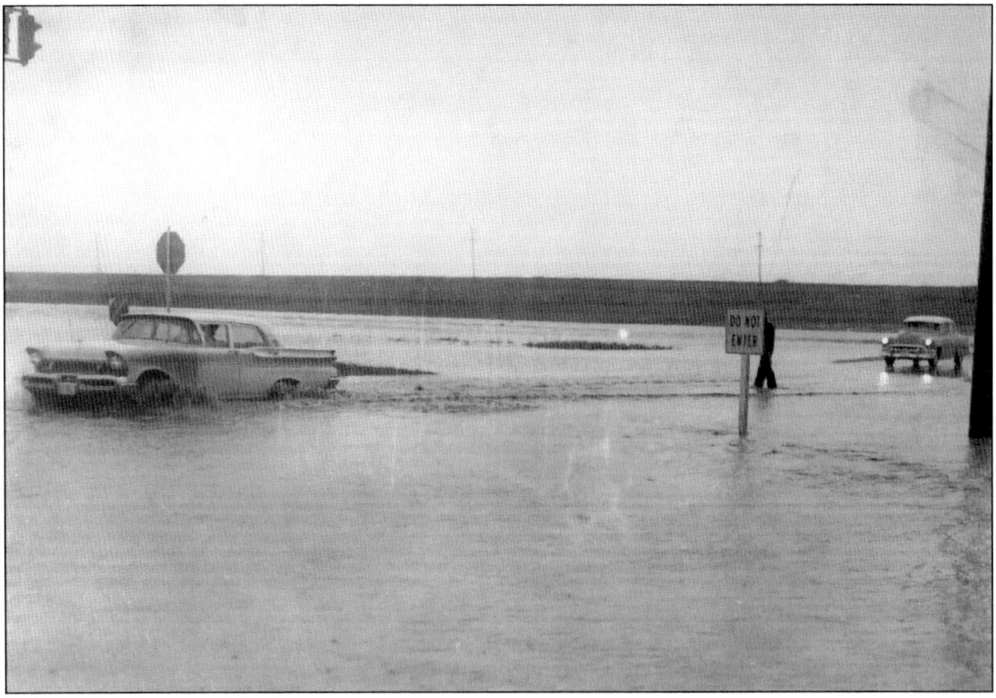

Four

Churches, Schools, and Community Service

For residents of Royse City—from the earliest settlers to those living in town today—dedication to church, school, and the community has been a constant. Diehard Royse City High School Bulldog fans, devout churchgoers, and citizens dedicated to community service have formed the bedrock of this small-town Texas community.

The first church to organize in Royse City was the First Christian Church in July 1884. The First United Methodist Church of Royse City organized in 1887, followed by the First Baptist Church in 1888. All three congregations initially met in school buildings before constructing their own places of worship, and all three congregations are still active.

The first school in the city was a clapboard building constructed in 1887 and located on the south side of town. At the same time, dozens of country schools were established throughout Rockwall County, including several in the Royse City area. In the early part of the 1900s, independent school districts were formed, with Royse City, Rockwall, Fate, and Heath all having their own districts. Today, only the Royse City Independent School District (RCISD) and the Rockwall Independent School District remain.

Many Royse City residents have dedicated their lives to civic service at the city, county, and state levels. Royse City attorneys James Reese, Carl Miller, and, more recently, Bill Bell, all served as Rockwall County judges. Many Royse City residents have been elected county commissioners, including J.W. Terrell, John Pullen, and, more recently, David Magness. Dee Brown Walker, who was born in Royse City in 1912, was appointed the first judge of the 162nd Judicial District Court of Dallas County in 1963 and served until 1980. Although he moved to Dallas in the late 1920s, Judge Walker had a great love of family and was an integral part of the creation of the Royse City Cemetery Foundation. In 1998, Judge Walker returned to his birthplace, where he was named "Man of the Year" and given a golden key to the city. These are just a few examples of the many Royse City residents who have served their city, their county, and their country.

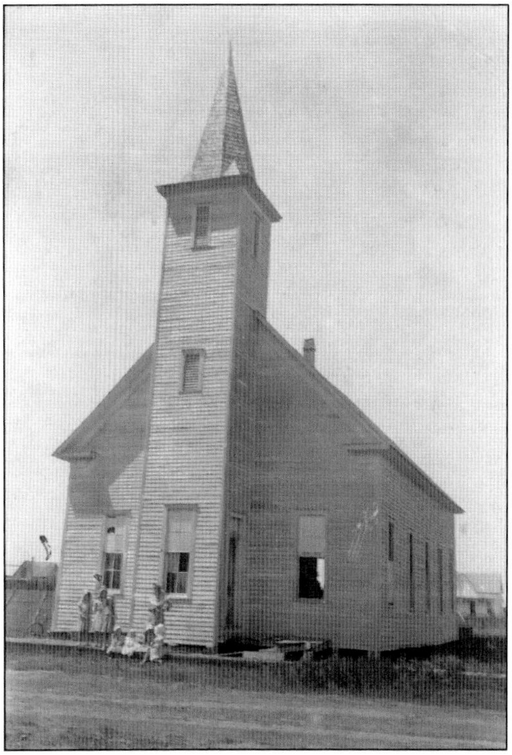

The First United Methodist Church of Royse City was organized in 1887 in a school building, which was subsequently used as a place of worship. In 1890, the members began making plans for a dedicated church building (pictured at left), which was erected on a lot across from the north entrance of the current sanctuary. The lot had been owned by the McCasland family, who donated it for the church building. In 1904, the current church (below) was constructed in a style called Trinity Western Gothic. The church's three towers represent the Trinity: God the Father, God the Son, and God the Holy Spirit. The sanctuary is built in the form of a cross.

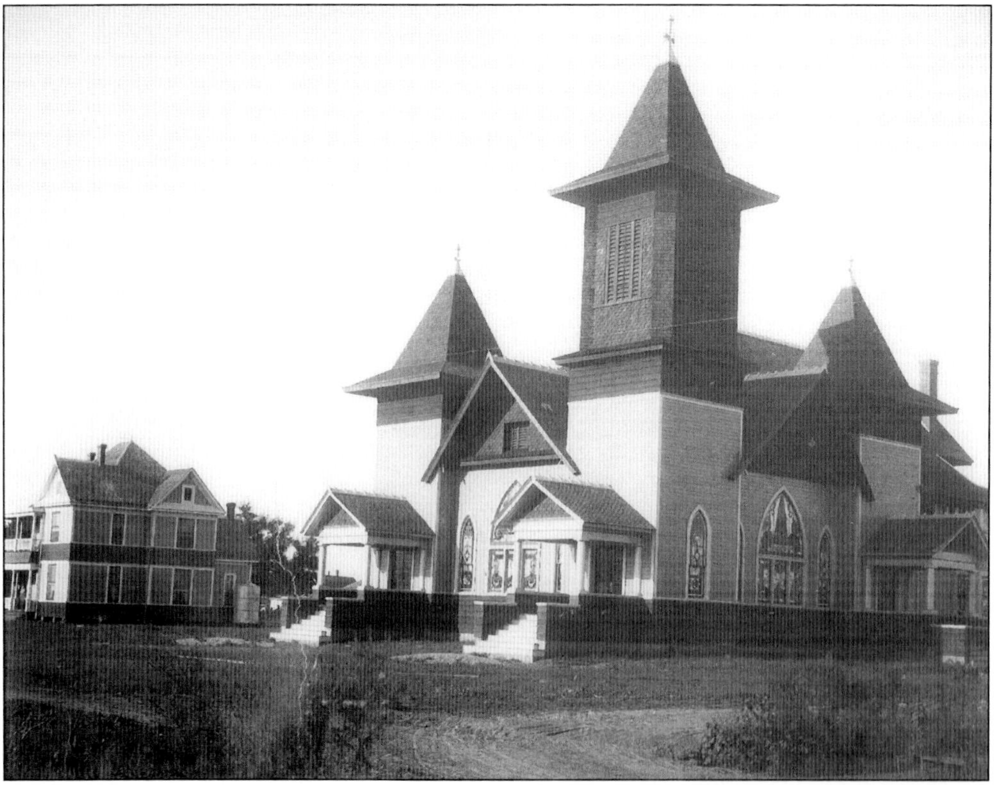

The first parsonage to serve the church was in Old Fate, but in 1904, when the new church was constructed, a new parsonage (the building at left in the photograph) was erected on the south side of the same lot using lumber from the old church. When the Bankhead Highway was built through town, the parsonage was in its direct path and was relocated to the west side of the church at a cost of $250.

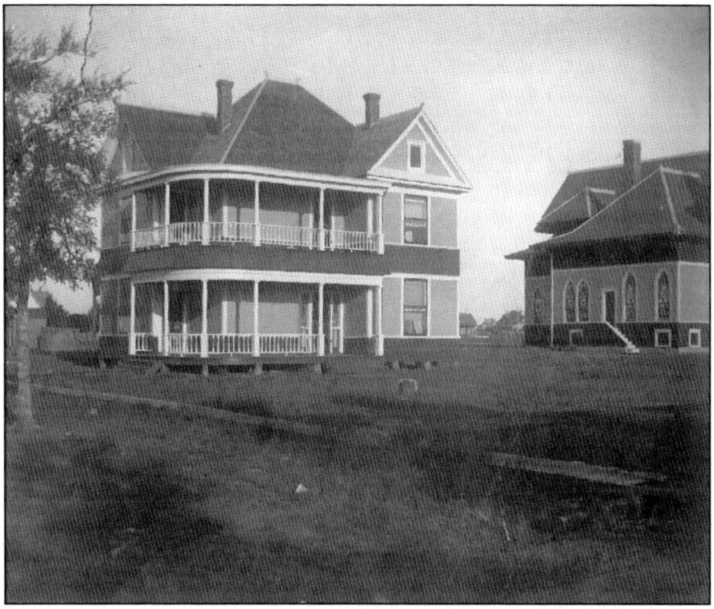

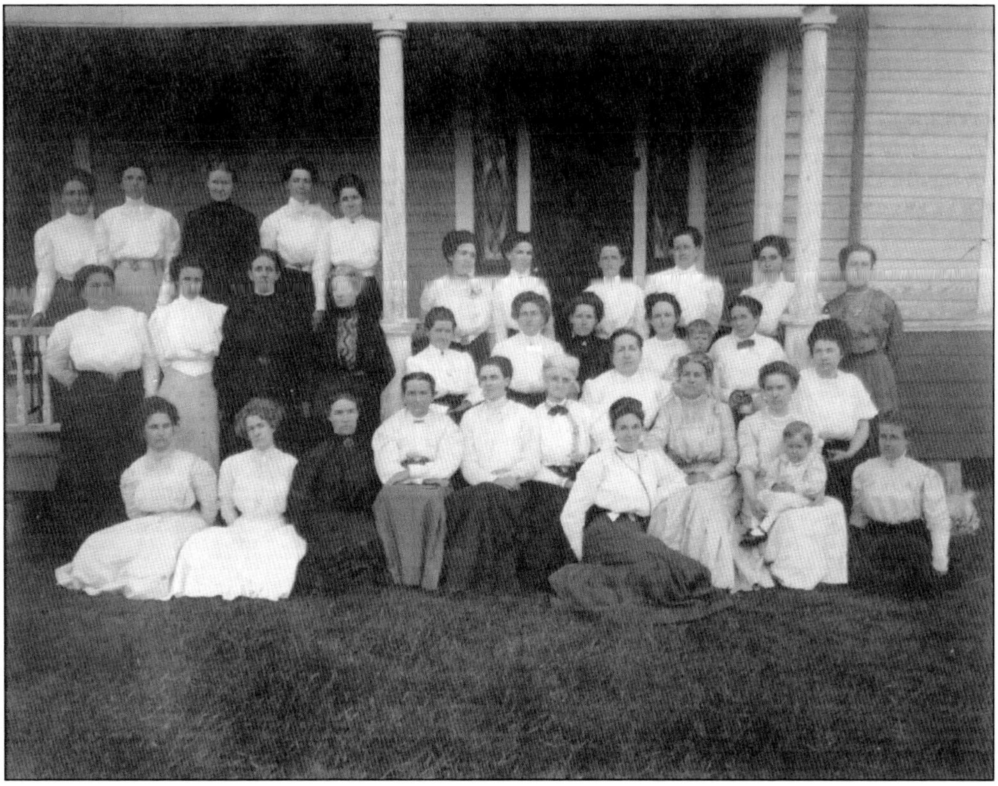

A written history of the First United Methodist Church records that from the beginning of the church, there was a missionary society, but it took them several years to be officially recognized. In 1910, the Methodist Home and Foreign Societies merged to become the Women's Missionary Society, and later the Women's Society of Christian Service. This photograph shows the First Methodist Women's Missionary Society.

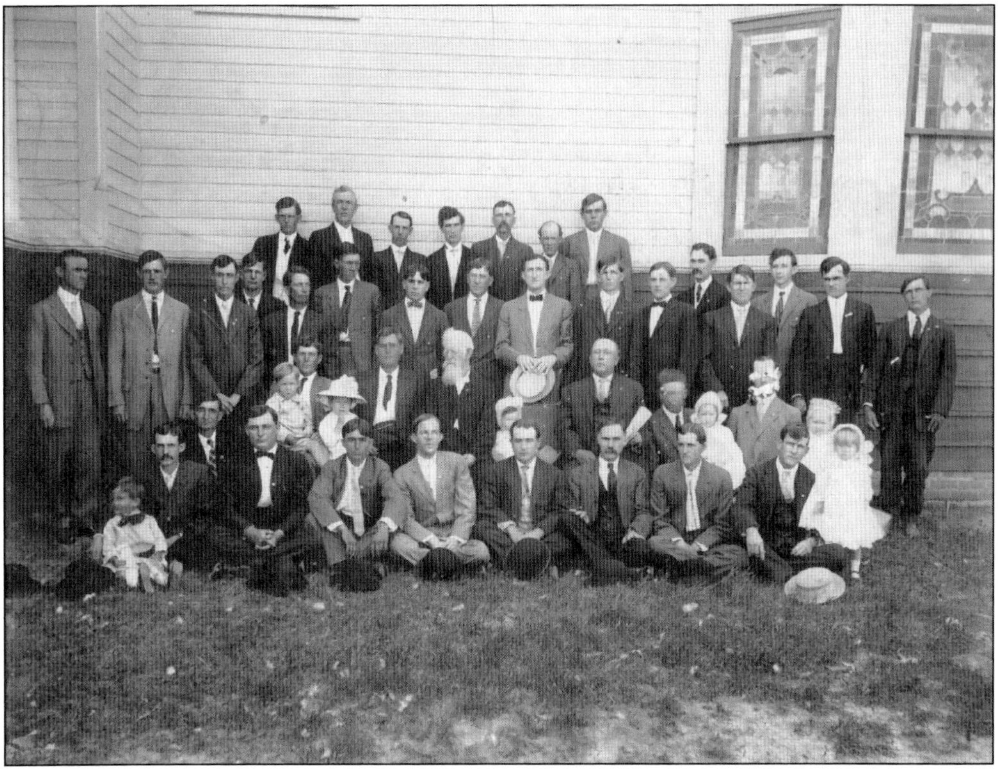

The charter members of the First United Methodist Church were well known in the community due to their civic and business involvement. Organizing members included the W.A. and J.R. Terrell families, the Reinhardt family, the Johnson family, and the Creel family. This image is an early photograph of the First United Methodist men's Sunday school.

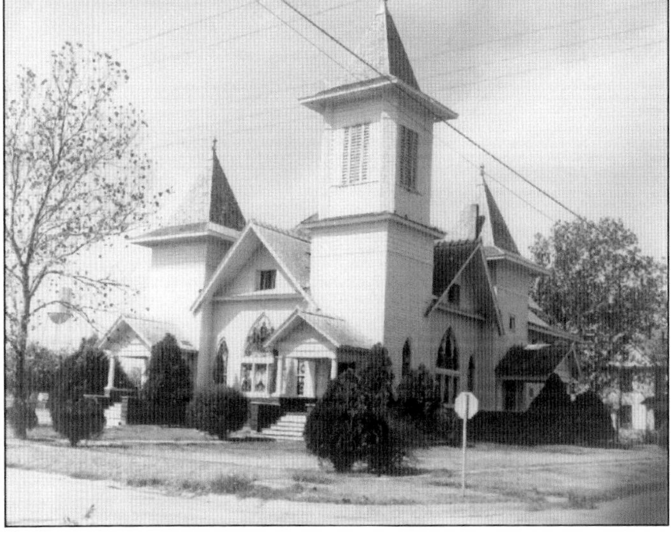

This c. 1950 image shows the First United Methodist Church painted white. The two large, visible stained-glass windows are part of the Gothic architecture and feature Bernhard Plockhorst's "The Good Shepherd" and Rembrandt's "The Resurrection"—these were given in memory of former pastors J. Marvin McKee and Dudley Brown. The other stained-glass windows in the church were given by members in memory of family and friends.

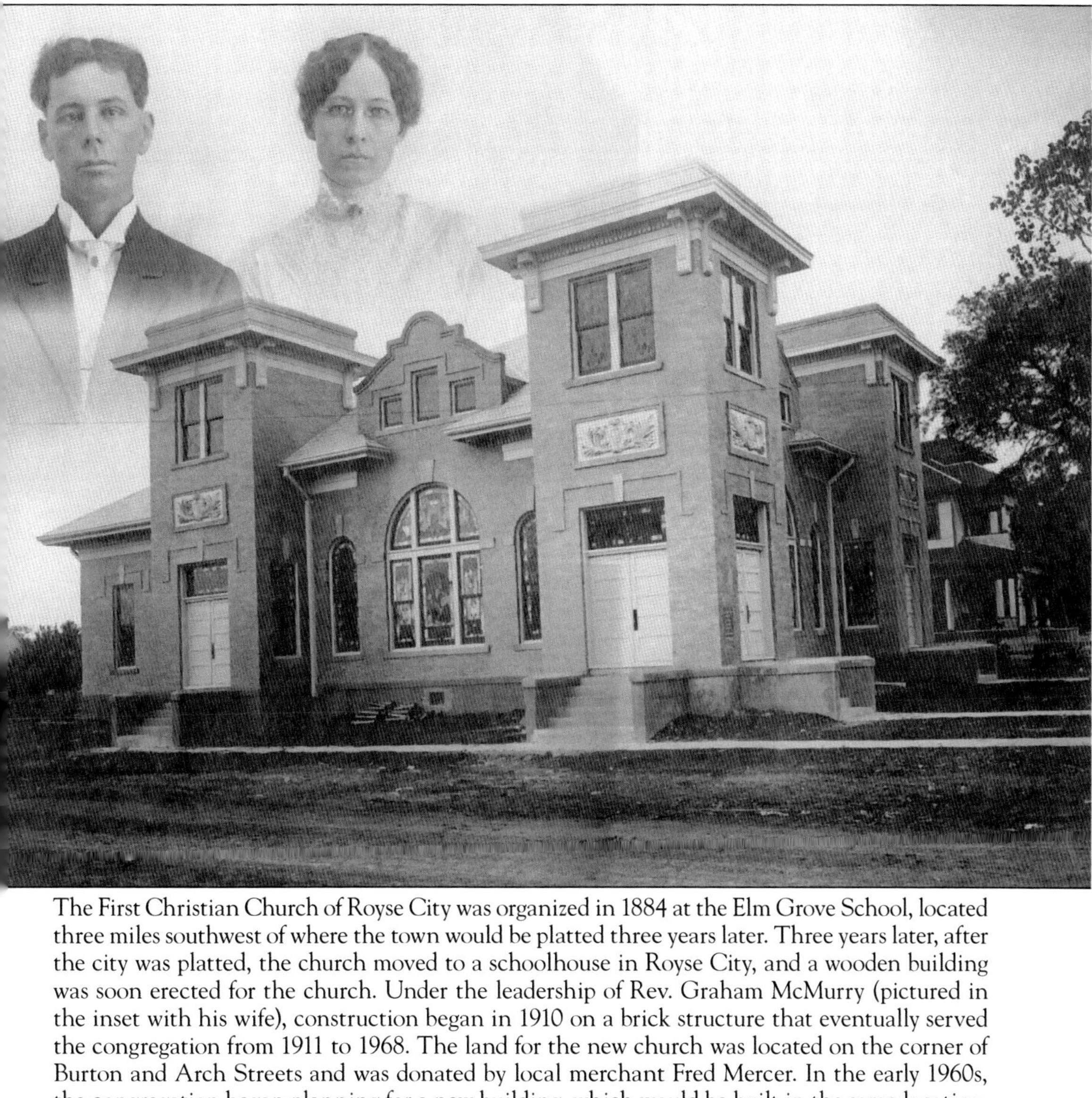

The First Christian Church of Royse City was organized in 1884 at the Elm Grove School, located three miles southwest of where the town would be platted three years later. Three years later, after the city was platted, the church moved to a schoolhouse in Royse City, and a wooden building was soon erected for the church. Under the leadership of Rev. Graham McMurry (pictured in the inset with his wife), construction began in 1910 on a brick structure that eventually served the congregation from 1911 to 1968. The land for the new church was located on the corner of Burton and Arch Streets and was donated by local merchant Fred Mercer. In the early 1960s, the congregation began planning for a new building, which would be built in the same location. The last service in the old building was held on June 2, 1968, after which it was soon demolished. The first service in the new building was held on February 9, 1969.

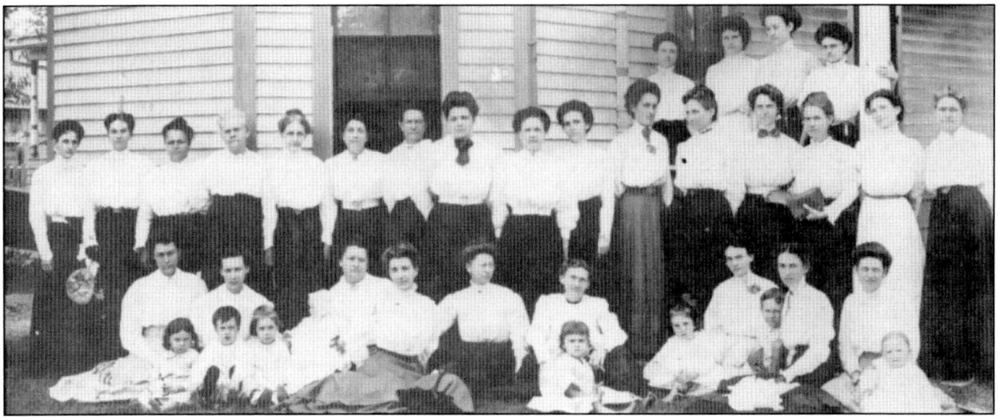

One of the earliest organizations formed at the First Christian Church was the Ladies Aid (pictured above in 1908). According to church history, members of the Ladies Aid would meet on Mondays for devotionals and Bible studies. They would also have quilting days, when they enjoyed social time during covered-dish luncheons while constructing quilts that were often given to the needy. The organization is now known as the Christian Women's Fellowship. Below is a postcard of the First Christian Church soon after its construction in 1911. The stained-glass windows that adorn the church were given in honor of family members and friends. The Miller home is partially visible at right.

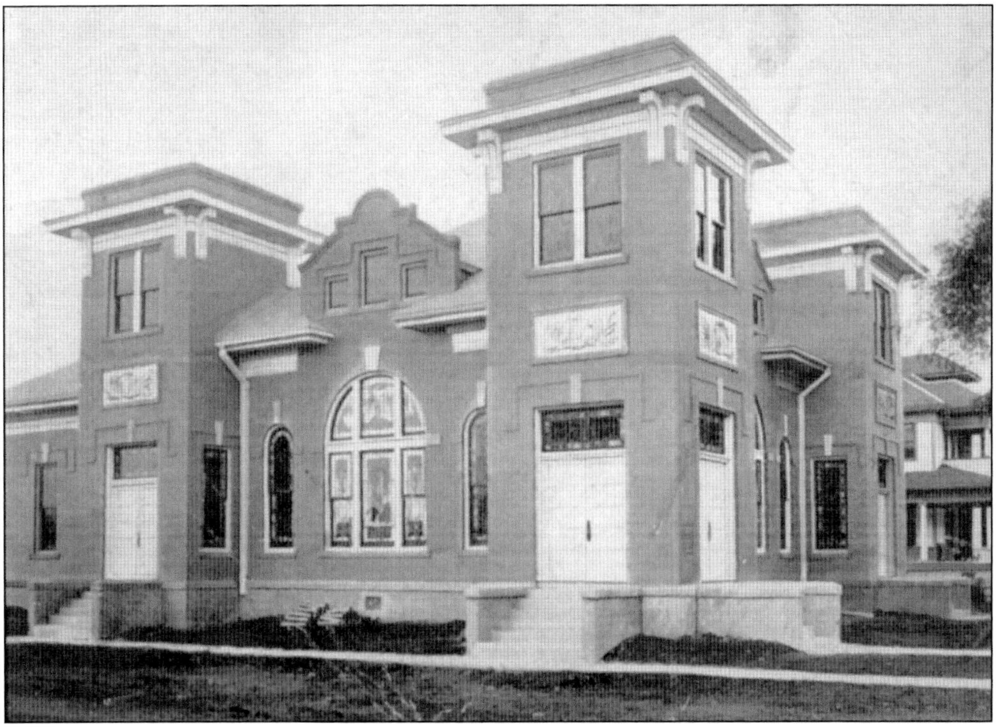

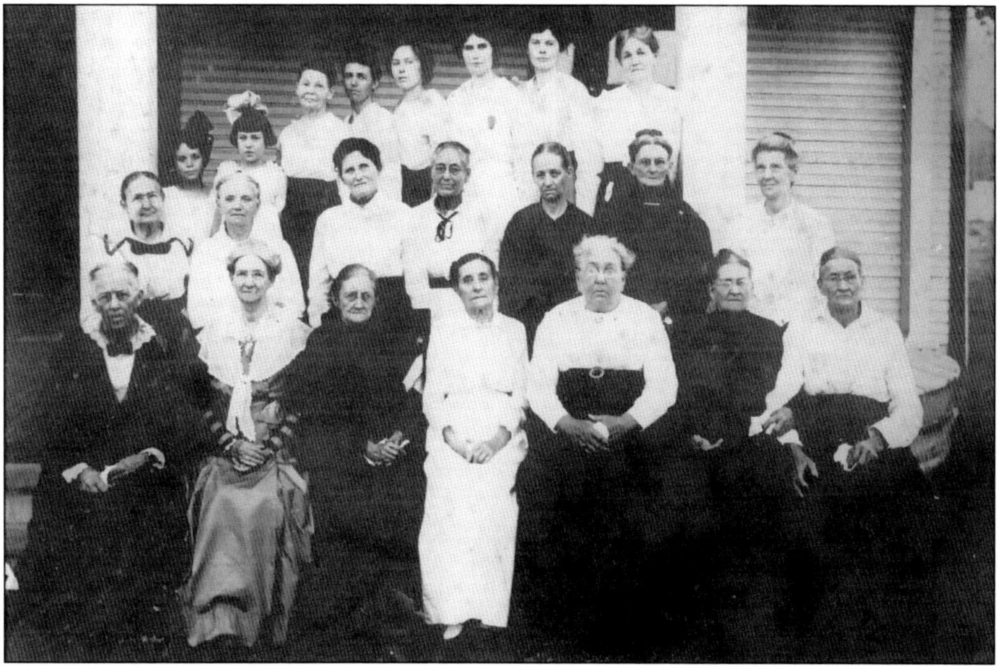

The First Christian Church Ladies Aid is pictured above in the early 1900s and below in 1937. From left to right in the photograph below are: (first row) Stewart Loftis, Bonnie (Crowell) Gentry, Dale Dowell, Alta (Walker) Banks, Joy Banks, Mrs. Campbell, Kenneth Noel, and Tommye Louise Dowell; (second row) Pearl Bounds, Daisy Blair, Mrs. A.C. Pedigo, Mrs. V.B. Harris, Joe Loftis, Mrs. Joe Dowell, Mrs. Joe Morgan, Buck Green, Mrs. S E. Cooper, and Mrs. A. Cavitt; (third row) Mrs. Buck, Cordie (Walker) Green, Nell (Dowell) Loftis, Rob (Benbrook) Dowell, Orpha (Bailey) Cross, Mrs. Tom J. Bailey, president Mr. Lamberson, Pearl Walker, Mae Anderson, and Jessie Noel.

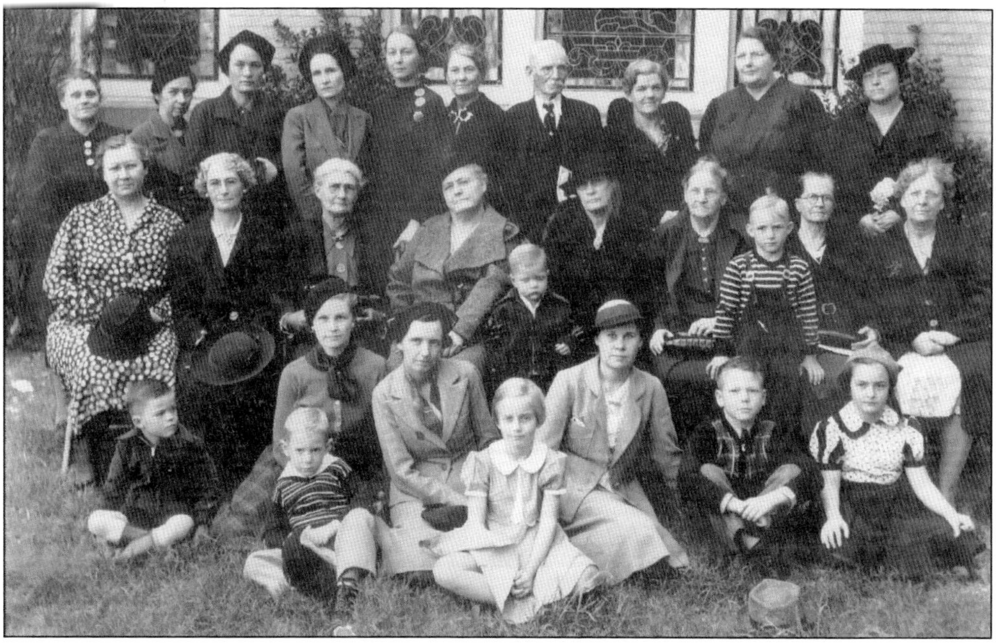

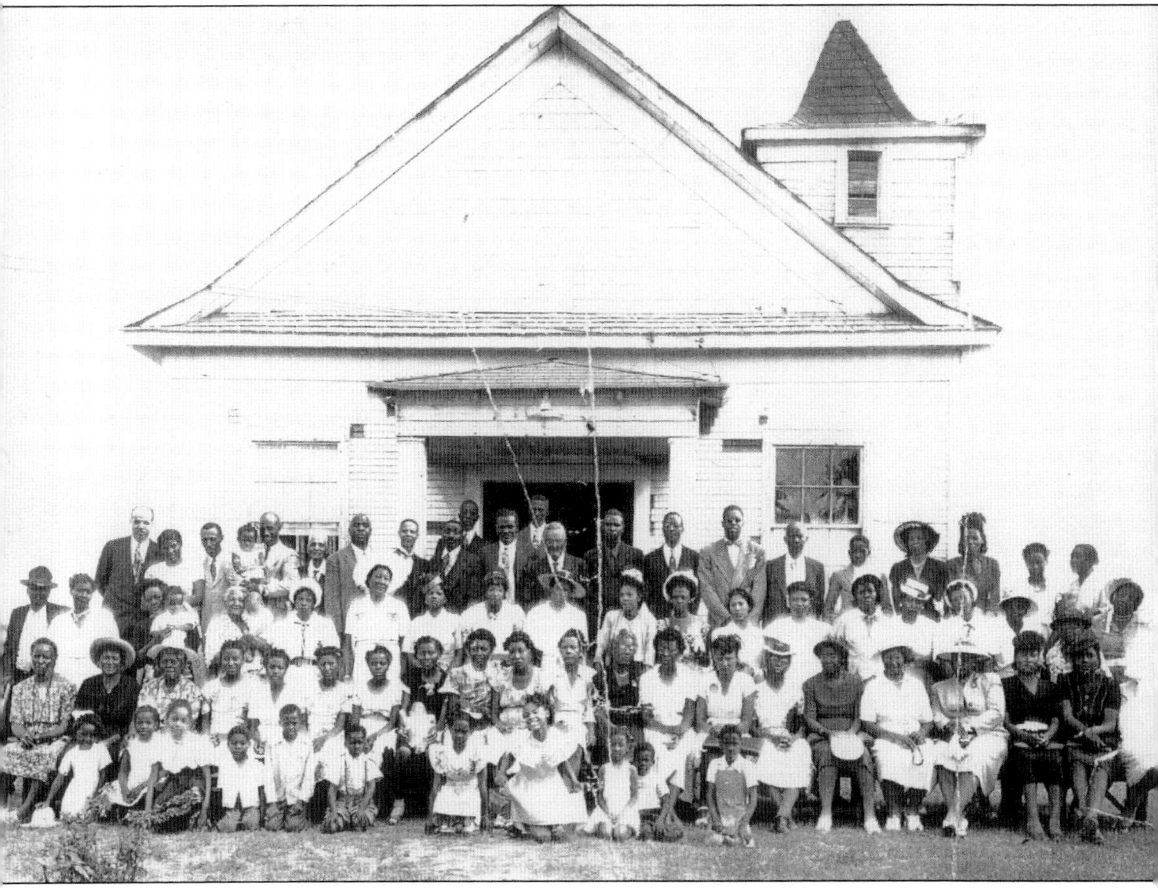

According to a written church history, it was 1859 when a group of former slaves joined together in worship near Royse City. Their first "church" was a brush arbor. In 1906, Lewis Rice donated land for the construction of a church, and the church's name was changed from a name that has been lost to history to New Hope Baptist. Several years passed before the congregation was able to build, but in 1914, 25 members built the frame structure that would serve the congregation as a house of worship until February 1953, when it was demolished to make room for a new building. The doors of the new church opened in May 1953. A complete remodel of this building was completed in 1974, followed by construction of a new building in 1994, which still serves the congregation. Here, members of the New Hope Baptist Church are pictured front of the first church building.

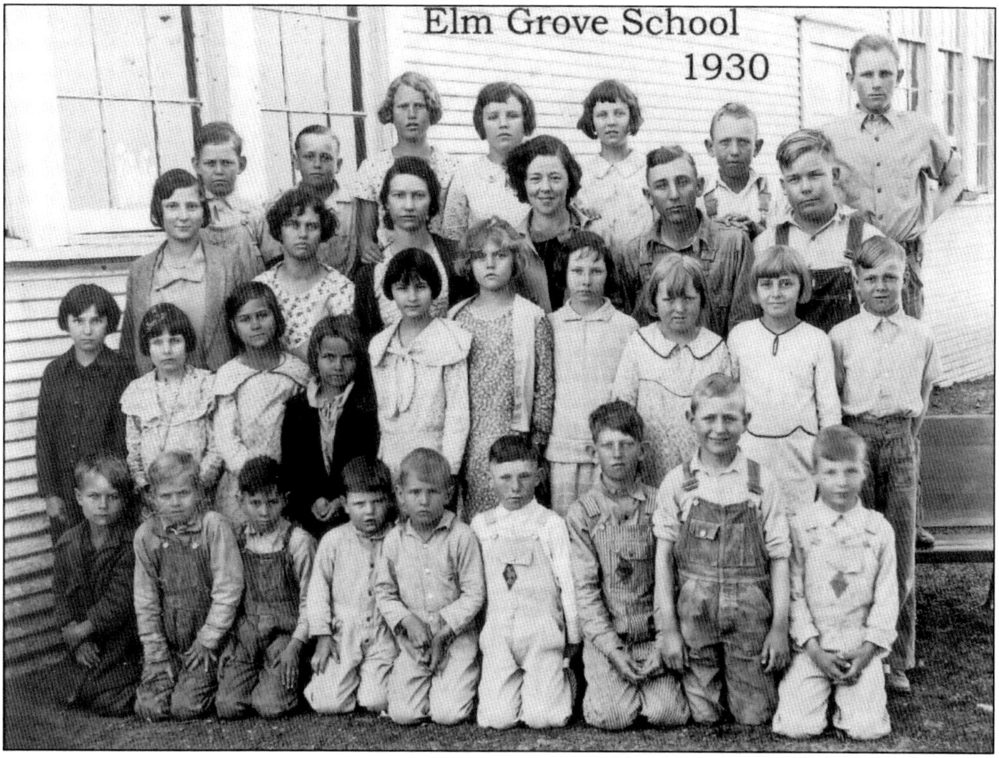

Around the start of the 20th century, there were more than 60 country schools throughout Rockwall County. These were usually one-room schoolhouses, located three to four miles apart, with one teacher instructing all grades. In 1894, a printed list of area schools included the Royse City School as part of School Community No. 5, which included only two schools—Elm Grove (pictured above in 1930) and Royse City (pictured below around 1900). The first formal mention of a Royse City school district was in 1897, when it was noted in a list of 18 school districts in Rockwall County as Royse City Common School District No. 18.

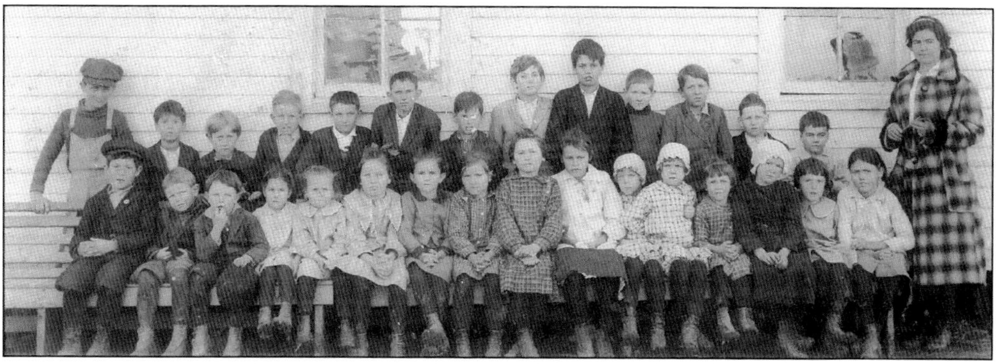

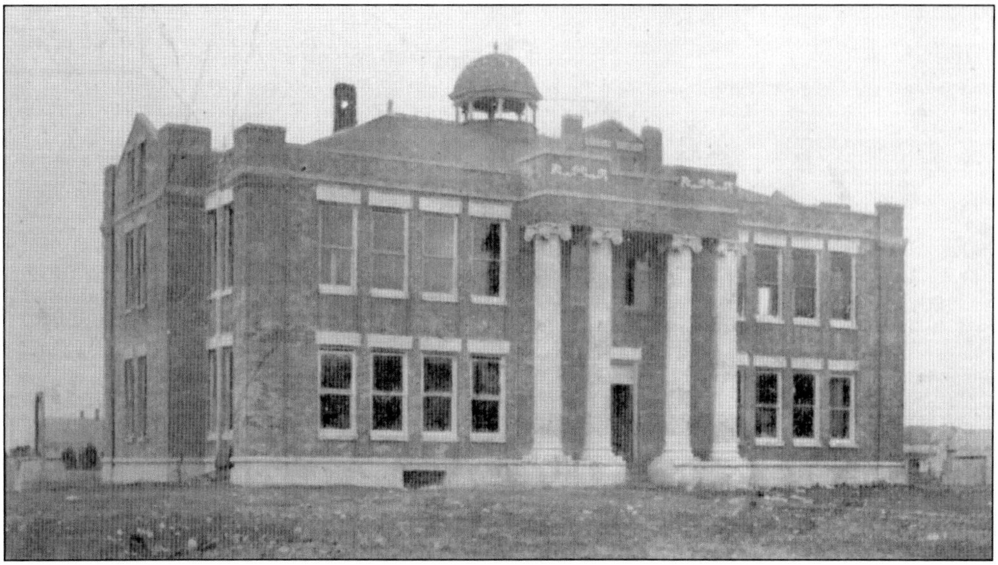

Royse City Common School District No. 18 was organized into an independent school district in the late 1800s. In 1906, Royse City's first brick school building (above) was constructed south of the railroad. By 1913, the foundation on this building had become unstable, and it was deemed unsafe. The school building was demolished, and students were temporarily housed in the upstairs part of the Woodmen of the World building. Some classes were even held in tents while the town waited for the new school to be completed. In 1916, a new, three-story brick building opened. Below is a photograph of the 1916 school that was printed in the 1938 *Bulldog* annual.

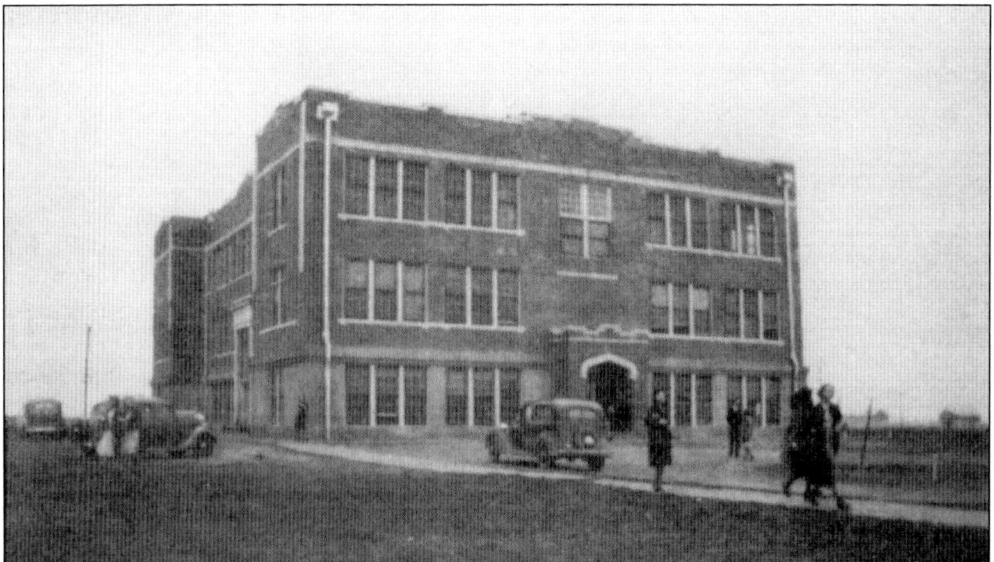

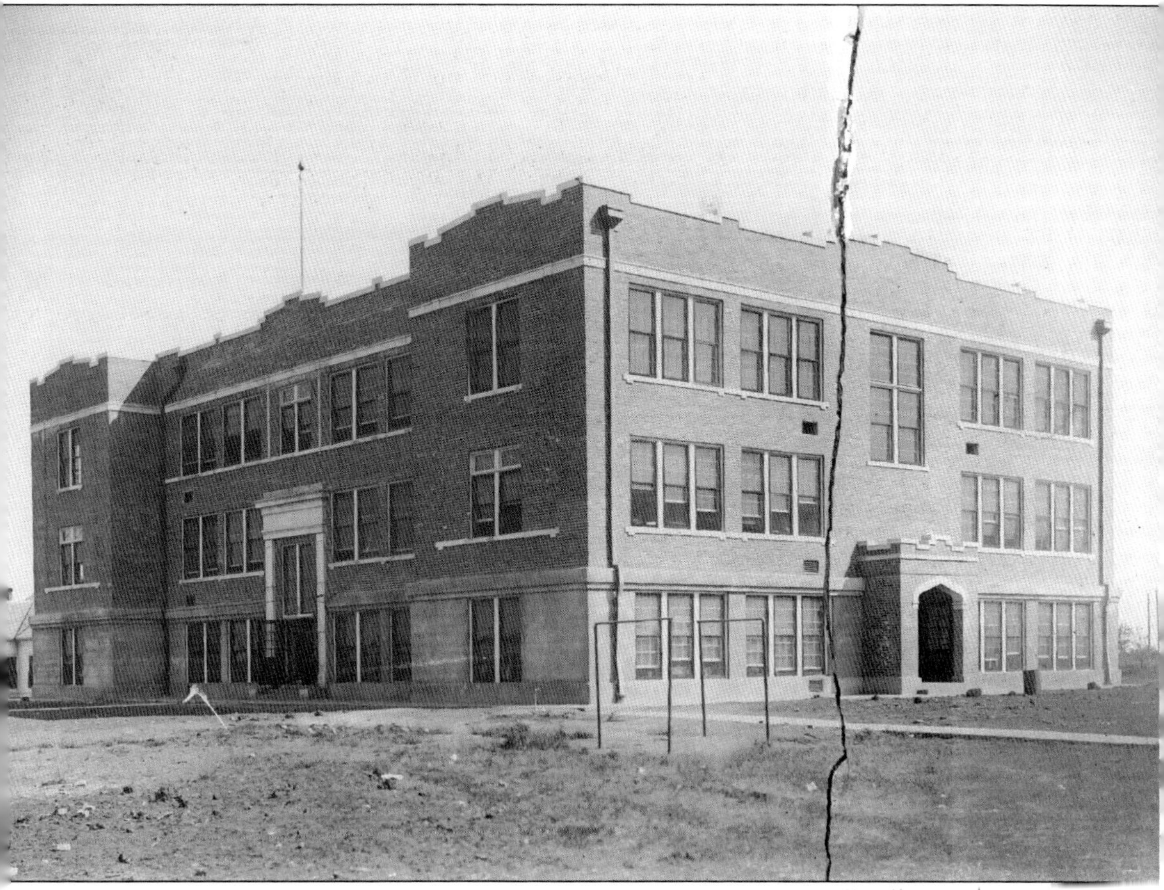

The 1916 Royse City Public School contained grades one through six on the first floor and grades seven through twelve on the second floor. The auditorium occupied most of the third floor, and music classes were held at the back of the stage. A separate wooden building housed a gymnasium. Martha Pullen was a teacher in this building from 1938 to 1943, and started out making a monthly salary of $80 over a nine-month term. Pullen had also taught in the country schools, including Elm Grove and Blackland, and in a written history, she described the amenities of the city school: "Here we had the conveniences of buses, lunchroom, janitorial services, indoor toilets, drinking fountains, and only one grade per elementary teacher." In her fifth year of teaching at Royse City, Pullen's salary increased to $90 per month. When she came to the Royse City Public School in 1938, the entire elementary faculty consisted of Martha Pullen, Ethel Hellams, Leila Price, Bonnie Gentry, Phoebe Hall, and Anita Scott.

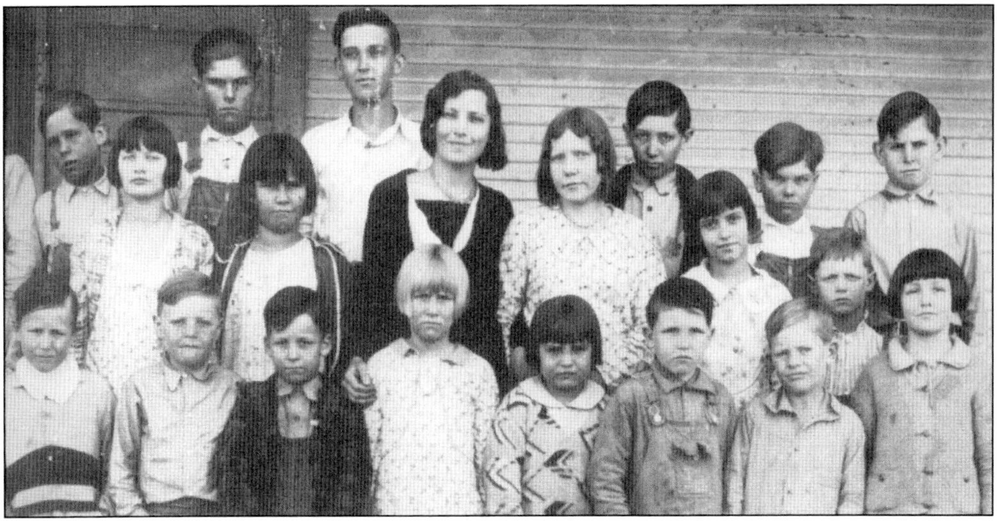

In the early part of the 1900s, the outlying one-room county schools enjoyed healthy levels of student enrollment. The school term often started in October, after most of the cotton had been picked. Students and teachers brought lunches to school and got their water from a well. The schools had only outdoor bathrooms and no electric lights, and a wood stove provided heat. One of the trustees would build a fire in the morning, and the teacher and students kept it going during the day. On the last day of school, there was usually a picnic for all families. Above, Martha Pullen (center) is pictured in 1930 with her students at the Blackland School. Below are students and teachers at the Elm Grove School.

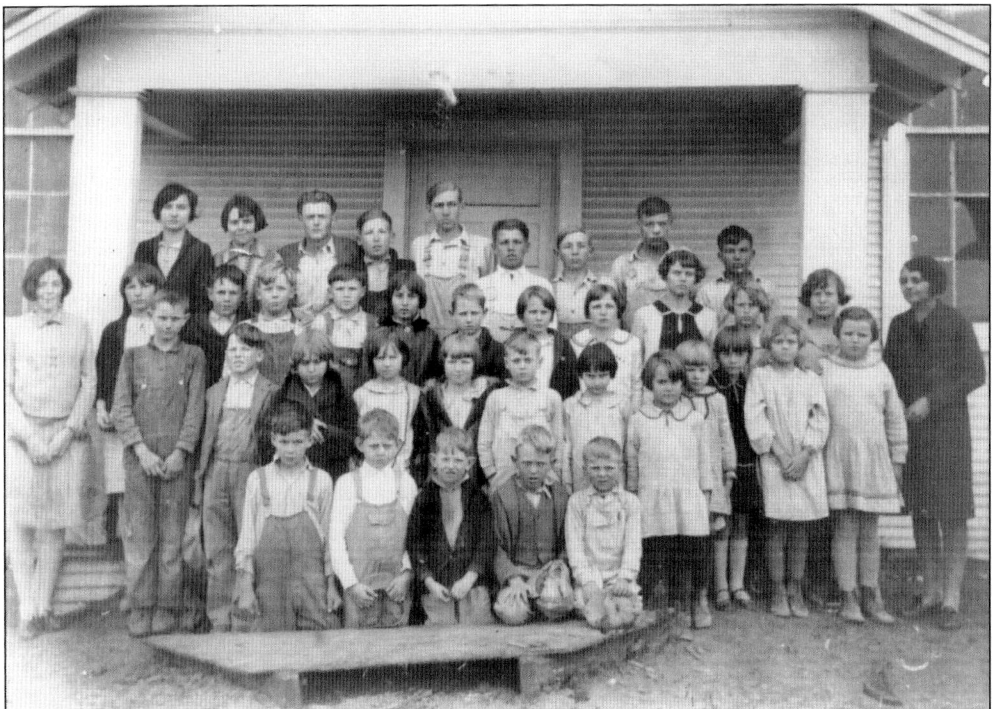

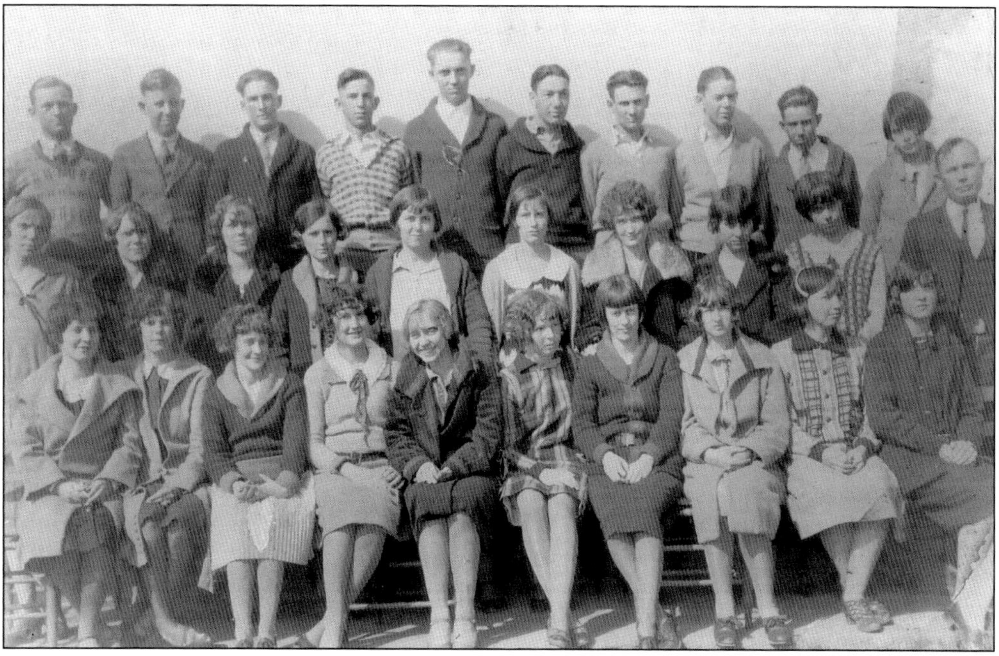

The student population at Royse City High School fluctuated greatly in the early part of the 1900s. In 1918, the high school had 12 graduates (six boys and six girls). The next decades saw ranges from a low of only seven graduates (three boys and four girls) in 1919 to a high of 30 graduates (11 boys and 19 girls) in 1938. In 1940, the number of graduates was 23 (13 boys and 10 girls). Above is the 1925 senior class from Royse City High School. Below, the 1938 graduates strike studious poses in their caps and gowns.

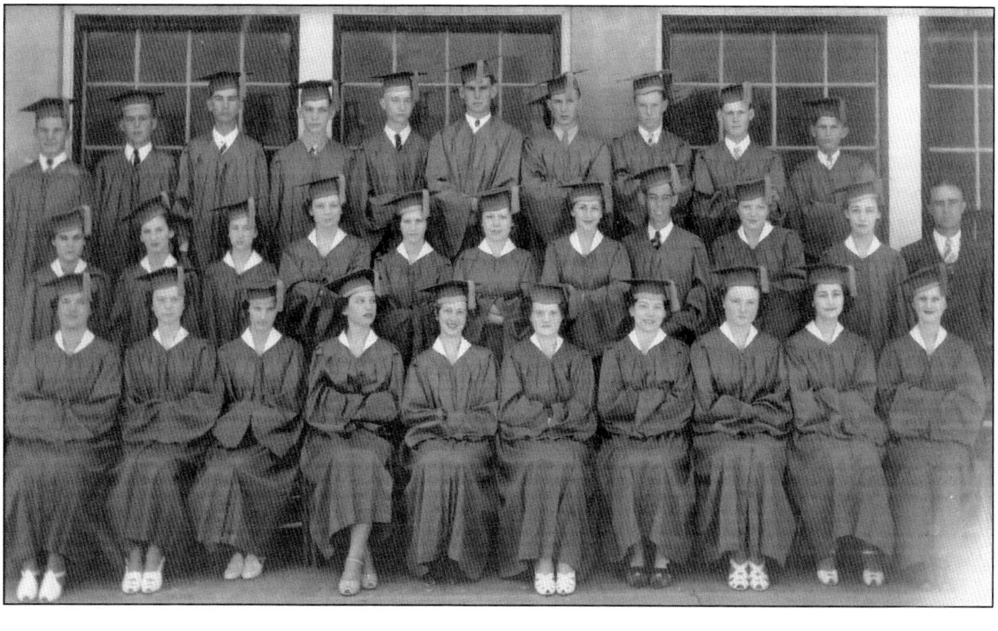

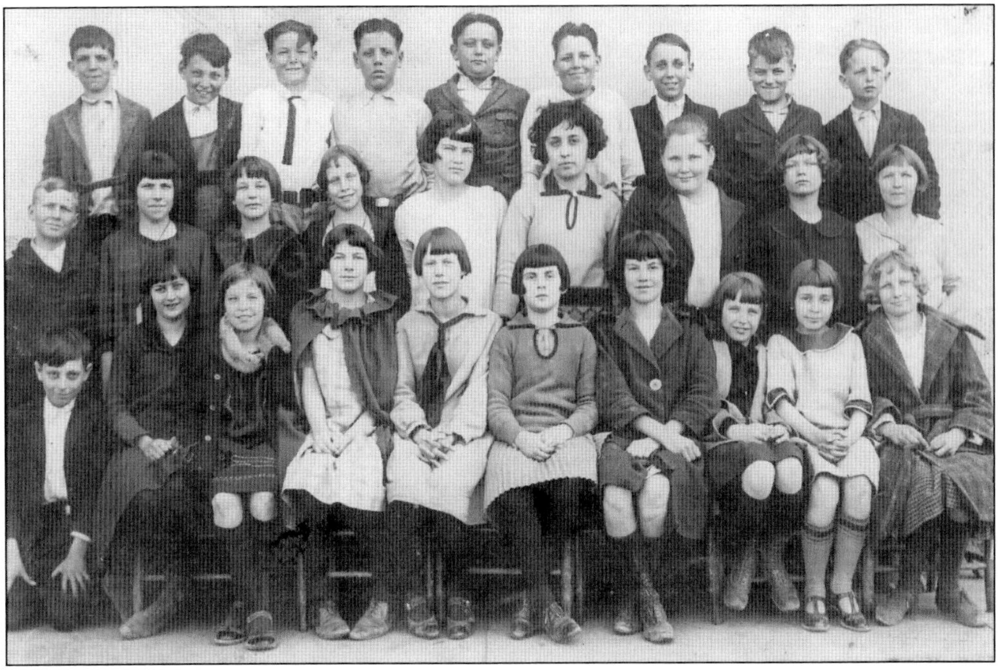

Throughout the 1930s and 1940s, many of the country schools were consolidated into the Royse City Independent School District (RCISD). These included Burrow, Munson, Union Valley, Sabine, Graham Point, Blockdale, Blackland, Elm Grove, and part of Fate. Transportation had become easier, especially after the addition of a school bus in 1937. John Crenshaw, a 17-year-old student at Royse City Public School, owned and operated the first school bus in Rockwall County for the RCISD. He altered a 1928 Ford Model A Coupe and transported students from Elm Grove and Mt. Zion. The bus charge—$2 per student—was paid by Rockwall County. A fifth-grade class from the 1930s is pictured above. Below, a 1930s high school class poses in front of the school.

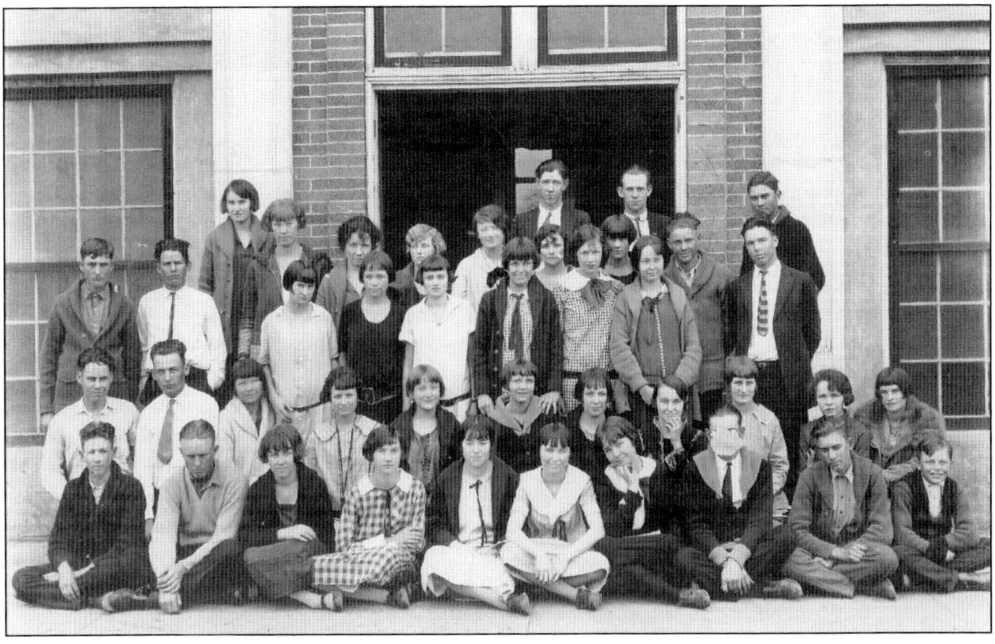

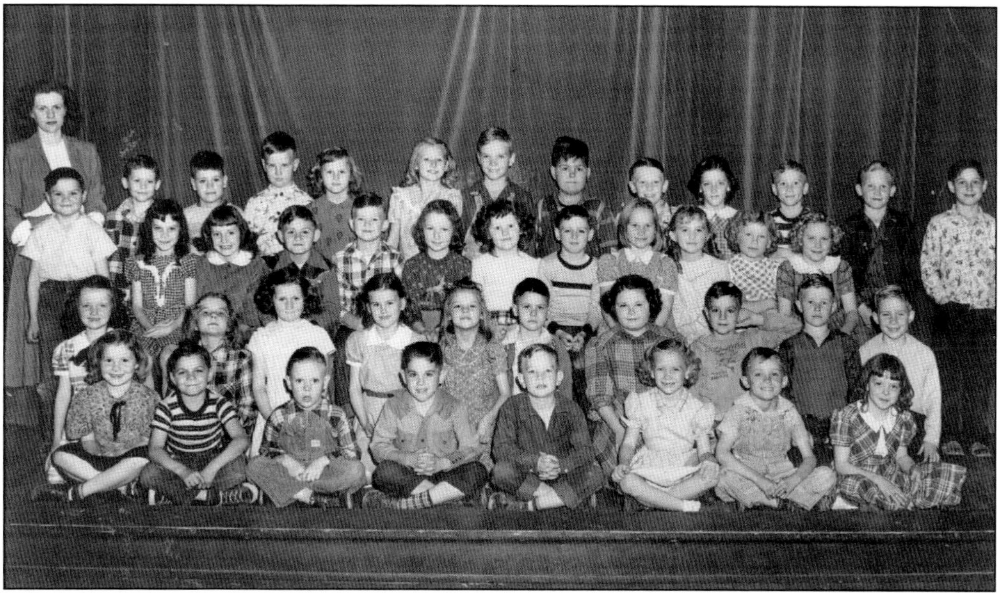

Throughout the 1930s, Royse City public schools added many amenities and strived to offer courses that would benefit the growing student population. A 1941 newspaper article notes that the high school "has continued to strive for efficiency and an increase in the number of affiliated credits." Junior business training, commercial law, and typewriting were added to the course schedule between 1934 and 1939. In the 1939–1940 school year, both homemaking and vocational agriculture were added. The 1948–1949 second-grade class at Royse City Elementary is pictured above. The 1950 senior class from Royse City High School is pictured below.

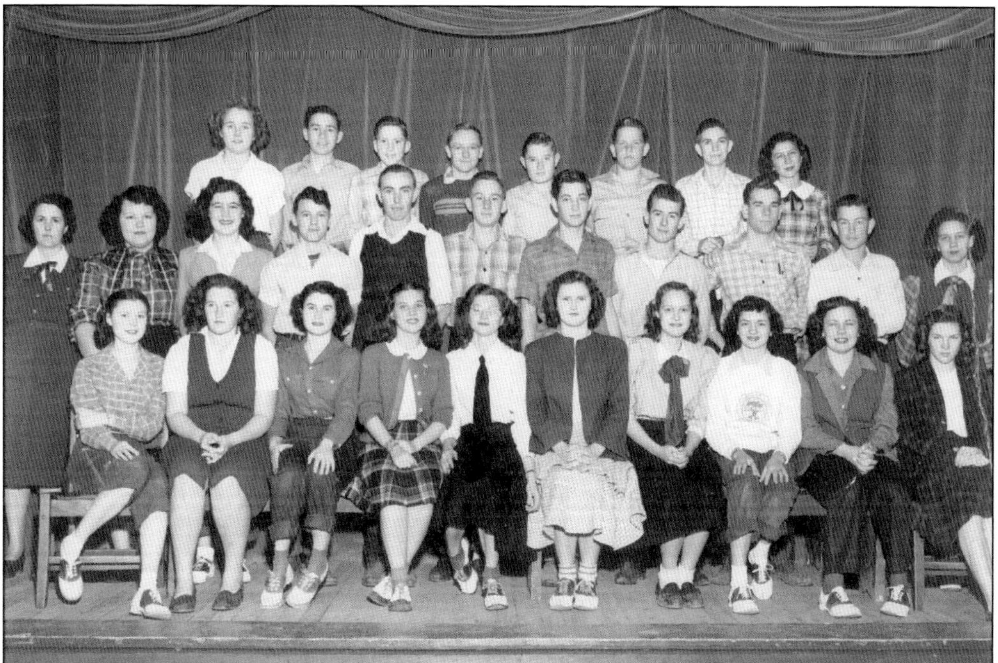

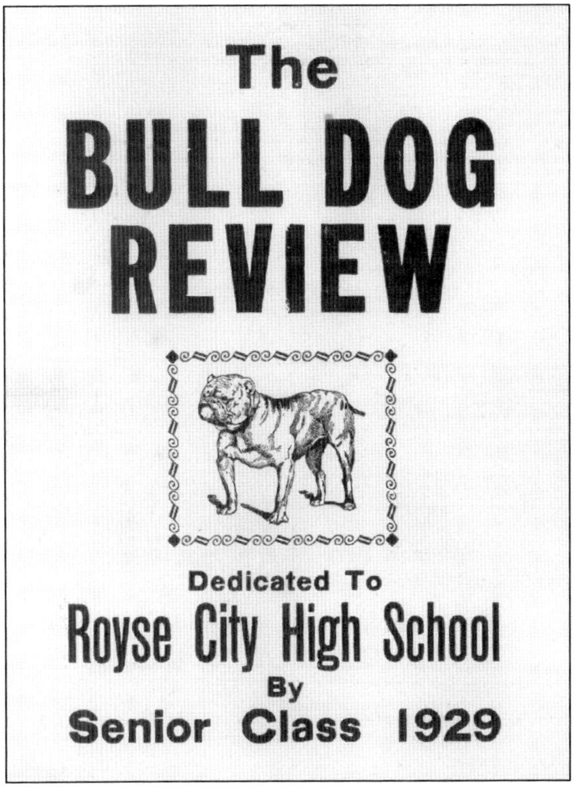

The
BULL DOG
REVIEW

Dedicated To
Royse City High School
By
Senior Class 1929

Royse City High School received enormous support from the business community as shown in this 1929 publication, *The Bull Dog Review.* In addition to articles, this eight-page newspaper contains advertisements from the First National Bank, Mills & White Sanitary Meat Market, J.V. Wood & Bro. Lumber, Houser Drug Company, Burton Motor Company, Lyon Gray Lumber Company, and the Royse City Ice Plant.

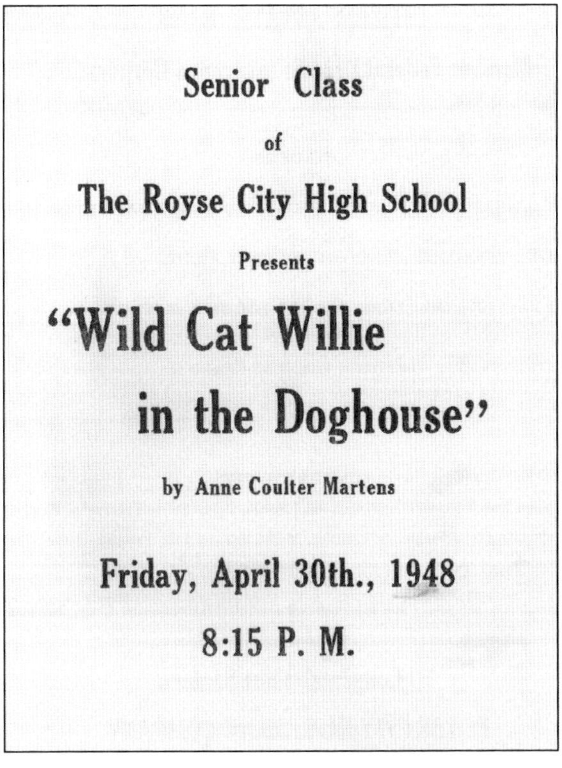

Senior Class
of
The Royse City High School
Presents
"Wild Cat Willie
in the Doghouse"
by Anne Coulter Martens

Friday, April 30th., 1948
8:15 P. M.

For many years, the senior play was a highlight of the school year. At right is the program cover of the 1948 senior class play, *Wild Cat Willie in the Doghouse.* The play was directed by Mrs. Ben Branch and starred Rodney Shaw as Wild Cat Willie, with supporting actors including Orvie Lee Cantrell, Buck Green, Joe Mae Lemmons, Truett Sledge, Bobby Pierce, Charlie Jo Nowlain, Johnny Shelton, Frances Loftis, Doris Lee Hall, and Helen Leinart.

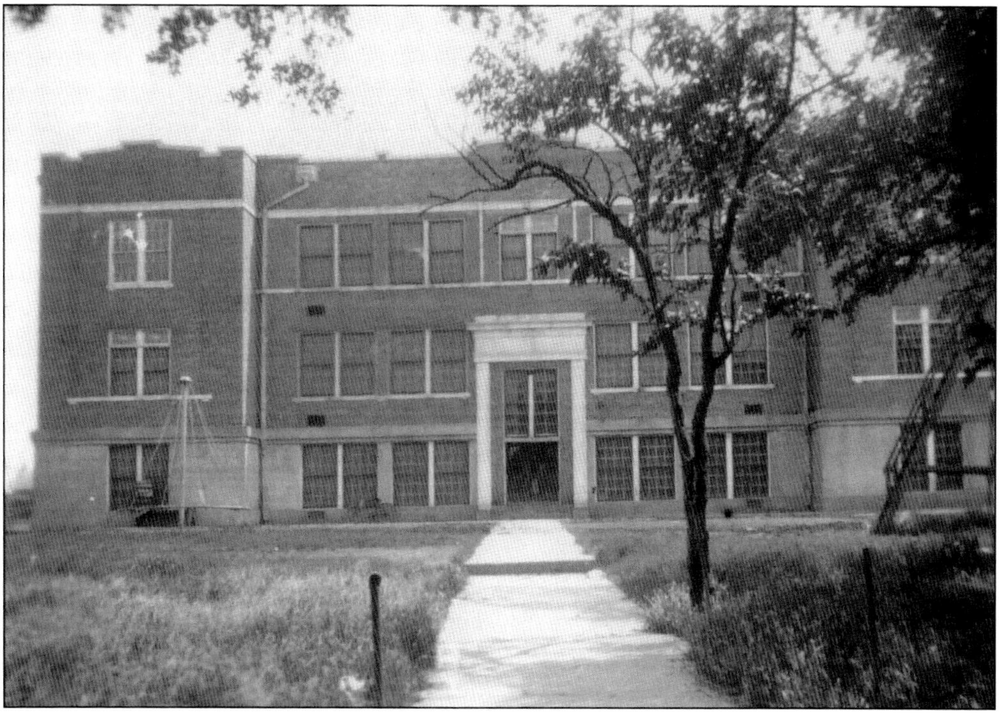

In 1953, the second and third floors of the 1916 school building (above) were declared unstable, and construction began on a new school just north of the old building. The basement portion of the 1916 building was used in the new building as the cafeteria, the band room, and the agricultural workshop. Below, the new Royse City High School is shown in the 1950s. This school was used until 1975, when a new building was constructed on FM 1777. The summer before students arrived at the new building, someone set the old school building on fire, resulting in the loss of irreplaceable trophies and awards that had not yet been transferred to the new school.

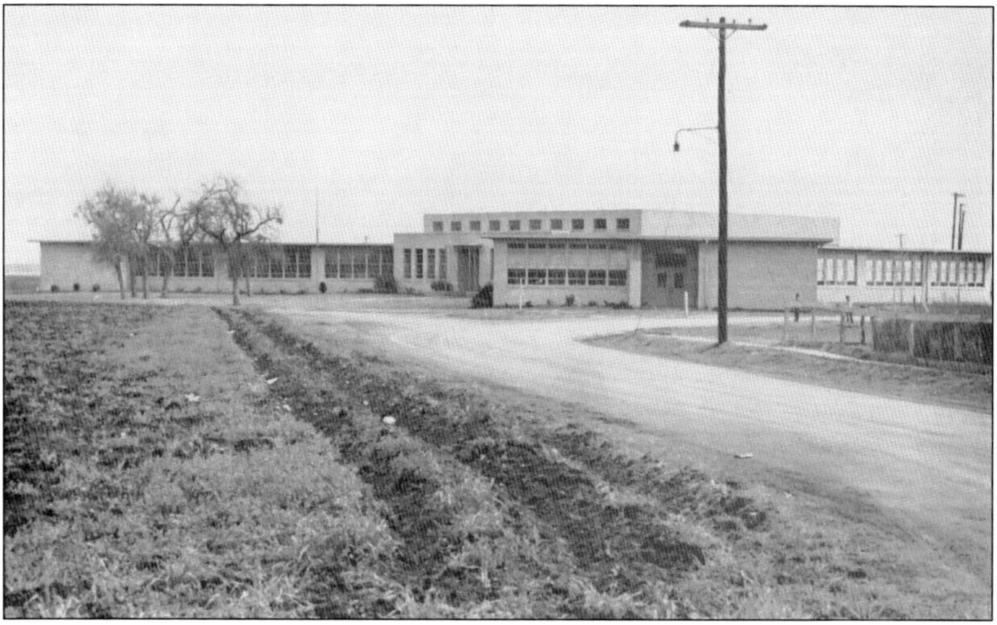

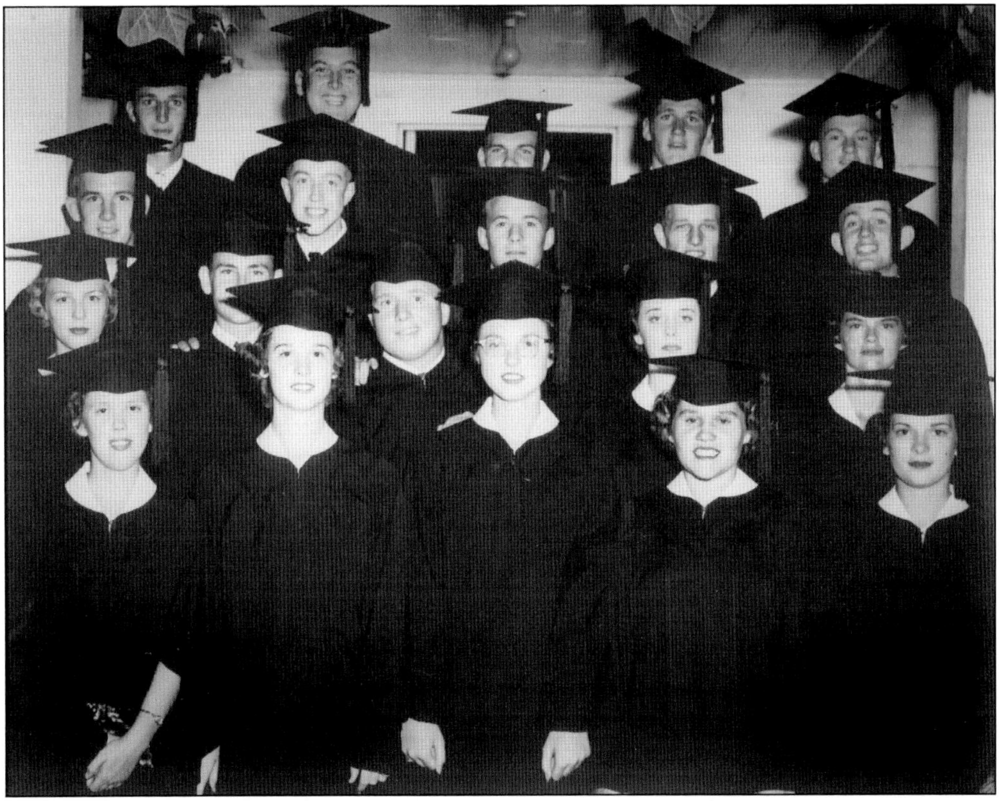

The 1955 graduating class at Royse City High School (pictured above) included a mere 20 students. The 2012 class, with approximately 200 graduates, had nearly 10 times as many. Today, RCISD educates more than 4,400 students at eight regular campuses and one alternative learning center. Below, a 1955 Royse City High School diploma belonging to James Cornelius denotes a May 27, 1955, graduation date and was signed by school board president R.S. Crowell, school board secretary Carl Edwards, principal Ted Jowers, and superintendent of schools M.L. Johnson. In the above photograph, Cornelius is second from right in the fourth row.

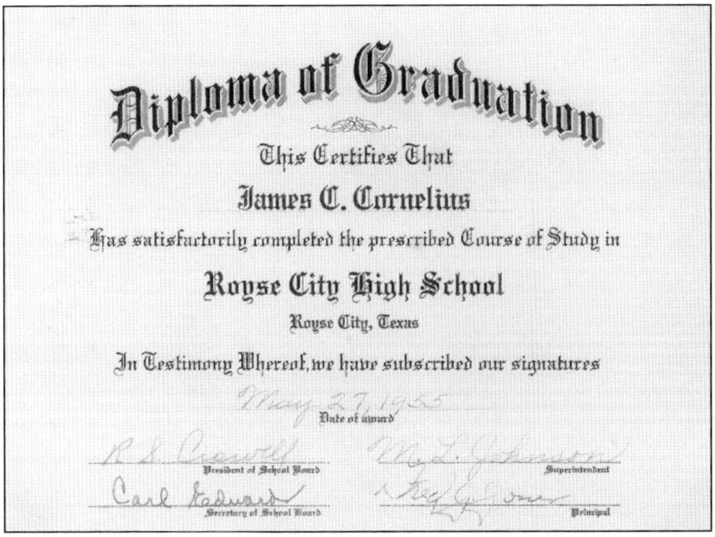

Diploma of Graduation

This Certifies That

James C. Cornelius

Has satisfactorily completed the prescribed Course of Study in

Royse City High School

Royse City, Texas

In Testimony Whereof, we have subscribed our signatures

May 27, 1955

Date of award

R. S. Crowell — President of School Board

M. L. Johnson — Superintendent

Carl Edwards — Secretary of School Board

Principal

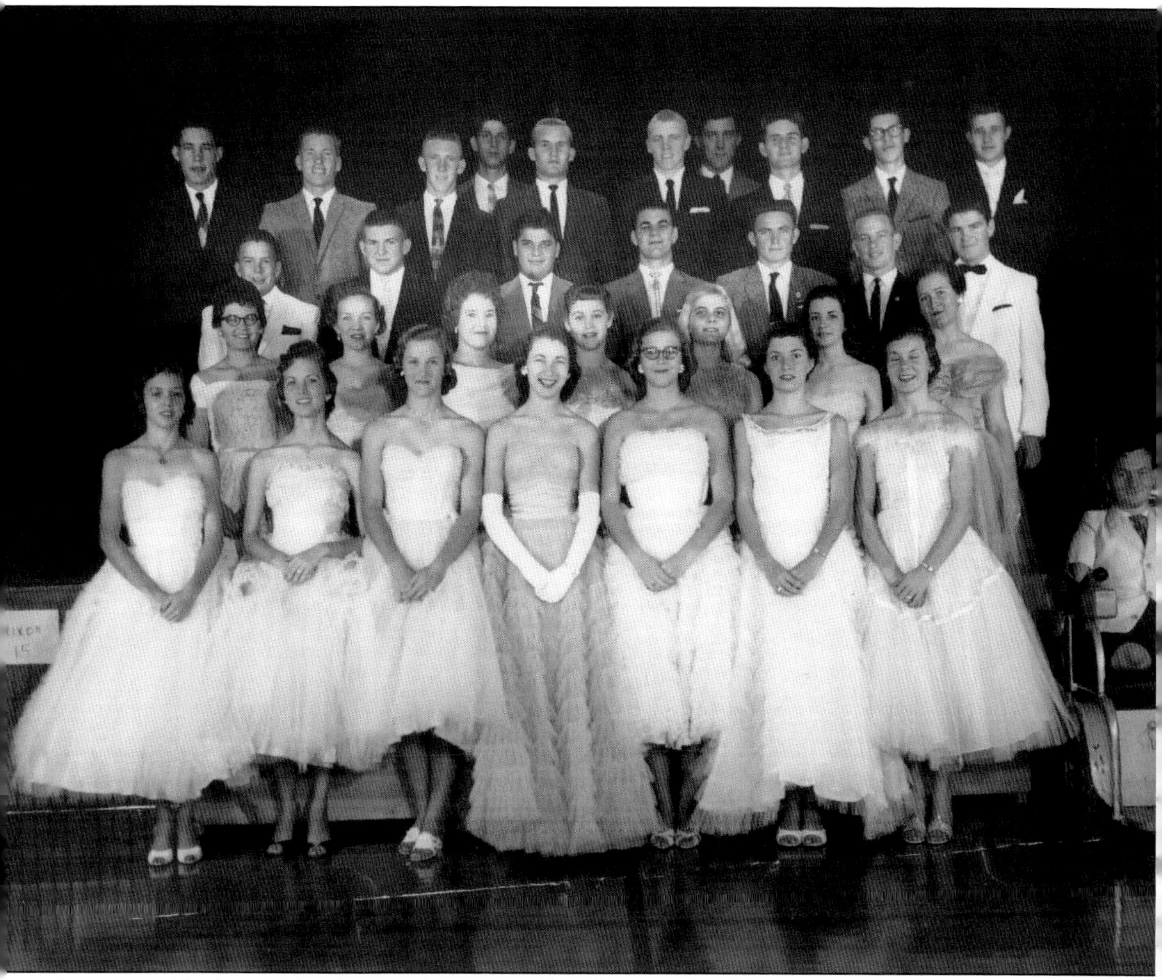

Strapless tulle dresses clearly were the rage in this photograph of the 1959 senior class of Royse City High School. Mass-production had made clothing more affordable, and families were able to buy modestly priced eveningwear inspired by designer fashions. This popular dress style featured a tight bodice, a small waist, and a flared skirt that exuded a soft, feminine style. Although white was the most popular color by far, tulle dresses could be found in other soft colors such as pink, blue, or yellow. Fashion historians credit the expansion of senior proms as the number-one reason that teenage girls became one of the main market segments for evening wear purchases in the 1950s. Although senior dances and proms were mentioned in high school yearbooks in the 1930s and 1940s, it was not until the postwar economic boom that proms expanded to become more elaborate, elegant events.

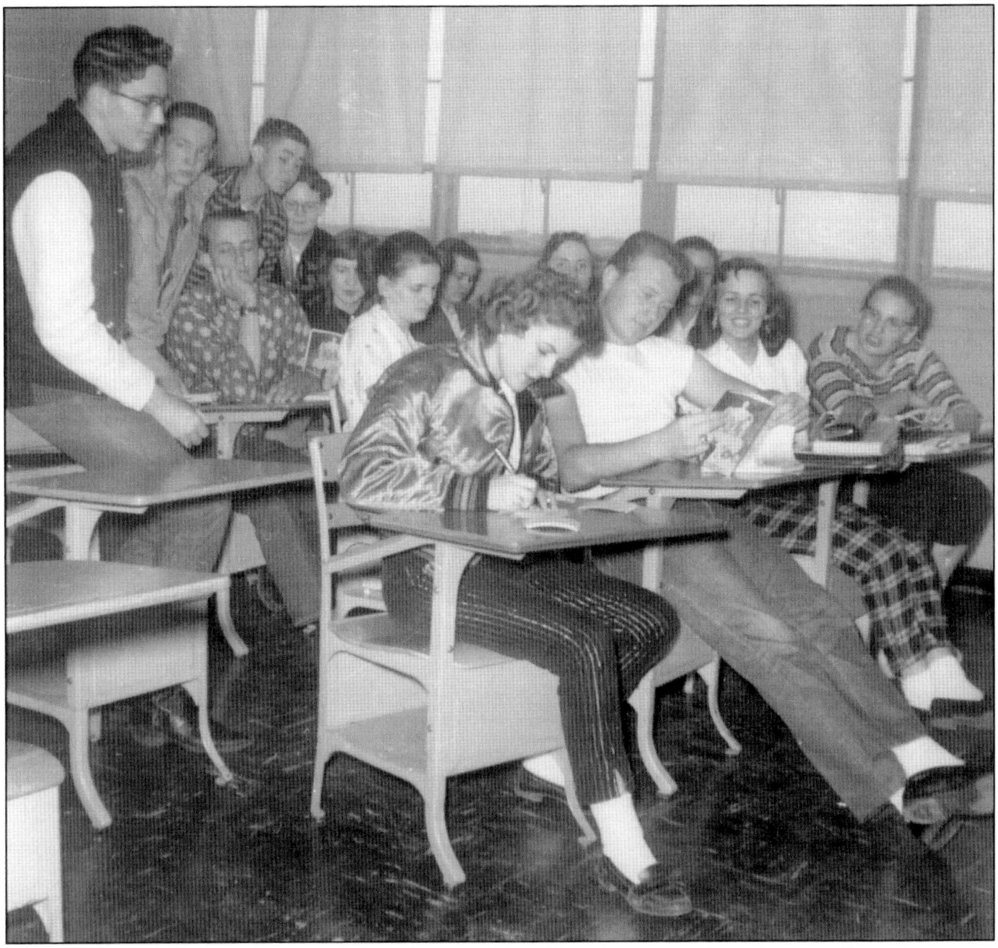

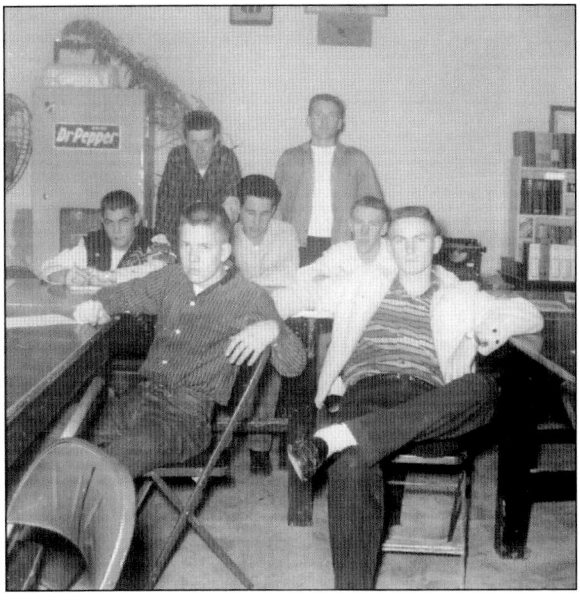

As in many other small towns around the country, the postwar 1950s were ideal times for Royse City. High school students in particular seemed to revel in the prosperity. Deloris Cross, a photographer for the Royse City High School (RCHS) yearbook, captured dozens of images of students enjoying the "Fabulous Fifties." "It was like growing up on the Happy Days TV program," said Cross (now Deloris Ballard). "There were only 220 in the Royse City school system, and with only 80 of us being in high school, we were just like brothers and sisters." Above and at left are Cross's photographs of RCHS classrooms in the 1950s.

Leather jackets, letter jackets, slicked-back hair, and penny loafers were all fashionable looks for young men in the 1950s. The leather jacket gained popularity after the 1953 release of *The Wild One*, starring Marlon Brando. These 1950s teenagers display the popular fashions of the day.

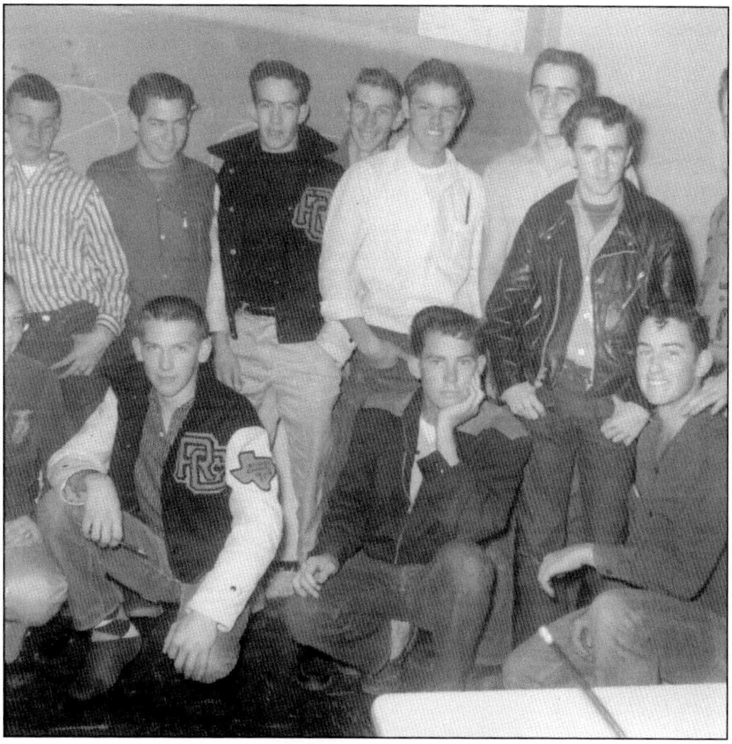

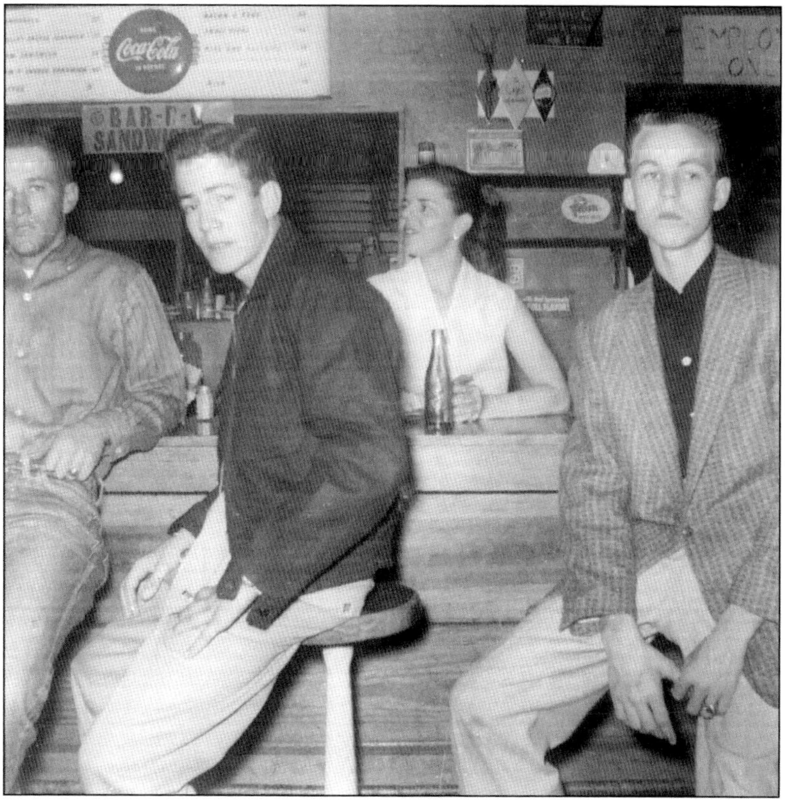

Malt shops and hamburger joints enjoyed a swift after-school business in the 1950s. In Royse City, Blakeway Drug was a popular spot to stop and have a malt or a soda on the way home from school. A local hamburger place also proved popular, as it had a jukebox and room for dancing. At left, a photograph taken by Deloris Cross captures the Royse City soda shop experience.

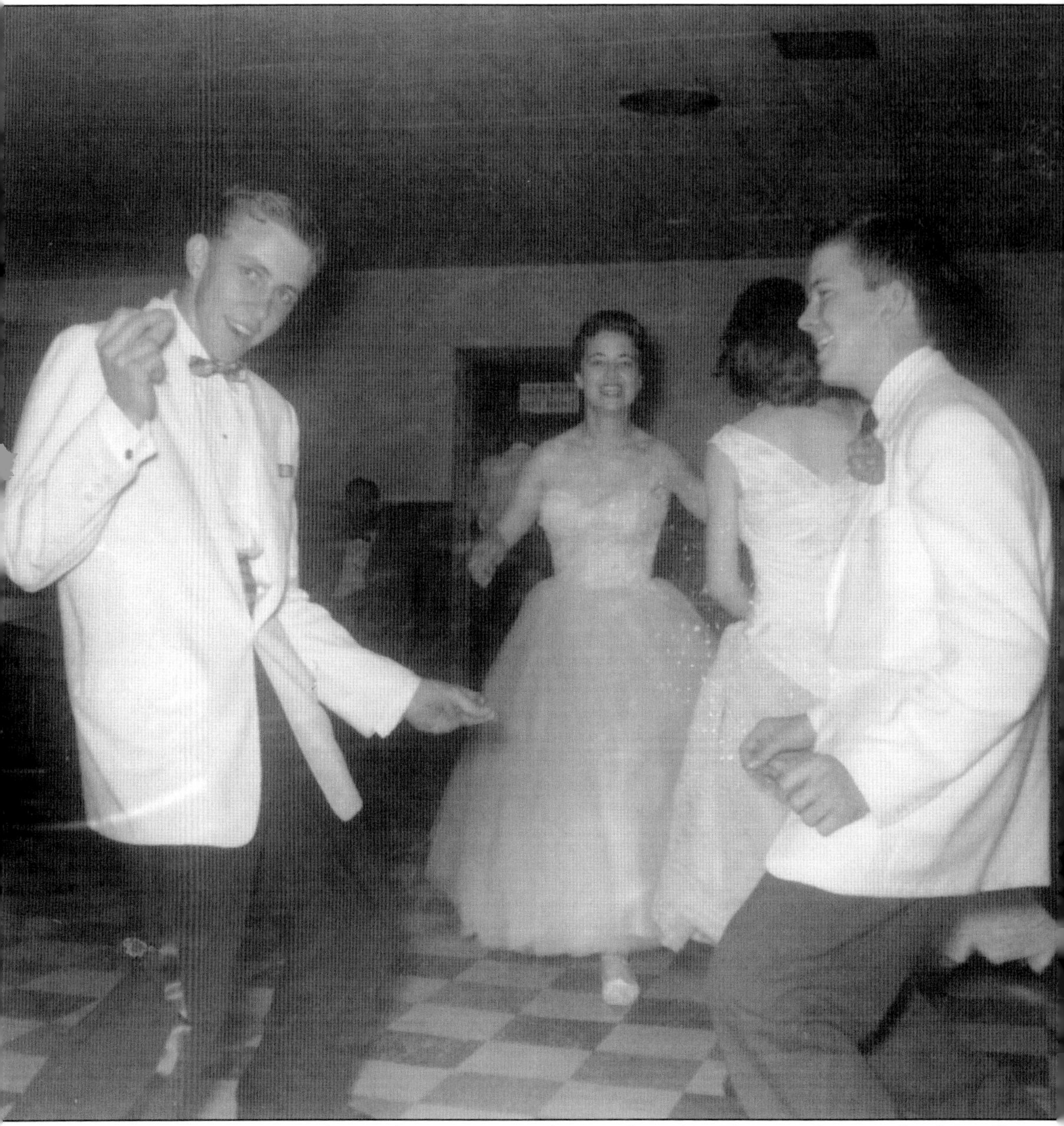

Dancing was an essential part of most teenagers' lives in the 1950s. The introduction of rock 'n roll into the culture had an effect on even the smallest of towns—including Royse City. Sock hops, a 1950s invention, were so named because students had to remove their shoes before dancing on slick, wooden gym floors. Proms, which were merely dances in prior decades, became elaborate affairs for which gentlemen wore tuxedos and ladies wore evening gowns. Prom locations also shifted from school gyms to hotel ballrooms, country clubs, or restaurants with dance floors. Dancing was also part of many teenagers' social lives during this period. Royse City High School students frequented a Dallas dance hall on Greenville Avenue called Louann's, which often showcased live music and catered to a family crowd. Here, Royse City High School students are all dressed up for the dance.

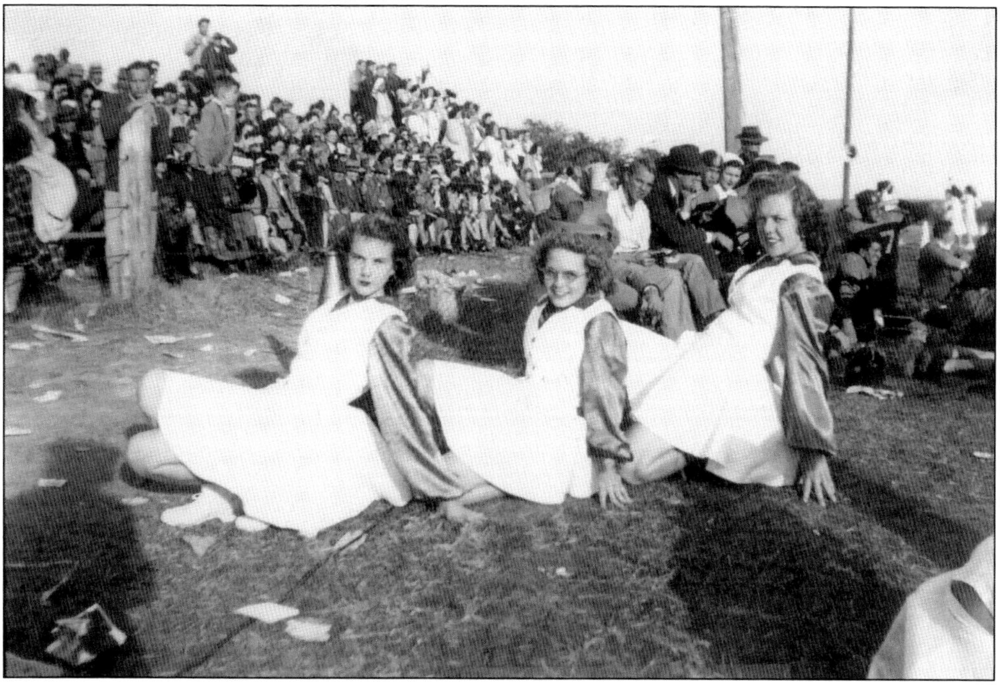

Starting in the 1930s, football became a central interest for both Royse City High School students and community supporters. Former teacher Anita Scott recalled, "When football first originated at school, the principal not only coached the boys, but played on the team as quarterback. Of course, there were no uniforms, no helmets, no padding." Between 1935 and 1940, a football field was obtained, fenced, lighted, and laid with sod. Around 1939, a band was organized, with a 1941 newspaper article noting that "a bass horn, a bass drum and seven uniforms were purchased recently." Majorettes and cheerleaders supported the teams, and Friday night football became a community event. Above, Royse City High School cheerleaders are pictured in the 1940s. Pictured below at the Royse City Stadium ("Home of the Bulldogs") are, from left to right, students Ann Rutherford, unidentified, Nanalee Smith, Fran Harvey, and Peggy Van Cleave.

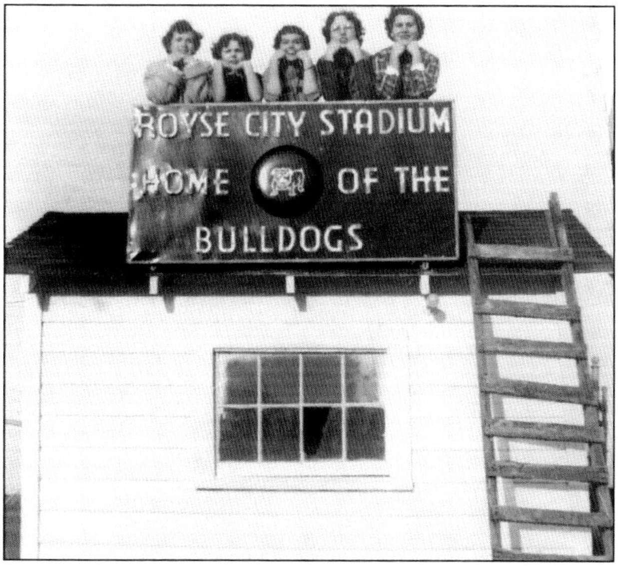

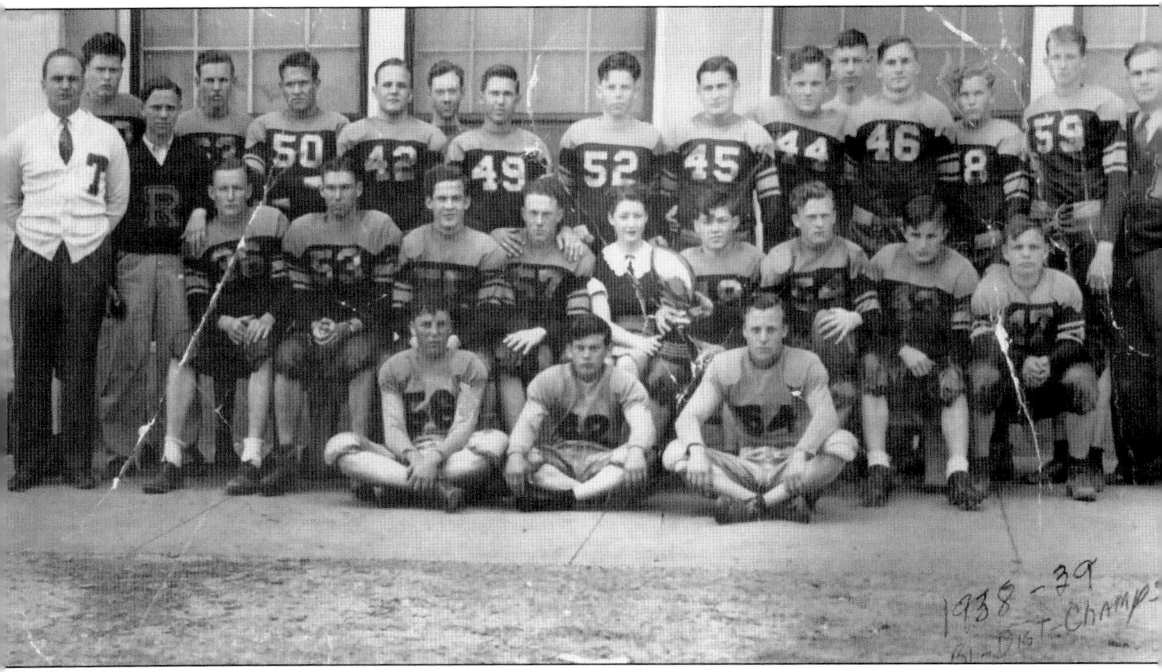

The University Interscholastic League (UIL) was formed in 1913 to oversee and coordinate extracurricular academic, athletic, and music contests. In 1920, the UIL began sanctioning playoff games for Texas high school football. As football increased in popularity around the state, so did the desire to secure a playoff berth. According to state football statistics, as of 2011, Royse City High School has made it to the playoffs 28 times, with the team's first appearance being in 1930. During the 1930s, Royse City was considered a "Class B" team, which had no state championship, but did have bi-district and regional titles. Above, the 1938 Bi-District Championship football team shows off their trophy after beating Leonard. The winning score was 92-0. The RCHS Bulldogs did not earn another playoff spot until 1943, but made seven playoff showings in the 1950s.

The BULLDOG

OUR AIM: "SUCCESS" OUR HOPE: "TO WIN"

Volume 1 Tuesday, Septem ber 22nd, 1953 No. 1

Bulldogs Smother Yellowjackets 20 to 6

BON-FIRE GIVES BOYS CONFIDENCE

Much school spirit was shown at the bon-fire Thursday night before the Rockwall game. The enthusiastic crowd was led in several yells by two of our capable cheer leaders, Deanna Wester and Nan McDaniels. We are sorry to report that Joy and Peggy could not attend.

Afterwards the football boys proceeded to the football field for a very thorough workout by Coach Drennan. The pep-rally proceeded to the football field to where they watched the work-out from start to end.

We missed seeing many of the students faces at the bon-fire. Next time let's all go out of our way to back up the Bulldogs. Remember they're working for our school so lets do our part too. Back the Bulldogs! ! !

WELCOME

We wish to welcome to Royse City High Schools our two new faculty members, Mr. Fred Jones and Mr. Ralph Beck.

Mr. Jones, who is filling the place of principal, is also teaching the courses in science. Mr. Jones comes to Royse from Pittsburg, Texas.

Mr. Beck, who is our capable band director, also teaches world history. Mr. Beck comes to us from Dallas.

Once again we say welcome to R. C. H. S.

Pat Nowlain had a job in Dallas and was living with a friend. Bobby asked her how he could get to her house and Pat gave these directions: "It's 81 East 19th Street. You press the button with your elbow, you go inside and you'll see my name on the mailbox—then you press the button with your elbow.

"When you reach my door you press that button with your elbow and . . . "

"Buttons with my elbow?" asked Bobby.

"Well for the love of Mike," said Pat, "You're not coming up empty handed are you?"

ROYSE CITY WINS OPENER

The Bulldogs took their first opening game against Plano Friday night, Sept. 11. It was the Bulldogs all the way. Royse City received and went down inside Plano's 40 but Plano took possession of the ball there. They couldn't do a n y t h i n g either. In the second quarter, Jerrell Shaw ran over for a touch down from the nine. Bobby Patterson's try for the point was blocked. At the half Royse City was ahead by 6 to 0.

The second half was filled with excitement when Shaw again went over from the seven yard line. The final score was 13 to 0.

The stars on offense were Shaw, Clark, Cook, Marcus James. The defense was sparked by Burks, Clark and Coleman.

PEP RALLY

The entire high school assembled in the high school auditorium Friday afternoon for the best and most important pep rally of the season. The football squad filled in the front rows while the cheer leaders led the student body in several peppy yells.

Mr. Johnson gave the "Bulldogs" a great pep talk. Coach Drennan aroused the enthusiasm of the entire school with a talk and report on both the Rockwall and Royse teams. His speech ended with the audience and 15 RAHS for the coach. After several yells and the school song, the students, with the exception of the football boys, were dismissed to r e t u r n to class.

The cheer leaders for this season are Peggy Smith, Nan McDaniel, Joy Houser and Deanna Wester.

Everyone was wondering why Lynn Houser carried a ladder to school with her the first day of school. Well, it's really very simple. Lynn didn't know what they meant by high school.

ROCKWALL-ROYSE HALF-TIME ACTIVITIES

The Rockwall Band and Pep squad performed at the half in their colorful uniforms. The Pep squad made a large "R" while the band played a number. The majorettes entertained the large crowd with a routine of twirls.

Royse Activities

Joan Shaw playing the part of the teacher, brought the band onto the field by ringing a large school bell. They went into the words, "The Cat Saw the Rat." The band then formed the letters "RC" and played the Royse City school song. After forming an 'R" for Rockwall and giving a yell the band marched off the field playing "Our Director."

The Royse Band, after the game, marched around the square in Rockwall playing "Our Director." The happy members and football squad then came back to Royse for a very gay party. The team and band will long remember the game and the after-effects.

BAND UNDER DIRECTION OF NEW LEADER

The Royse City High School Band began the school term with a new capable director, Mr. Ralph Beck of Dallas. Many changes have been made in the band since last year.

There are new band members which bring the total to about forty-two students.

The new drum majorette is Miss Patricia Bass, a senior at Royse High; assistant drum majorette, Miss Peggy Van Cleave, a junior; and the majorettes are: Misses Rose Jones, Pat Nowlain, Mari Adams, all seniors, and Miss Patsy Welch, a sophomore.

Flag carriers are: Myra Smith, Ann Retherford, both juniors, and Lurline Watkins, a senior.

The band has already started off with many new pieces. The first game the band was ready to present a nice comedy skit

(Continued on back page)

In the first quarter Rockwall kicked to Royse City. Royse City fumbled on the 40 yard line. Rockwall took the ball and scored on the first play to pull ahead 6-0. In the second quarter Cook took the ball on the 30 and scampered for a T. D. At the half the score wos 6 to 6.

In the third quarter Shaw bulled over from the one to pull Royse City ahead 13 to 6. Later in teh fourth quarter Jerrell Shaw again rambled from the twelve Royse City then led 20-6. Cook took a punt on the 50 and ran it back but it was called back and a clipping penalty was the result. There were some good runs by Clark also.

The defense was sparked by Coleman, Burks and Archer.

PUPPY FOOTBALL TEAM GETTING LINED UP

Coach George Mason announces this week that the Puppies are really working hard and if you have never seen them play you should attend some of their games as they will be our Bulldogs in a few years

Following are the list of candidates:

Seventh Grade—Danny Davison, Rudy Don Walker, Bobby Crowell, James R. Jackson, Clarence Ray Nixon, Hugh Sexton, Amon Burton, Jackie Houser, Teddy Bailey, Roy George Rhodes, Carl Wayne Smith, Buddy Thomas, Joe Windham.

Eighth Grade—Dannie Clark, Eugene Tanner, Karon McCreary, David Wayne Smith, Bobby Ishmael, Gerald Gray, Martin Harvey, Windell Brockaway, Gene Burks, Carl Nettles, Morris Lynn Johnson and Jamie Buck.

Among some of their games are with Caddo Mills, Greenville B team of Junior High, Rockwall and Wylie.

The Puppies Pepsquad is: Drum Major — Jane James; Asst. Drum Major — Runette Smith; Majorettes—Gerrie Tay-

(continued on page 2)

In 1953, the school newspaper, the *Bulldog*, featured the headline, "Bulldogs Smother Yellowjackets 20 to 6." For many decades, Rockwall High School (the Yellowjackets) was Royse City High School's top rival, and a victory was front-page news. Former RCISD teacher Anita Scott recalled the rivalry in a written account of her years with the district: "I remember quite vividly during the early years of my teaching career that probably the single most important event during each school year was the football game against the Rockwall Yellow Jackets [*sic*]. . . . This was always a hard-fought game. During this time, there were not enough people left in town to put out a fire." A *Bulldog* article recounting the pep rally prior to the game stated, "The entire high school assembled in the high school auditorium Friday afternoon for the best and most important pep rally of the season." Other front-page articles include an overview of the game's halftime show and postgame activities, which included the RCHS band marching around the square in Rockwall and playing one of the RCHS signature songs, "Our Director."

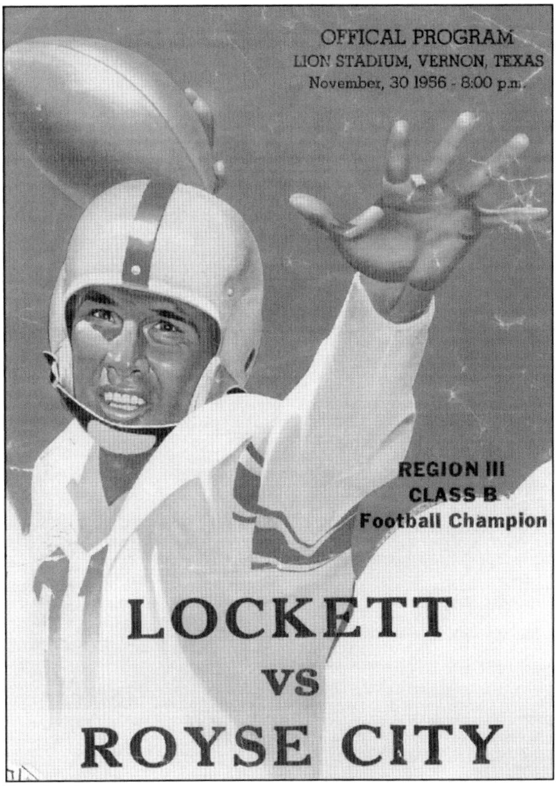

By the 1950s, colorful football programs that listed lineups and advertised products (such as Coca-Cola) became keepsake items for students and spectators, as well as great marketing tools for the companies that provided them to the schools. At left is a program cover from the November 30, 1956, regional championship game between Lockett and Royse City. Royse City had advanced to the regional game by beating Ladonia 33-6 in the bi-district game. The RCHS Bulldogs won the Region III, Class B, title by beating Lockett with the exact same score—33-6—of the game against Ladonia.

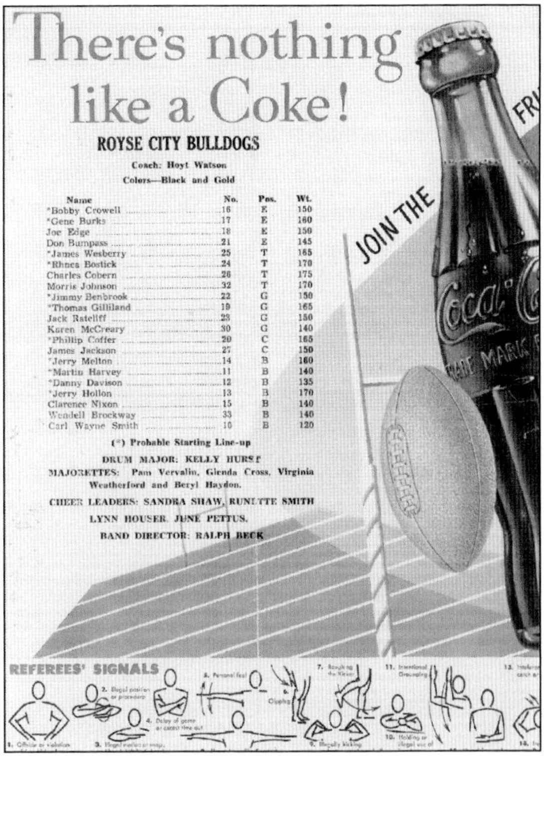

ROYSE CITY BULLDOGS

Coach: Hoyt Watson

Colors—Black and Gold

Name	No.	Pos.	Wt.
*Bobby Crowell	16	E	150
*Gene Burks	17	E	160
Joe Edge	18	E	150
Don Bumpass	21	E	145
*James Wesberry	25	T	165
*Rhnea Bostick	24	T	170
Charles Cobern	26	T	175
Morris Johnson	32	T	170
*Jimmy Benbrook	22	G	150
*Thomas Gilliland	19	G	165
Jack Ratcliff	23	G	150
Karen McCreary	30	G	140
*Phillip Coffer	20	C	165
James Jackson	27	C	150
*Jerry Melton	14	B	160
*Martin Harvey	11	B	140
*Danny Davison	12	B	135
*Jerry Hollon	13	B	170
Clarence Nixon	15	B	140
Wendell Brockway	33	B	140
Carl Wayne Smith	10	B	120

(*) Probable Starting Line-up

DRUM MAJOR: KELLY HURST

MAJORETTES: Pam Vervalin, Glenda Cross, Virginia Weatherford and Beryl Haydon.

CHEER LEADERS: SANDRA SHAW, RUNETTE SMITH LYNN HOUSER, JUNE PETTUS.

BAND DIRECTOR: RALPH BECK

At right, a page from a 1955 football program for a game between the Royse City Bulldogs and the Ladonia Rattlers notes the probable RCHS starting lineup, as well as the drum major, majorettes, and cheerleaders.

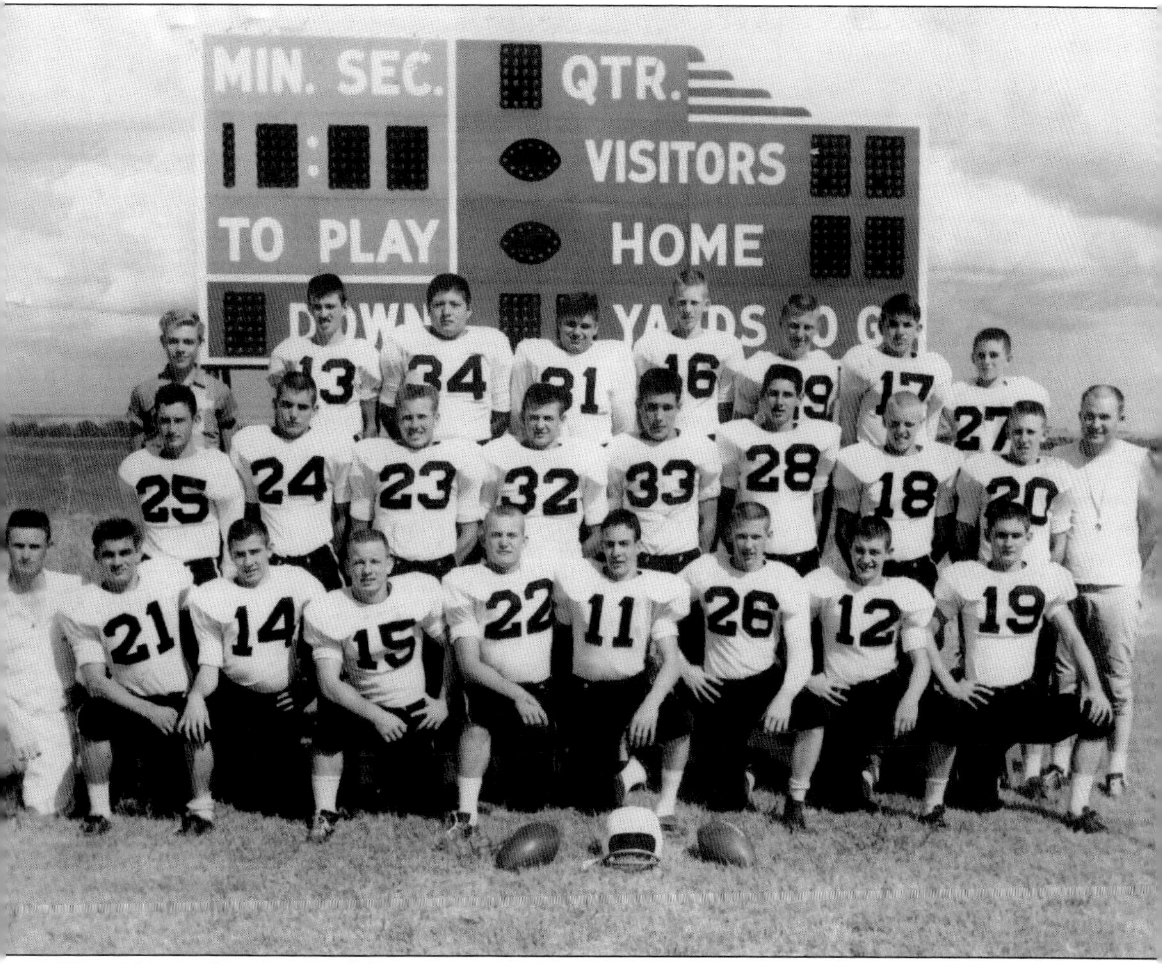

The 1950s produced some of the most successful teams in Royse City High School history. The seven consecutive playoff appearances during that decade have not been rivaled since, although the Bulldogs did earn five consecutive playoff appearances from 2004 to 2008—just two short of the 1950s record. To date, the Bulldogs have earned playoff spots in 1930, 1938, 1943 to 1945, 1951 to 1957, 1961, 1966, 1967, 1987 to 1989, 1997 to 1999, 2004 to 2008, and 2010 to 2011. The Bulldogs are also included in lists (kept since 1951) of the highest amount of points scored by one Texas high school team in a single game, with 98 points scored in 1956 against Bells (placing them fourth), and the highest amount of points scored by both teams in a game, with 130 combined points (Royse City scored 70 and Mount Vernon scored 60) in 2004 (placing them in a tie for sixth). The 1959 team pictured here symbolized the end of an era for RCHS football.

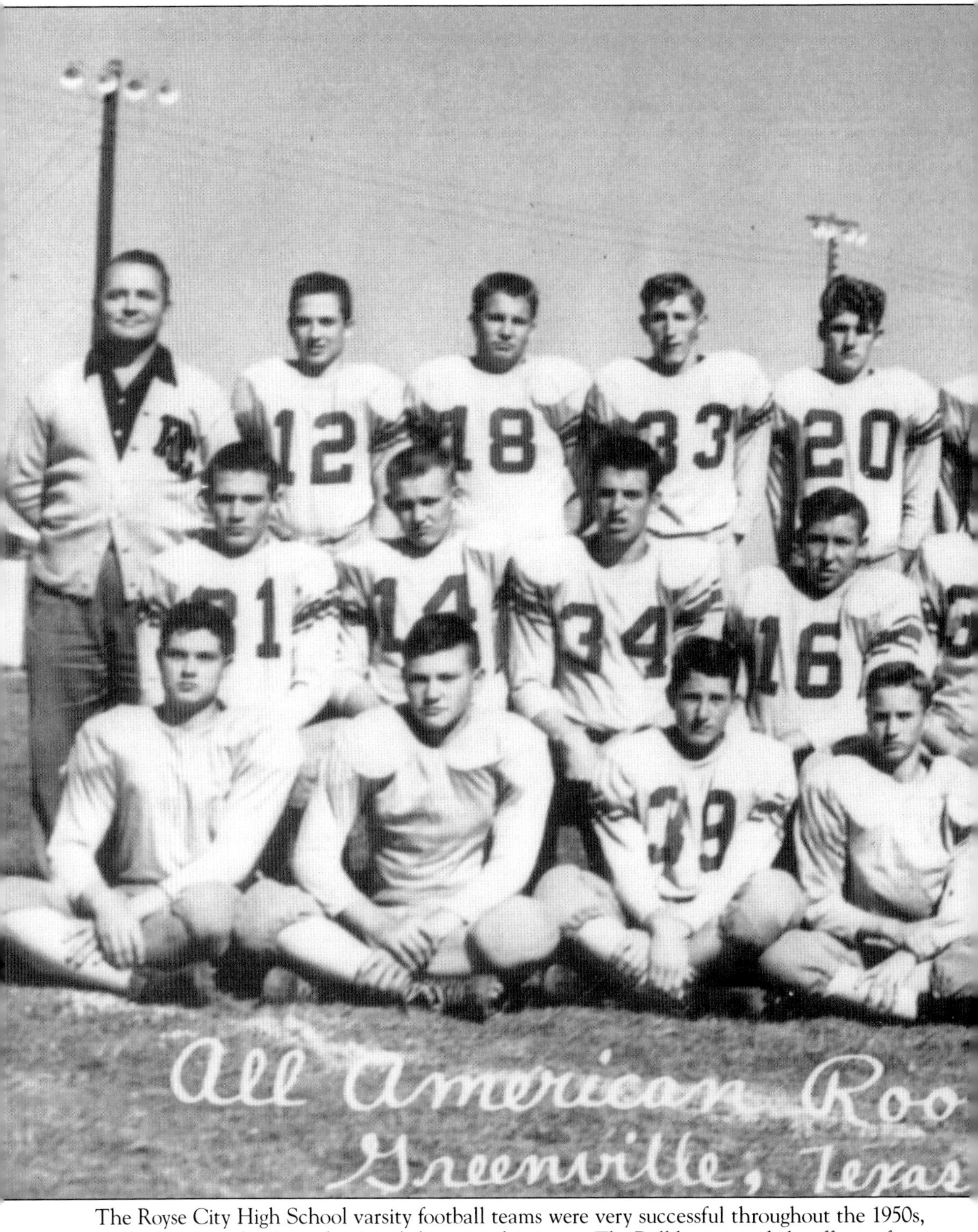

The Royse City High School varsity football teams were very successful throughout the 1950s, producing many district and regional championship teams. The Bulldogs earned playoff spots from 1951 to 1957, and from 1954 through 1957, the team won the Region III, Class B, championship. Since Class B schools did not play for state championships, these teams went as far as possible

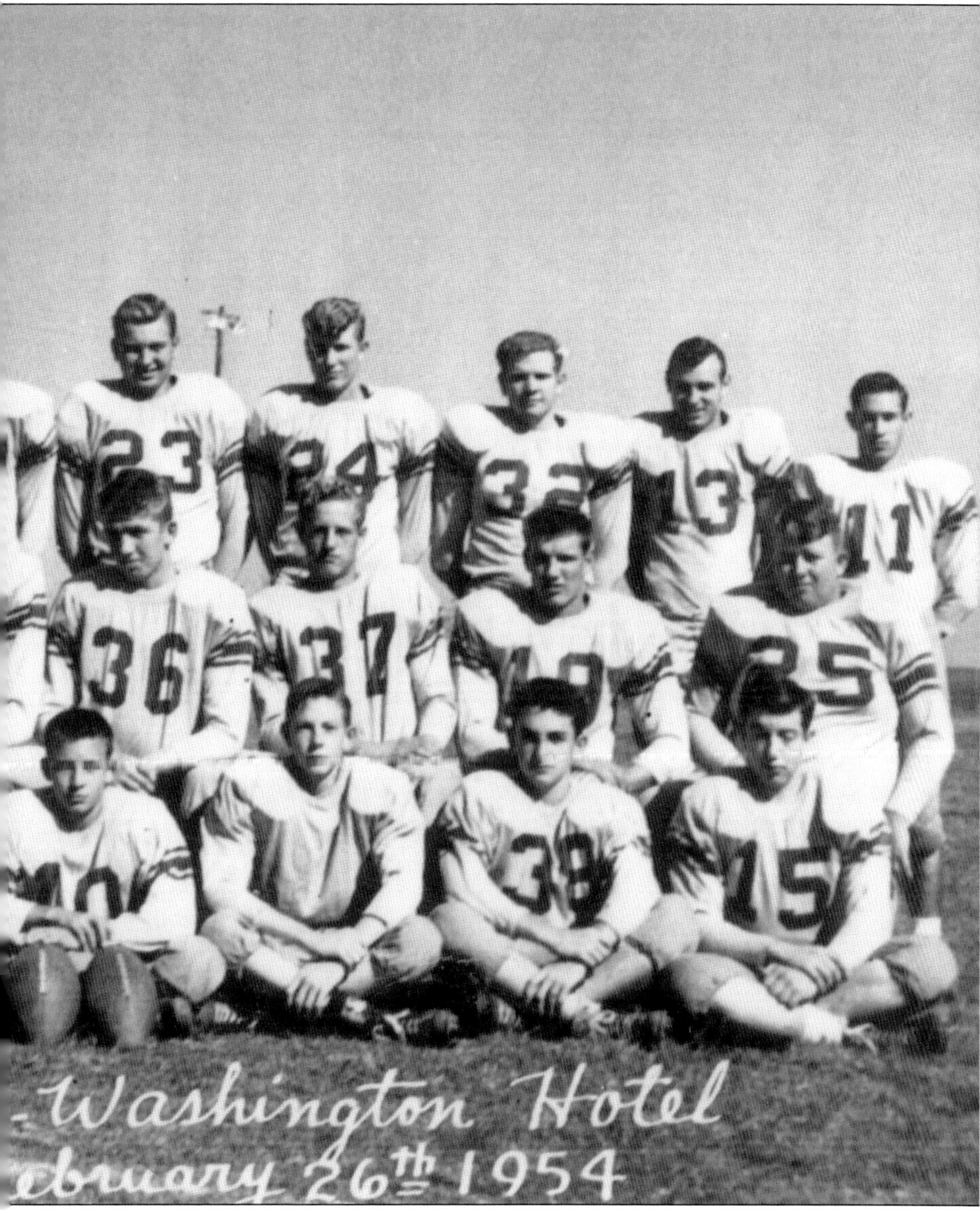

and were considered the top teams in the region. The 1953 Royse City Bulldogs captured the Bi-District title by beating Celeste 47-6. In the regional final, the Bulldogs were defeated 13-6 by Shelbyville. The 1954 RCHS team is pictured here.

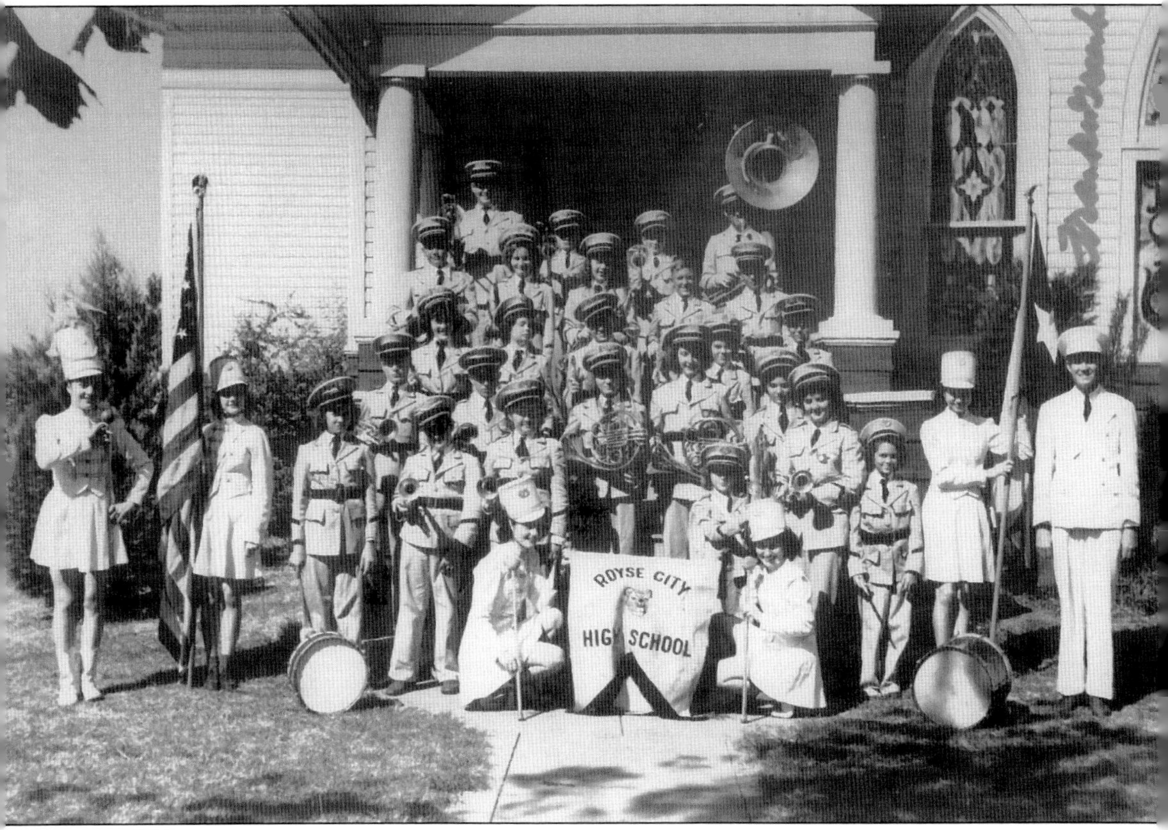

The Royse City High School Bulldog Band, pictured above in the 1940s, started in 1939 with just a handful of players and instruments, then steadily expanded. Since high school marching bands can trace their roots to military bands, it was common practice for early uniforms to have military styling, as shown above. A 1953 *Bulldog* article recounted the band's performance at the annual Royse City vs. Rockwall game: "Joan Shaw, playing the part of the teacher, brought the band onto the field by ringing a large school bell. They went into the words, 'The Cat Saw the Rat.' The band then formed the letters RC and played the Royse City school song. After forming an R for Rockwall and giving a yell the band marched off the field playing 'Our Director.'" Other news in the same edition of the *Bulldog* noted that the band had 42 members and that new band director (and world history teacher) Ralph Beck had just joined the faculty.

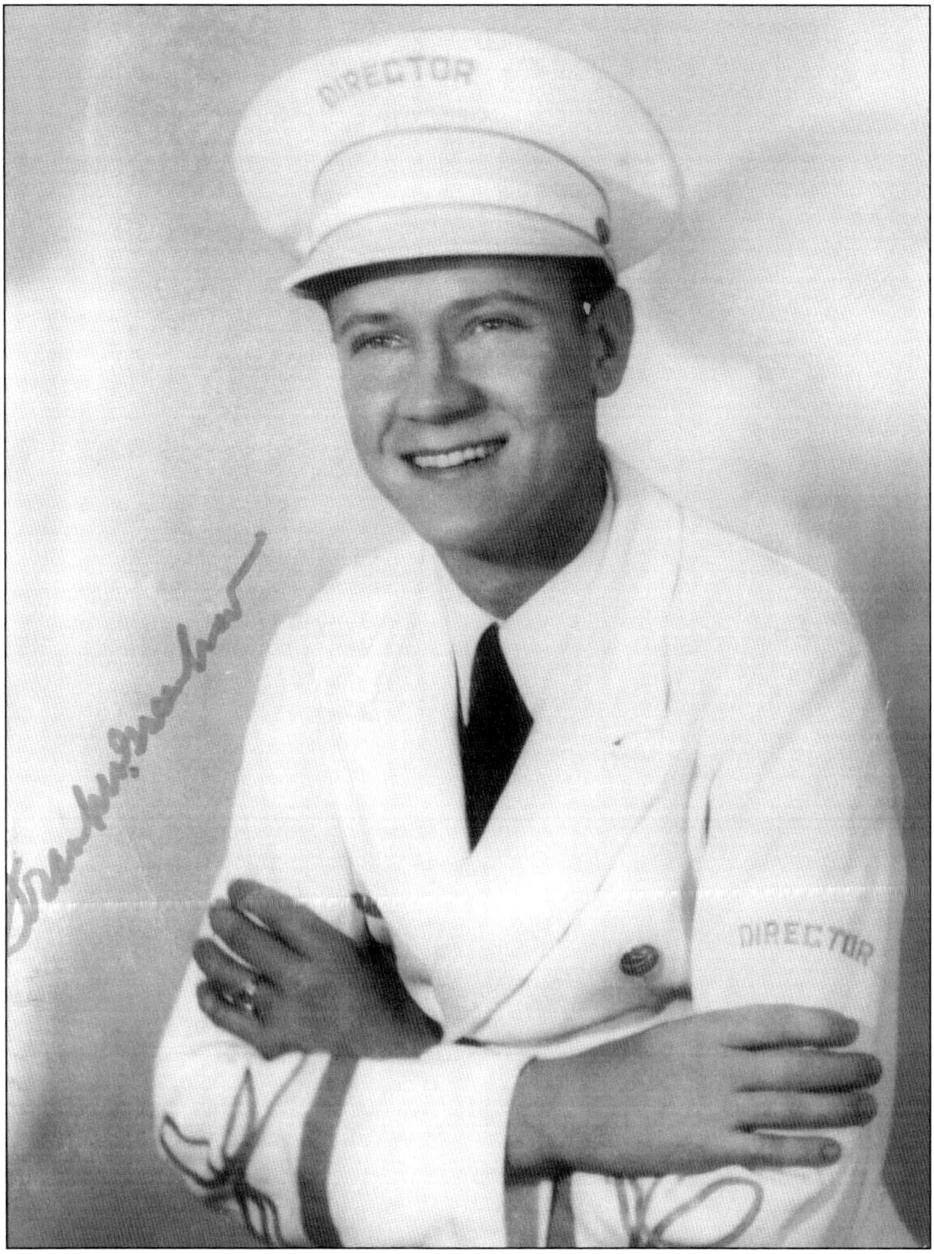

Frank W. Greenhaw was one of the early band directors for the Mighty Bulldog Band and wrote "We're True to Royse High School" during his tenure. Greenhaw graduated from Southern Methodist University with a bachelor's degree in music. After his time in Royse City, Greenhaw went on to be the band and choral director for the Mesquite Independent School District for a brief period of time. Greenhaw served as the director of music for the First Methodist Church of Mesquite for 38 years, becoming the longest-tenured music director in the church's history. He was also a member of the Mesquite ISD Board of Trustees from 1952 to 1961, serving seven of those years as president of the board. After retiring from the board, Greenhaw still sought ways to serve students, and through his family business, he began one of the region's first musical instrument rental programs.

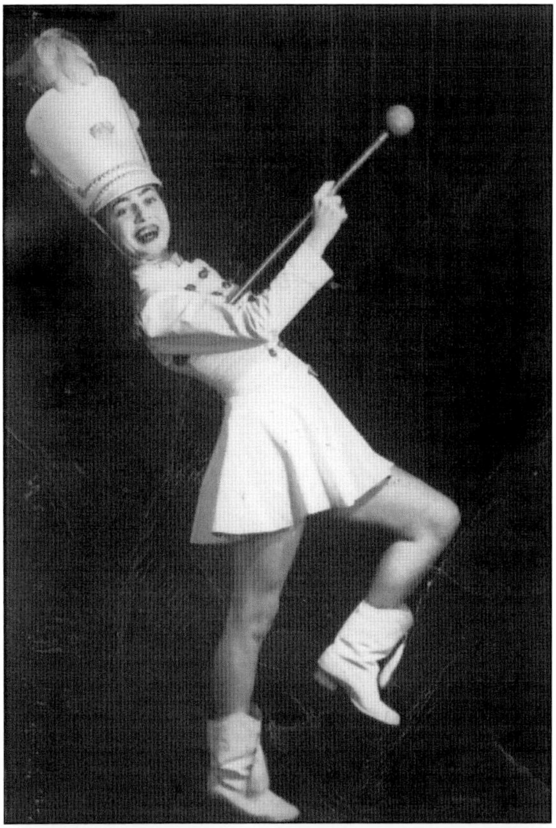

As high school football increased in popularity through the first part of the 20th century, cheerleaders and majorettes became an integral part of the football experience, but differed in purpose and origin. Majorettes marched with the band and twirled batons during halftime shows. Although the exact origin of majorettes is not known, one theory is that military bands were often accompanied by rifle twirlers, so when civilian marching bands began to gain popularity, baton twirlers were substituted for the rifle corps. The World Baton Twirling Federation states that female majorettes officially came into being at Millsaps College in 1889, when founder Reuben Millsaps established a twirling program. At left, majorette Sarah Burks is pictured in 1946. The 1957 majorettes below are, from left to right, the team's unidentified mascot, Pam Vervalin, Jo Ellen Archer, Beverly Tidwell, Bonnie Murry, Beryl Haydon, and Glenda Sue Cross.

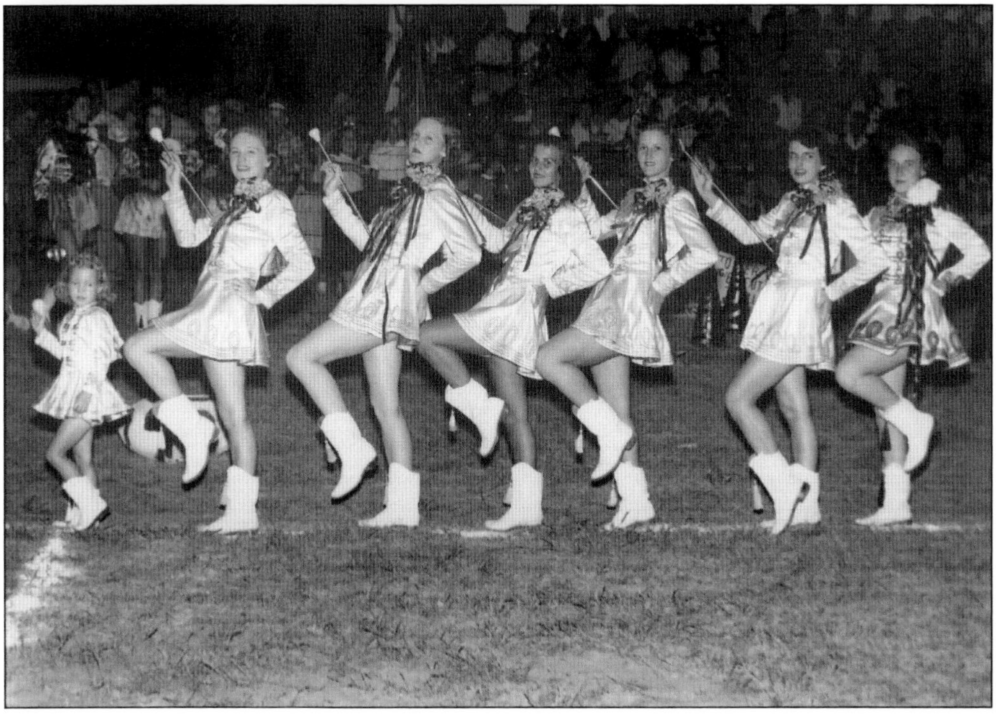

Although dedication to extracurricular activities seems to have remained a constant, in many ways, supporting the team in the first half of the 20th century was vastly different than it is today. For majorettes, costumes have evolved dramatically. At first, majorettes marched with the band and twirled batons. Their uniforms were militaristic, with tall, feathered hats; tasseled boots; and buttoned jackets. Some were embellished with sequins. At right, an unidentified Royse City High School majorette wears a traditional uniform.

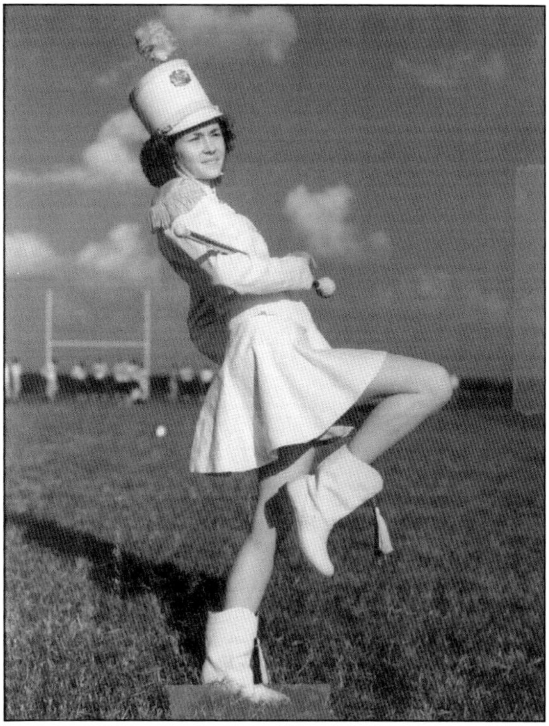

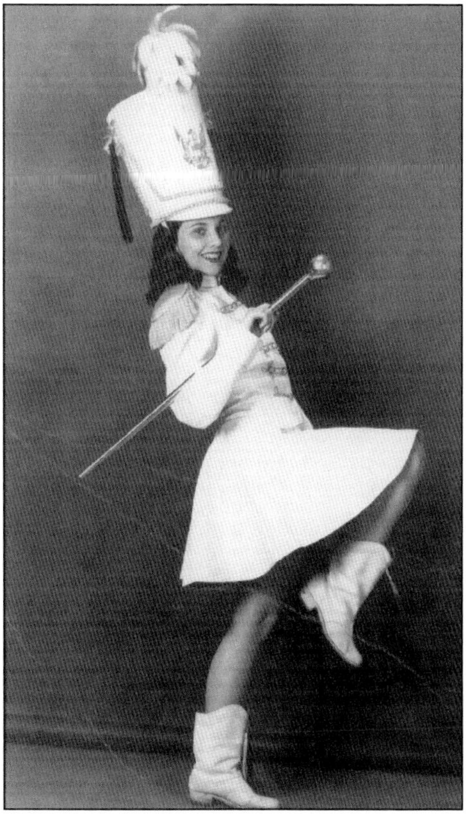

Today's high school marching bands often have separate baton twirlers and flag or rifle corps with uniforms that are more similar to dance wear. Here, majorette Joy Beene sports a high hat embellished with feathers.

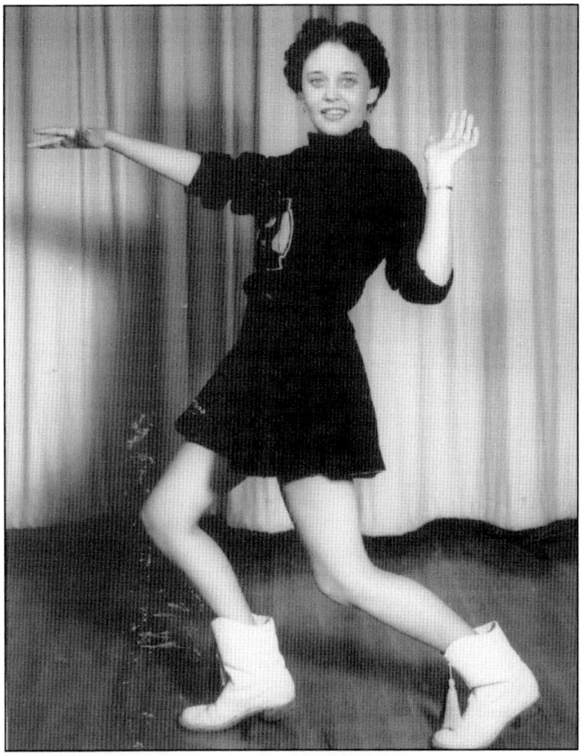

Cheerleading's origins begin with college football and Princeton University in the late 1800s. In 1898, the first organized cheer took place at the University of Michigan when a male student organized a small group to energize the crowd and used a megaphone to lead the cheers. From there, cheerleading spread rapidly from college campuses to high school fields. Initially, men dominated cheerleading, but in 1923, women were allowed to cheer for the first time at the University of Minnesota. By the late 1940s, even college squads were composed primarily of girls. Royse City cheerleader Deanna Wester is pictured at left. The 1953 "puppy" cheerleaders below provided encouragement for the seventh- and eighth-grade football teams. From left to right are Deloris Cross, Charlotte Sellers, Beryl Haydon, Marty Pullen, and Susan Prince.

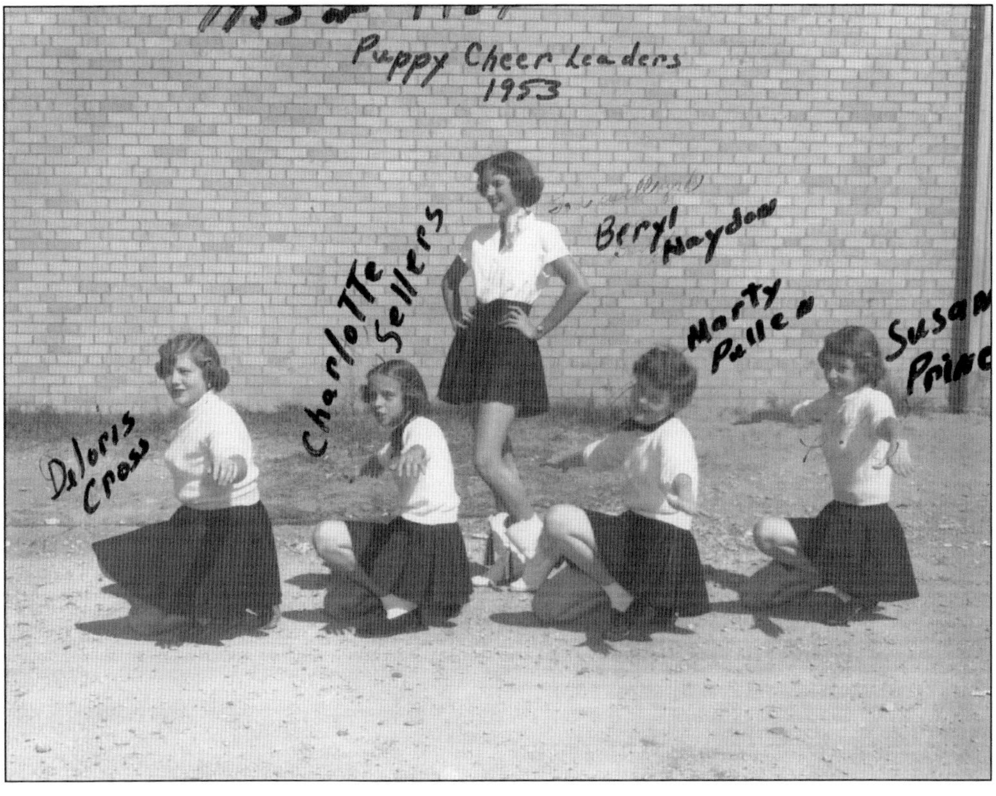

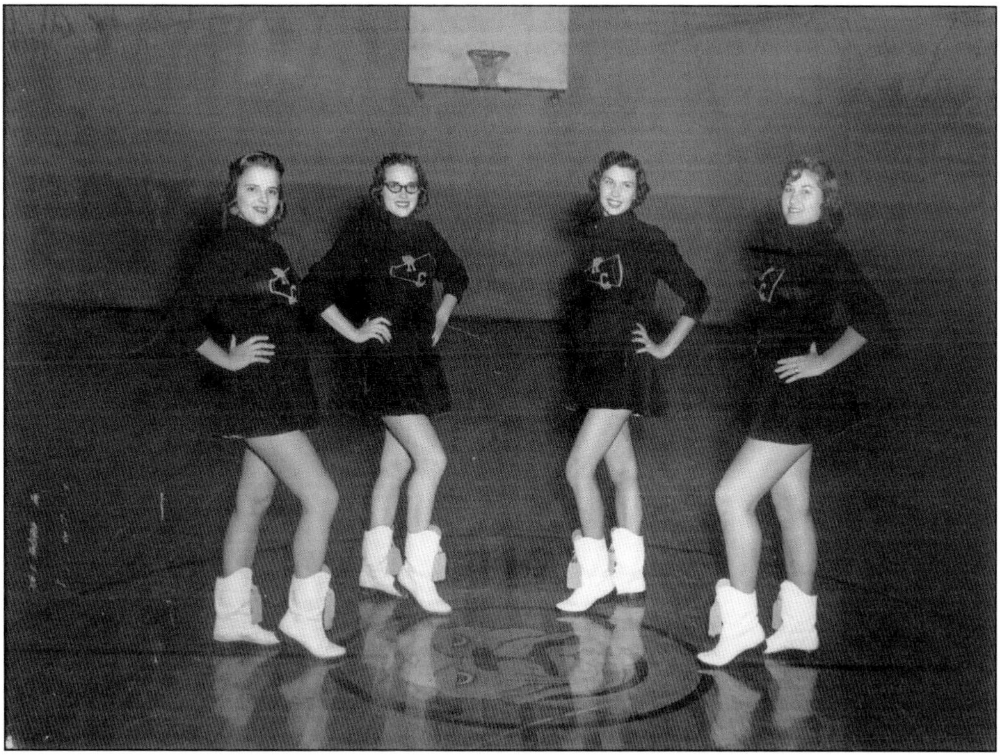

The first recorded homecoming game was held at the University of Missouri in 1911; the athletic director was concerned about attendance at a particular game and encouraged alumni to come. The concept was a huge success, and colleges and high schools across the country began scheduling homecoming games. The tradition of the "homecoming mum" (shown below as worn by Royse City cheerleaders) started as early as the 1930s, when young men gave chrysanthemum corsages to their dates for the big game. The tradition is considered uniquely Southern and is most commonly observed in Texas. Above, a 1950s cheerleading squad poses on the basketball court. In that era, cheerleaders concentrated on cheering (as opposed to the skillful stunts and jumps of today).

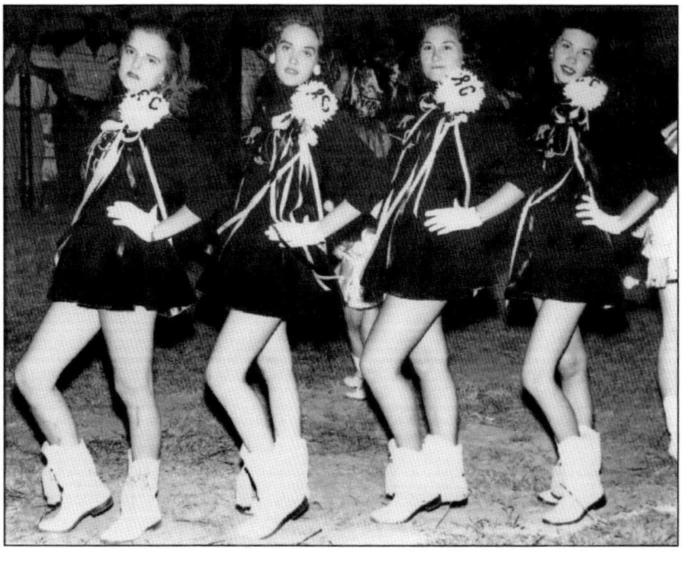

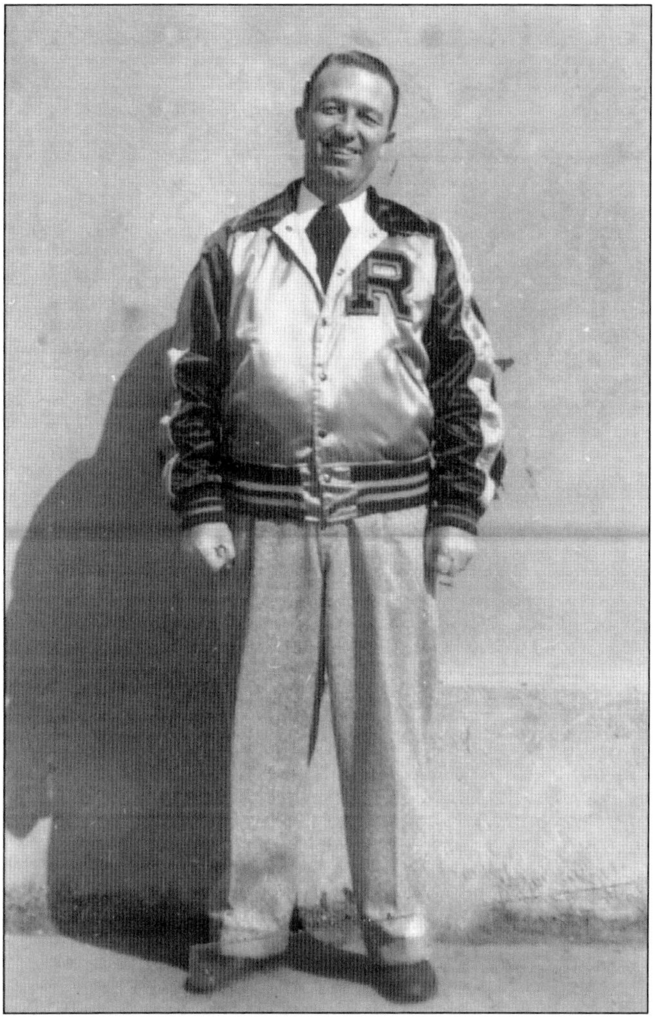

George Mason (left) was a math teacher and coach for many years. Coach Mason had a passion for boxing and organized a large, annual, weeklong tournament in Royse City. Teams from Greenville, Caddo Mills, Quinlan, and Dallas-Crozier Tech participated. Mason also coached what was known as the "puppy" (seventh and eighth grade) football team. One of Coach Mason's boxing teams is pictured below. They are, from left to right, (first row) Jimmy Don Edwards, David Kuykendall, Buster Brockway, Jeff Brockway, Buck Brockway, and Coach Mason; (second row) Ronald Melton, Donald Rex Kuykendall, Oscar Kuykendall, Donnie Melton, Harry Clark, and Windell Brockway.

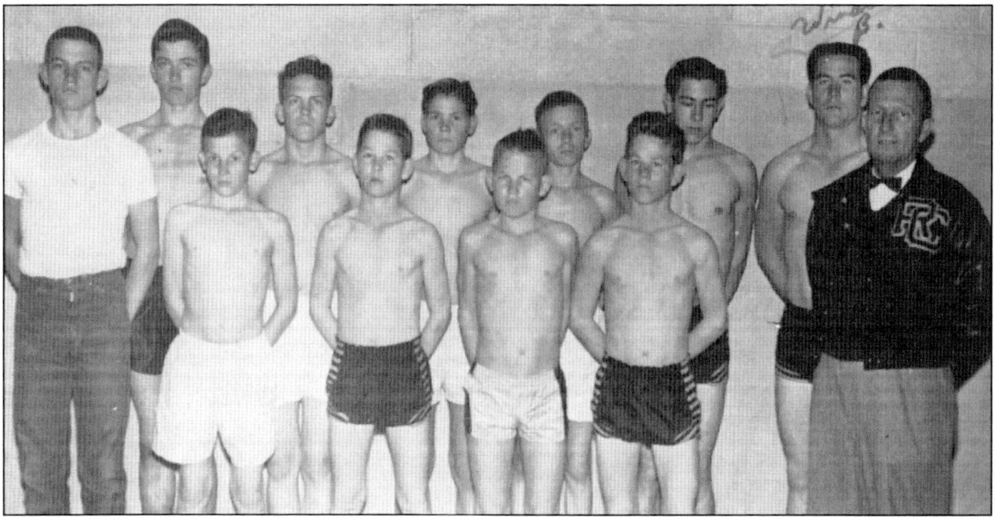

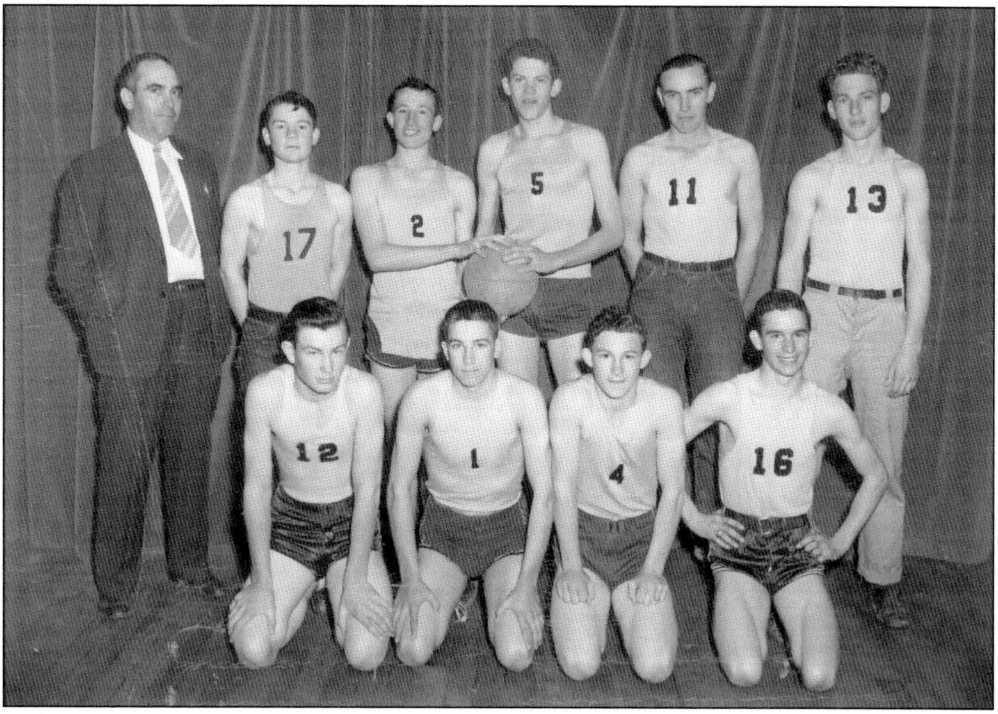

Although football reigned supreme in small-town Texas, other sports did gain prominence. Both girls' and boys' basketball enjoyed a loyal and dedicated following. Two Royse City High School basketball teams are pictured here. Pictured above are, from left to right, (first row) Billy Ray Bratton, Eddie Ansley, Burton Young, and Elbert Roan; (second row) unidentified, Jerry Houser, Billy Sisk, Bobby Price, T.E. Harrell, and B.L. Shoot. The gym floor's menacing Bulldog logo is partially visible in the image below.

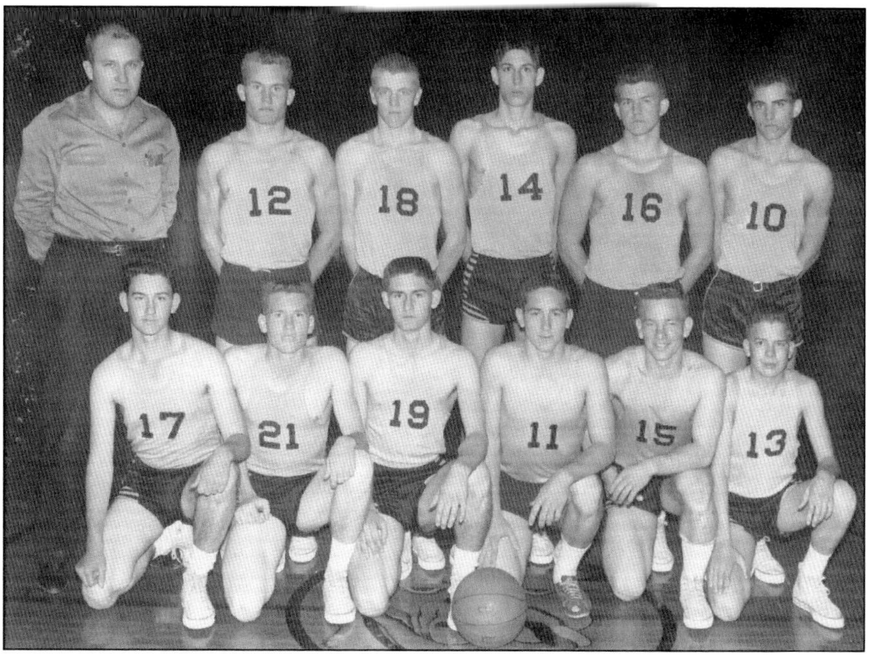

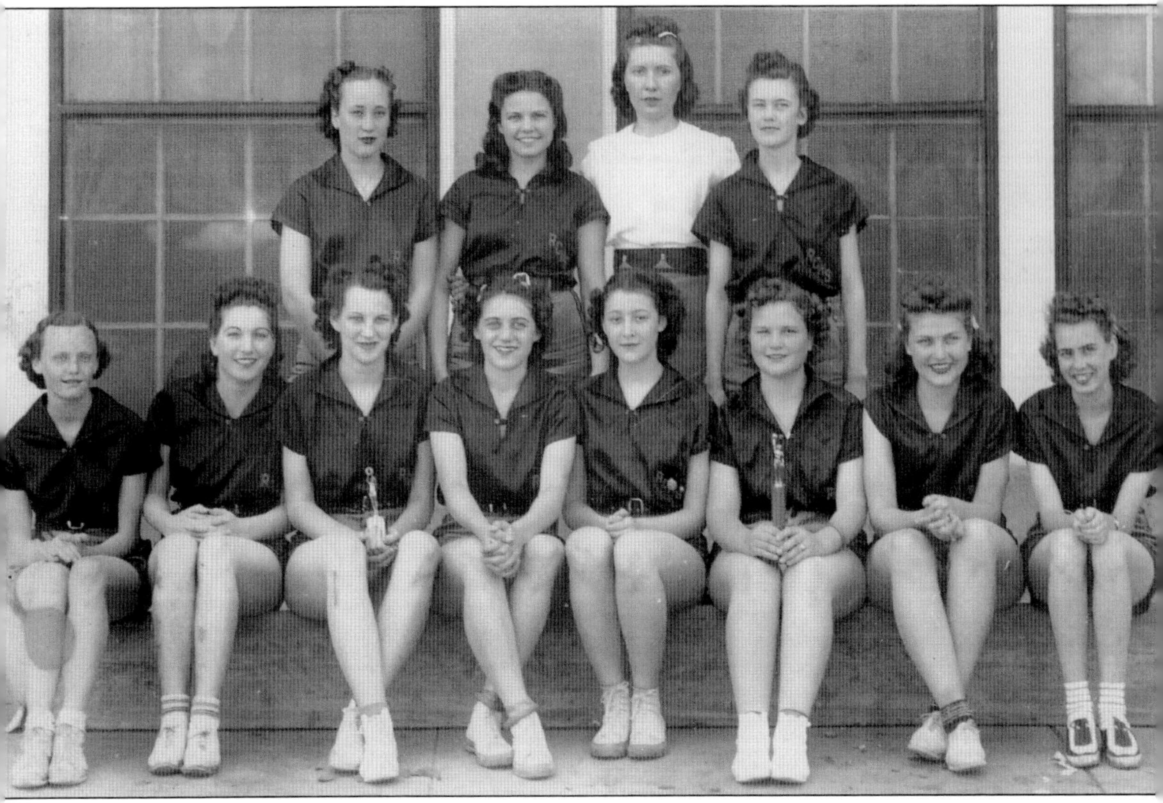

The origins of women's basketball can be traced to 1891, when the first interscholastic game was played between the University of California and a private girls' school. The sport soon made its way through the college and the high school ranks. In 1925, 25 recorded girls' varsity high school basketball tournaments were held in the United States. By the end of the 1930s, girls' basketball had gained popularity in terms of both participation and appreciation. The girls' teams at Royse City High School had a loyal fan base. The 1938–1939 Royse City girls' basketball team and their coach are pictured here. They are, from left to right, (first row) Donnelle Houser (forward), Ruth Williamson (guard), Bobbie Sue Hayles (forward), Florelle Cookston (guard), Ann Hurst, (guard), Dorrace Pullen (forward), Dorothy Lancaster, (forward), and Aurthur Jean Buck (guard); (second row) Annie Mae Lowrance (guard), Pauline Middleton, (forward), Frank Bicknell (coach), and Oleta Johnson (guard).

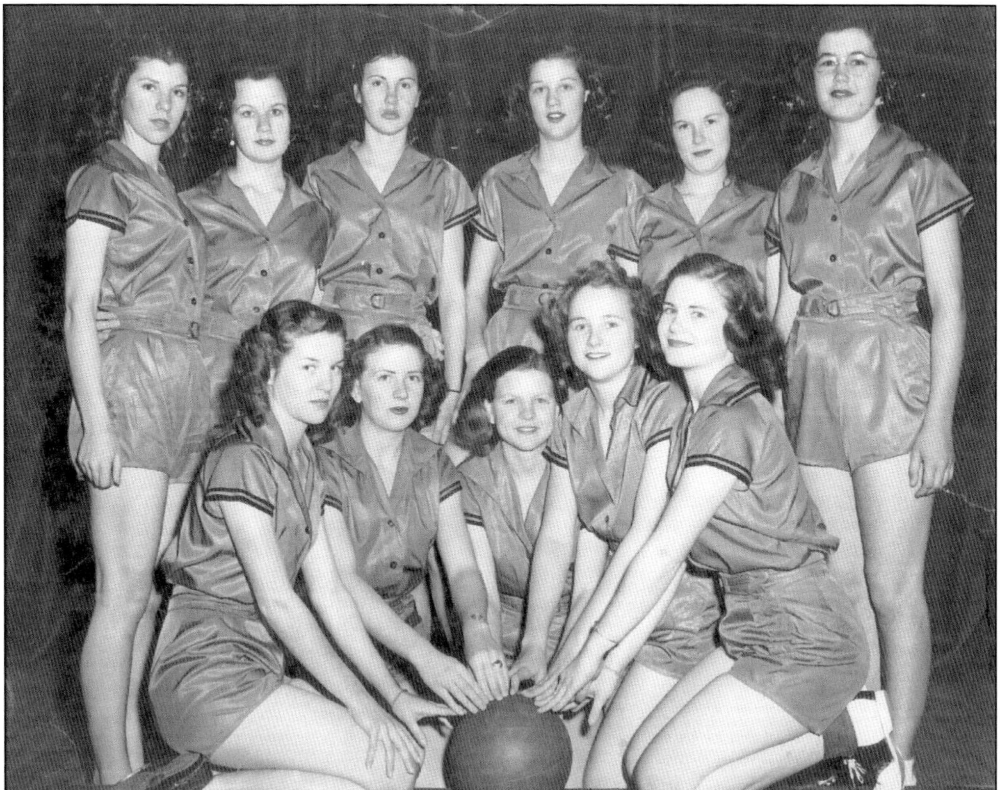

Things like "select" and "club" teams did not exist in the first six decades of the 20th century, and those are not the only differences between then and now. Coaches and teachers had an enormous amount of autonomy when it came to what they expected from athletes and students and how they should be disciplined. In a written history provided to the Rockwall County Historical Foundation, former Royse City teacher Anita Scott recalled, "Gobel Templeton was a coach vividly remembered. His favorite instrument that he used for disciplining his boys was a meter stick. It was said by those who were on the receiving end of this implement that no matter how many licks he administered, every single one hit the exact same spot." These images show two Royse City High School girls' basketball teams from the 1950s.

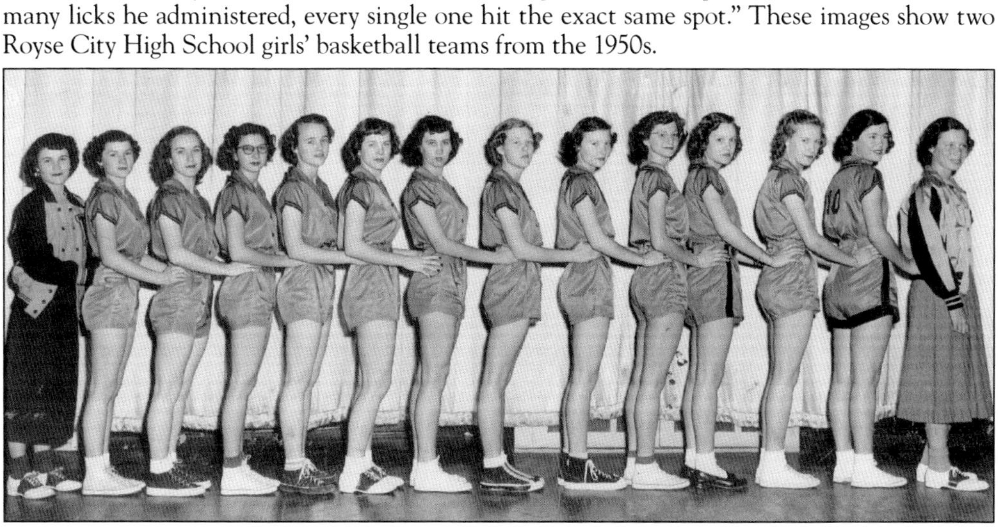

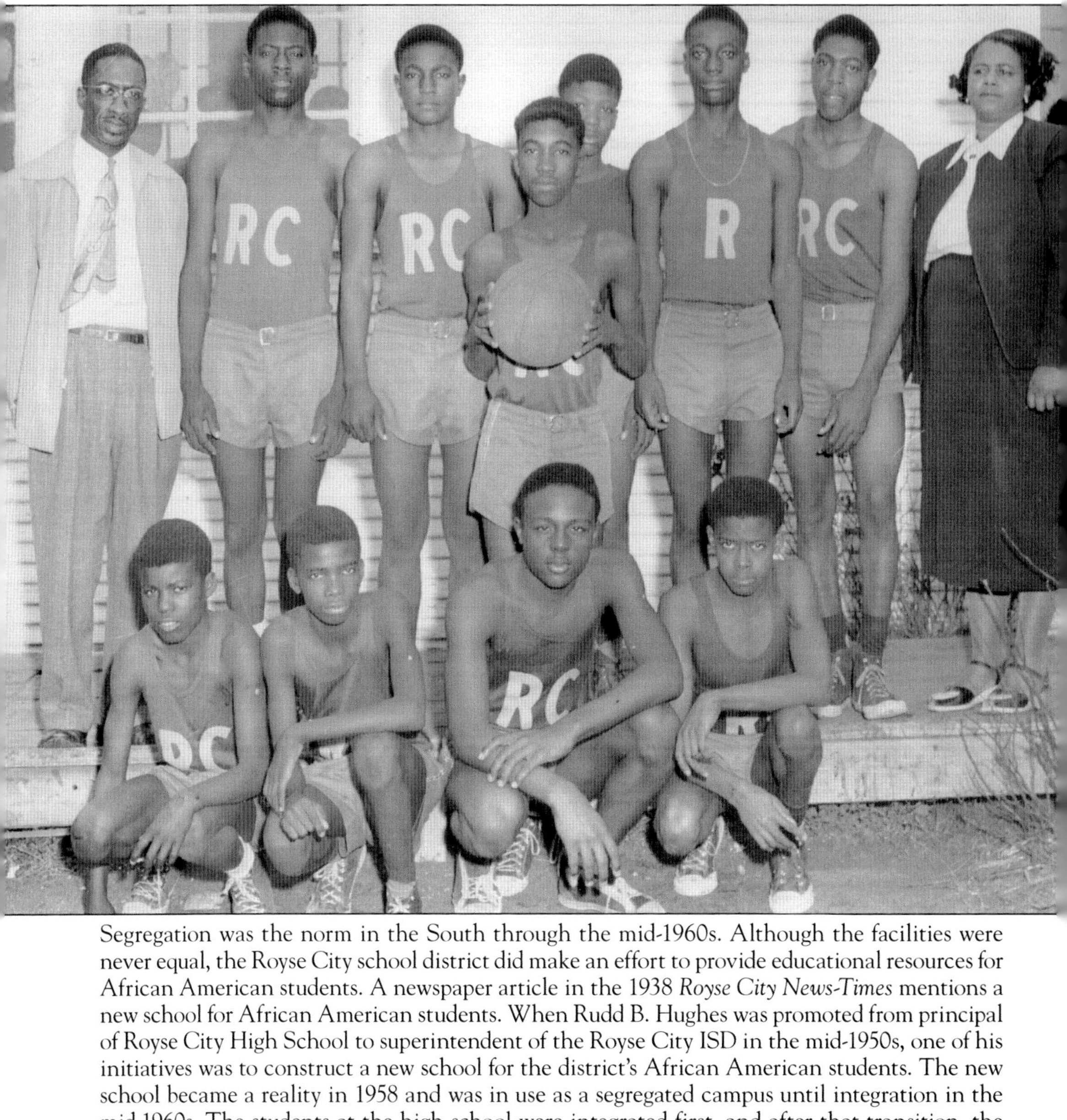

Segregation was the norm in the South through the mid-1960s. Although the facilities were never equal, the Royse City school district did make an effort to provide educational resources for African American students. A newspaper article in the 1938 *Royse City News-Times* mentions a new school for African American students. When Rudd B. Hughes was promoted from principal of Royse City High School to superintendent of the Royse City ISD in the mid-1950s, one of his initiatives was to construct a new school for the district's African American students. The new school became a reality in 1958 and was in use as a segregated campus until integration in the mid-1960s. The students at the high school were integrated first, and after that transition, the lower grades were also combined. This is a basketball team from Royse City's segregated school.

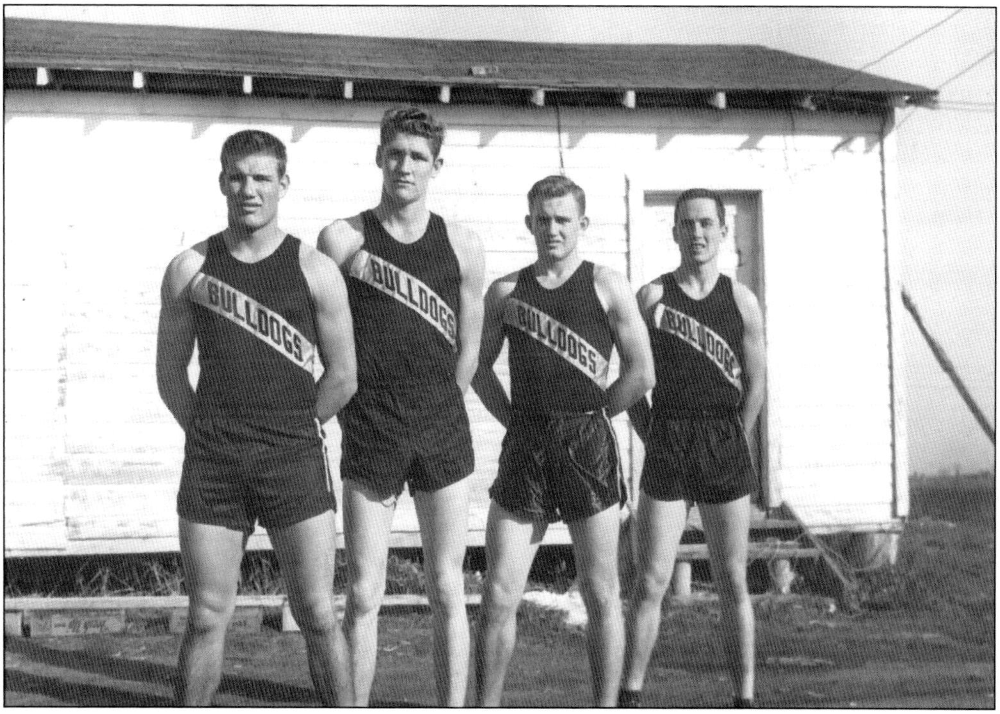

Although football was by far the most popular sport, basketball, boxing, and track also had loyal supporters. The Royse City High School track relay team is pictured above. Pictured below are, from left to right, (front row) Roy Roades and Danny "Dart" Davison; (second row) ? Henderson (coach), Bobby Crowell, Mike Hollon, Jerry Michael Burks, and Jerry Shaw.

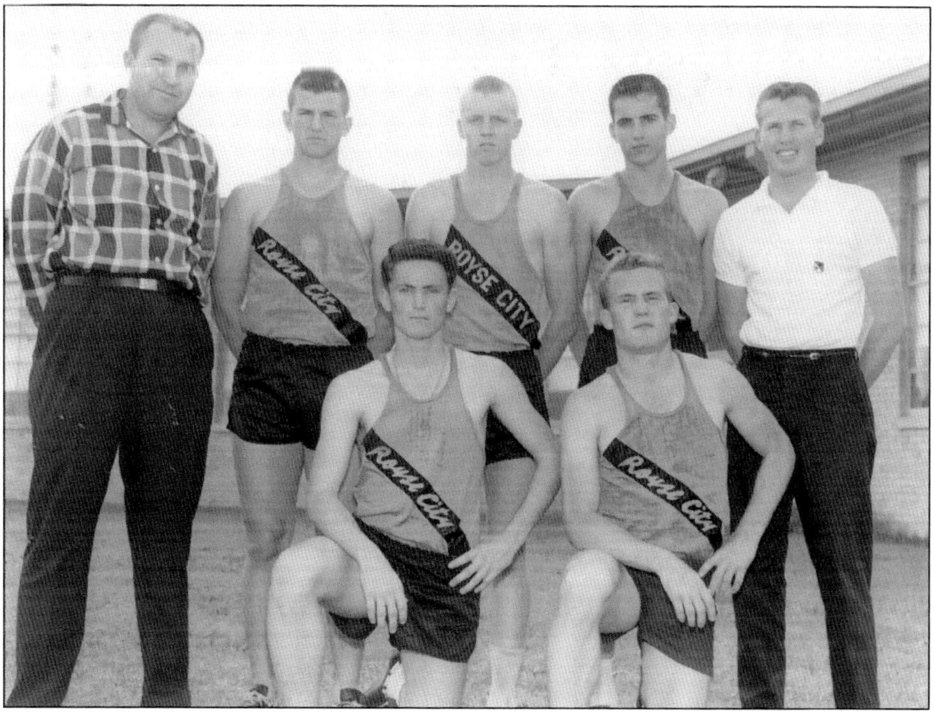

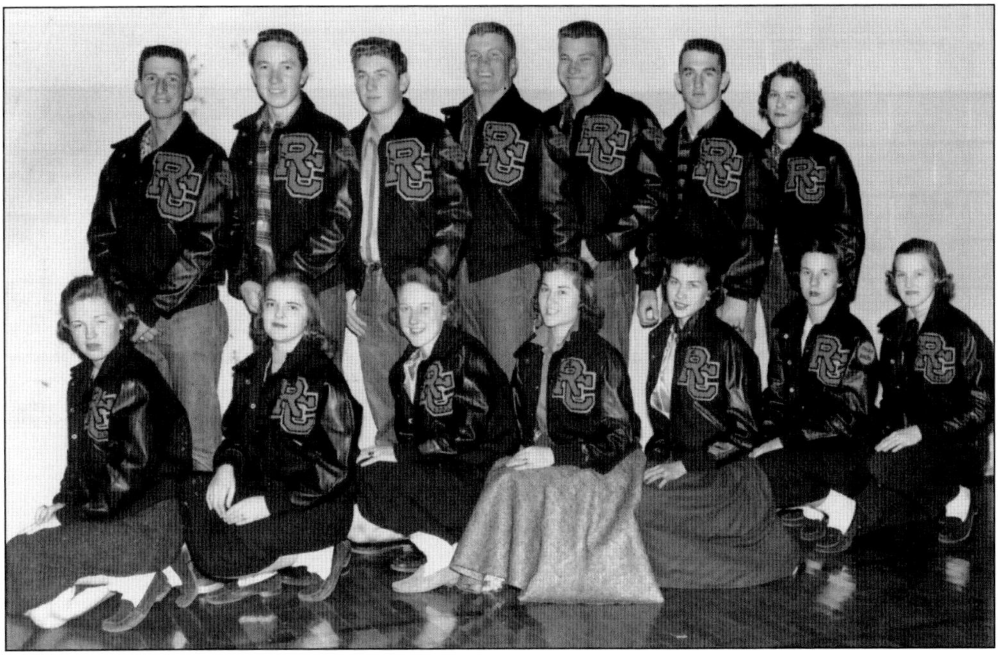

It is commonly believed that the tradition of the varsity letter jacket can be traced to 1865, when the Harvard University baseball team embroidered an Old English "H" onto a grey flannel shirt; Harvard players were able to wear the "H" uniform based on performance. Thus, the letter sweater was created, and, later, the letter jacket. At Royse City High School, the 1950s marked the height of the letter jacket's popularity. The 1957 senior football players and cheerleaders are pictured above on the day they were awarded their letter jackets. The 1958 senior football players and cheerleaders are pictured below on their letter-jacket day.

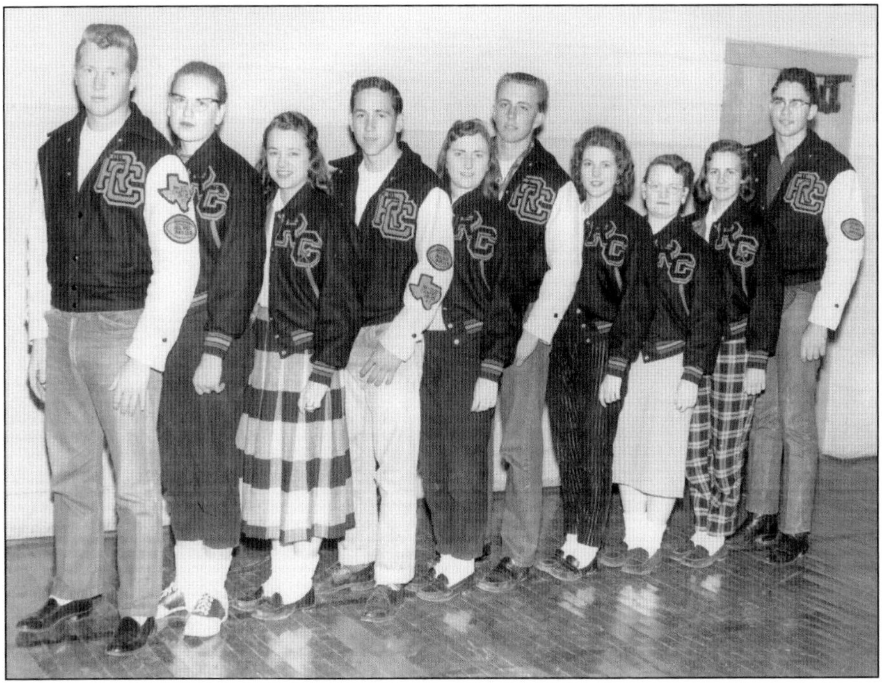

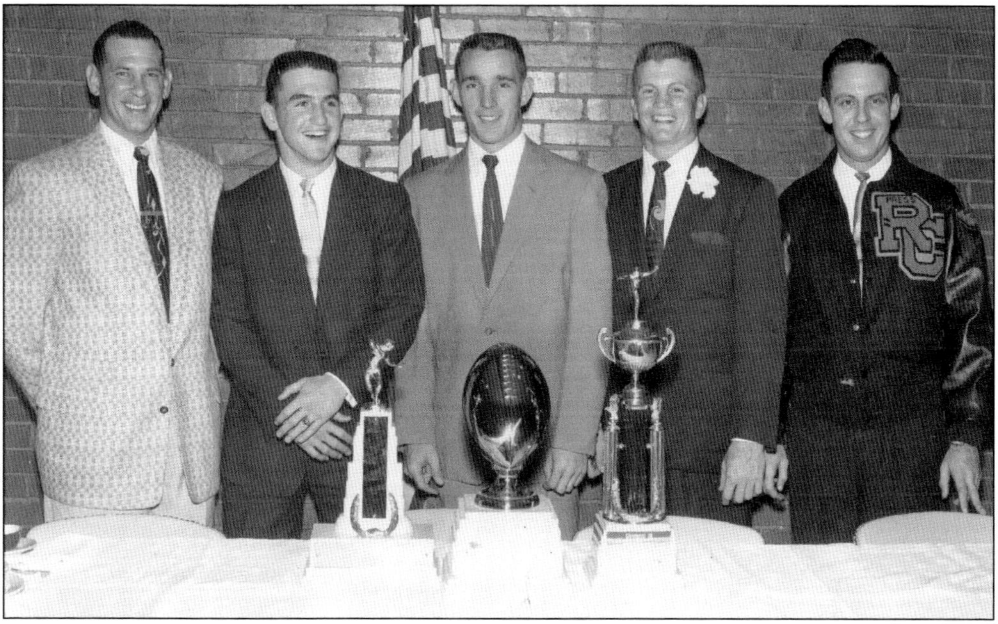

The annual spring football banquet celebrated the Bulldogs' outstanding season and featured players and coaches recounting the many accomplishments of the team. The players posing above with the evidence of their successful 1957 season as Region III champions are, from left to right, Hoot Gibson, Jim Benbrook, unidentified, Jerry Hollon, and Bill Betts. Below, from left to right, Lynn Houser, Jerry Hollon, unidentified (standing), Runette Smith, Jim Benbrook, and Glenda Cross (all students behind Cross are unidentified) listen to stories from the 1957 season, which ended with Royse City beating Wolfe City 58-6 to advance to the regional playoff game. Royse City won the regional title, defeating Lockett 19-0.

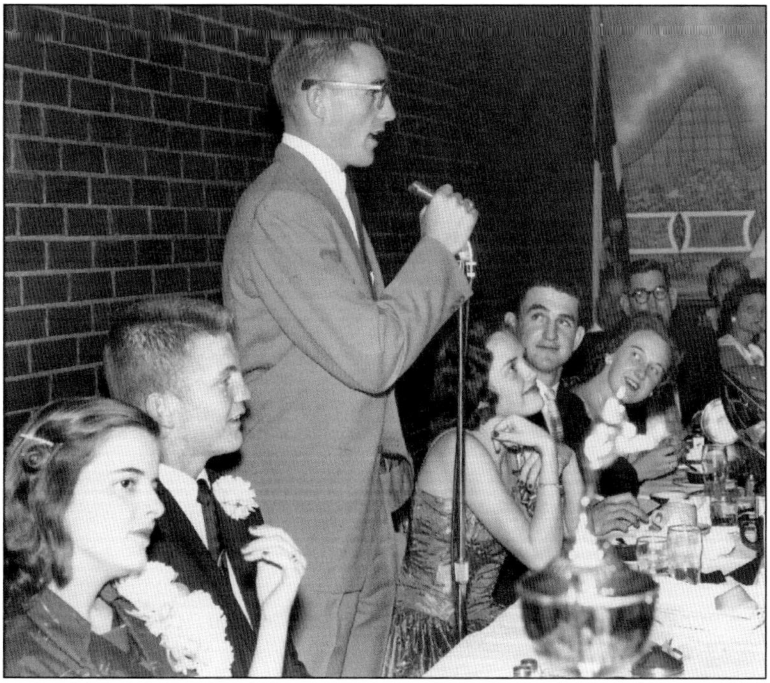

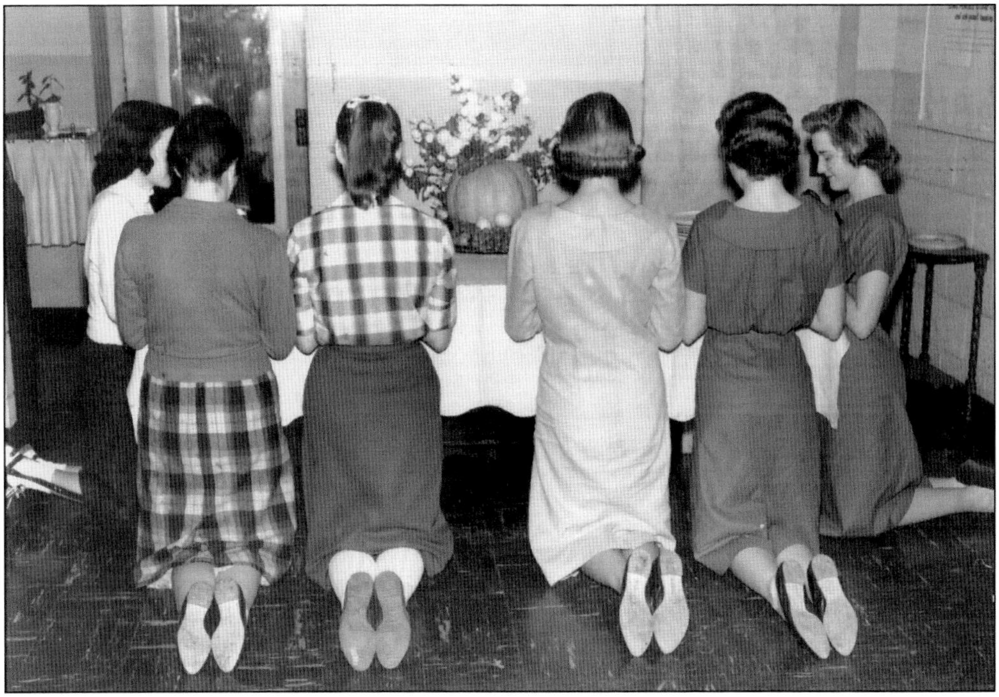

A 1941 newspaper article sang the praises of adding homemaking to the high school curriculum, stating, "Homemaking is also offered for our high school girls. They learn to plan meals, cook them and serve them. They also learn to sew. The homemaking girls have cooked and served the food for several banquets this year and the food seemed to be quite satisfactory. This course has proved to be very helpful to any girl that takes it." An early 1960s homemaking class is pictured above. Below, the Royse City High School annual staff works diligently to produce *The Bulldog*.

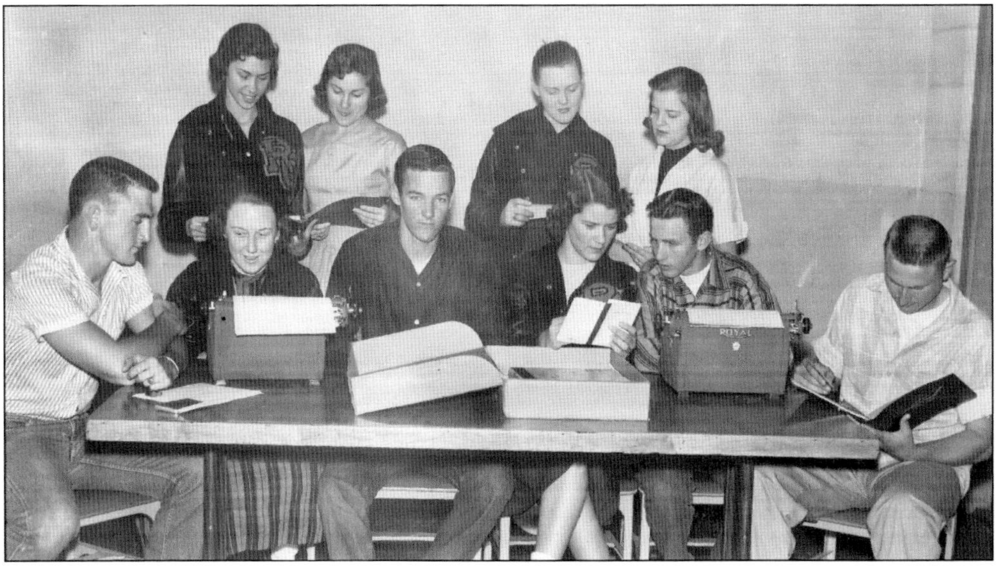

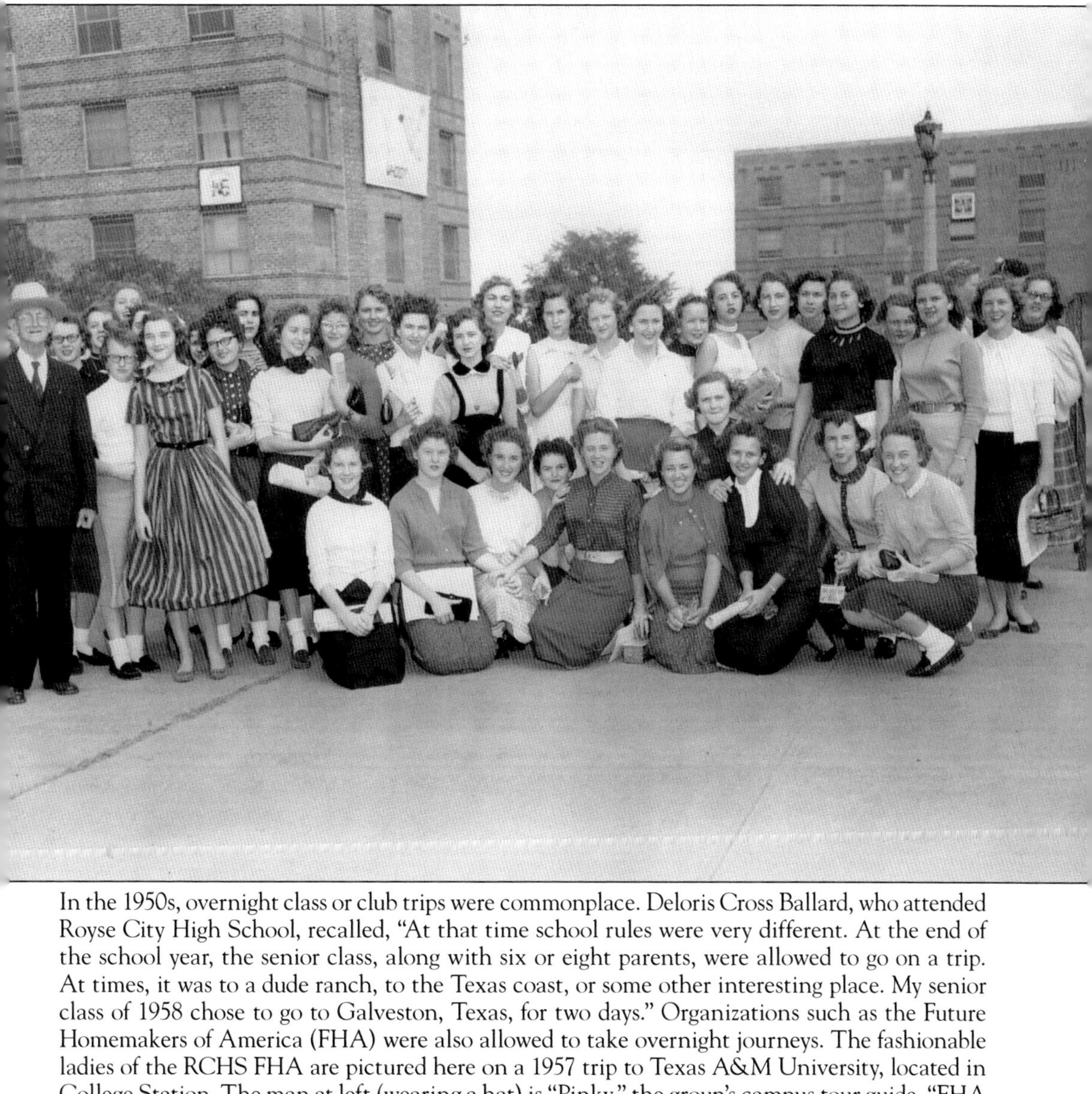

In the 1950s, overnight class or club trips were commonplace. Deloris Cross Ballard, who attended Royse City High School, recalled, "At that time school rules were very different. At the end of the school year, the senior class, along with six or eight parents, were allowed to go on a trip. At times, it was to a dude ranch, to the Texas coast, or some other interesting place. My senior class of 1958 chose to go to Galveston, Texas, for two days." Organizations such as the Future Homemakers of America (FHA) were also allowed to take overnight journeys. The fashionable ladies of the RCHS FHA are pictured here on a 1957 trip to Texas A&M University, located in College Station. The man at left (wearing a hat) is "Pinky," the group's campus tour guide. "FHA also took a trip each year," said Ballard. "It was basically all the girls in the high school, because we all took homemaking."

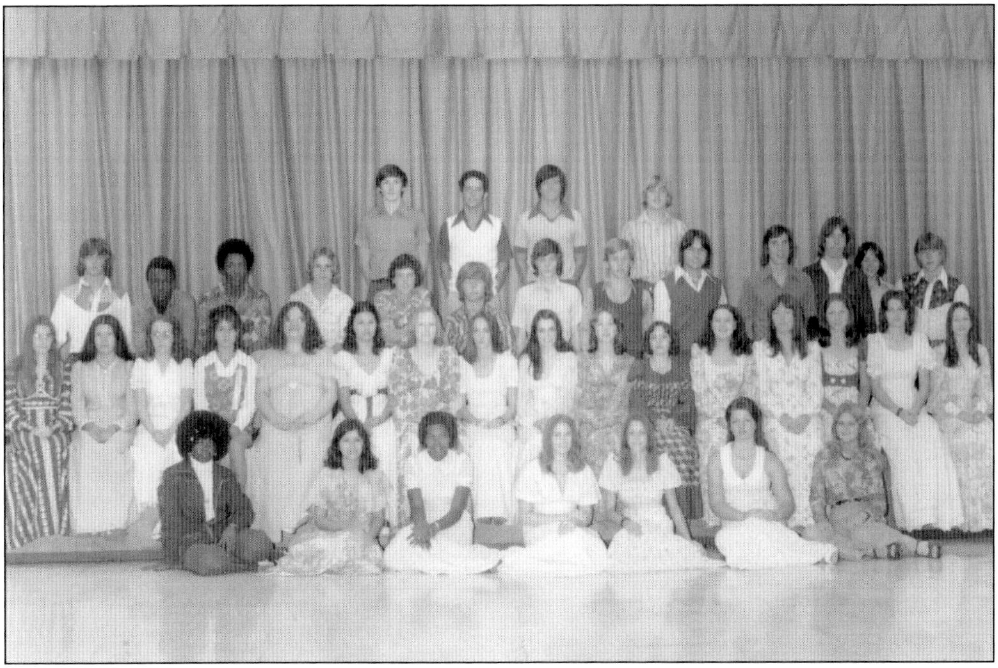

In 1975, under the guidance of Royse City ISD superintendent of schools James Holt, a new Royse City High School was constructed on 35 acres east of Royse City. Just prior to the completion of this building, a fire, which was intentionally set, destroyed the old building, resulting in the loss of textbooks, library books, furniture, and school records. In 1978, Randy Savage was named superintendent, followed by W.R. Fort in 1982. During the 1980s, construction was completed on a new football field, new tennis courts, and a new elementary school. The 1975 junior class is pictured above. Below is a 1970s Royse City High School Mighty Bulldog marching band.

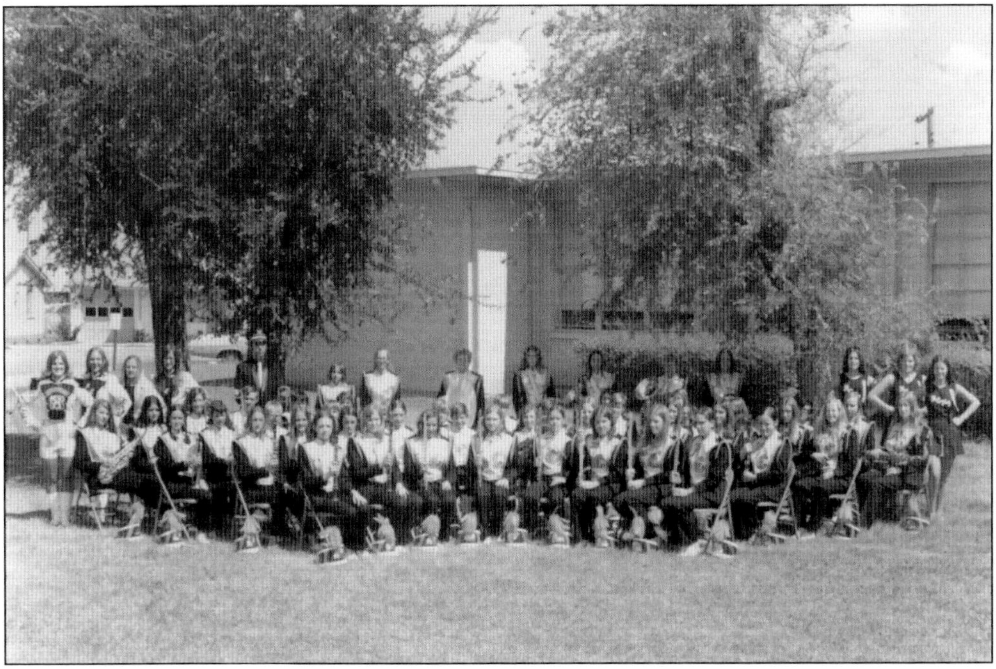

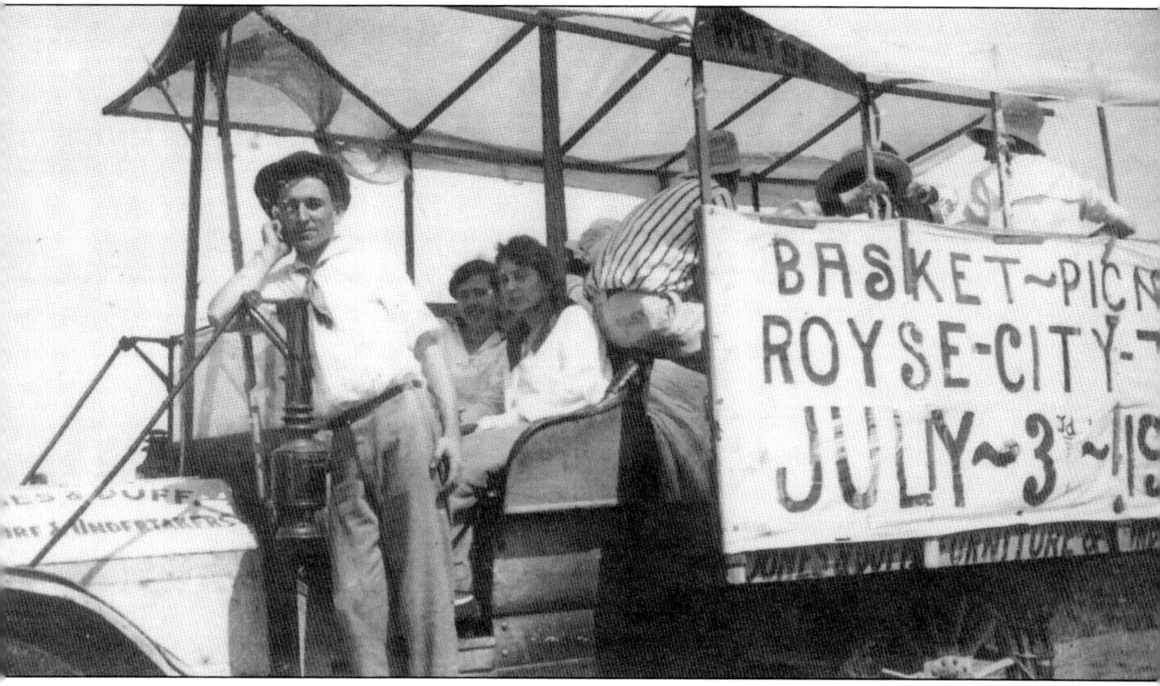

Royse City has planned many events intended to unite its citizens. Parades, festivals, trades days, and city celebrations began soon after the town was settled and continue into the present day. In the early 1900s, the Fourth of July was a large, community-wide celebration. From approximately 1890 to 1920, huge picnics were held at the city park—families would bring picnic baskets filled with homemade fare, bands would perform patriotic music in the bandstand, and contests and other festivities were organized. Parades were often a part of the day. This c. 1918 photograph shows a car decorated for the Independence Day parade and advertising (on the hood and under the picnic sign) "Jones & Duff Furniture and Undertakers." In the late 1800s and early 1900s, it was common for a furniture store to carry caskets and for the proprietor to perform the duties of an undertaker. At the time, there were few funeral homes; those who passed away lay in state in private homes, and services were held in the home or at a church.

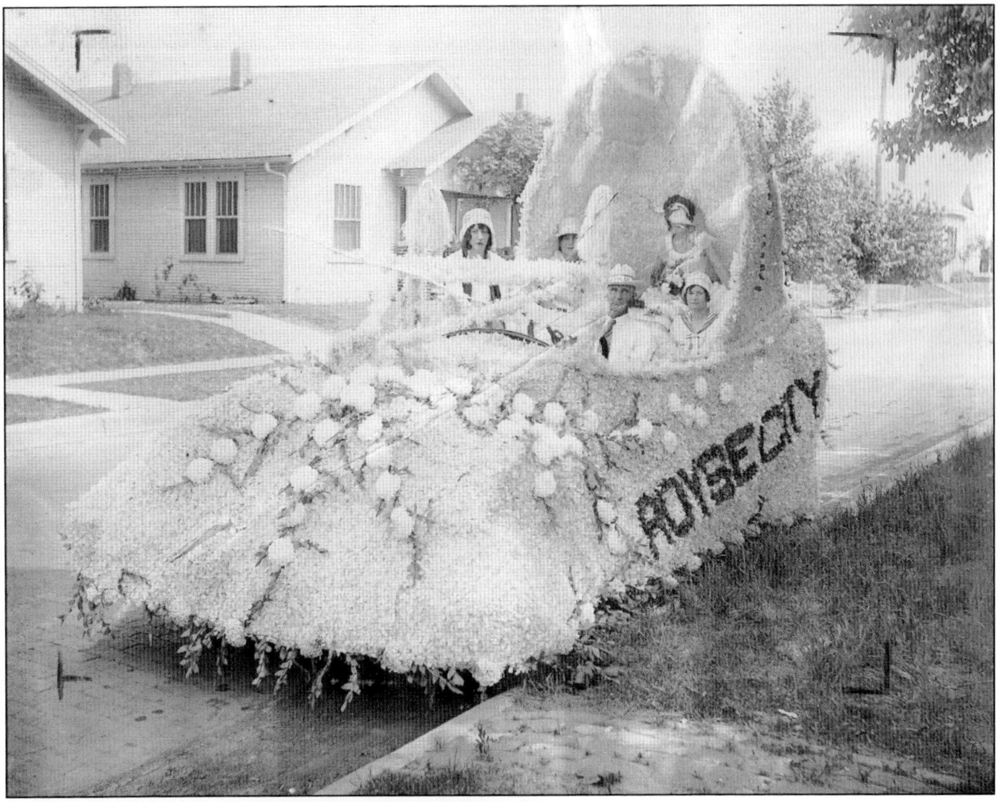

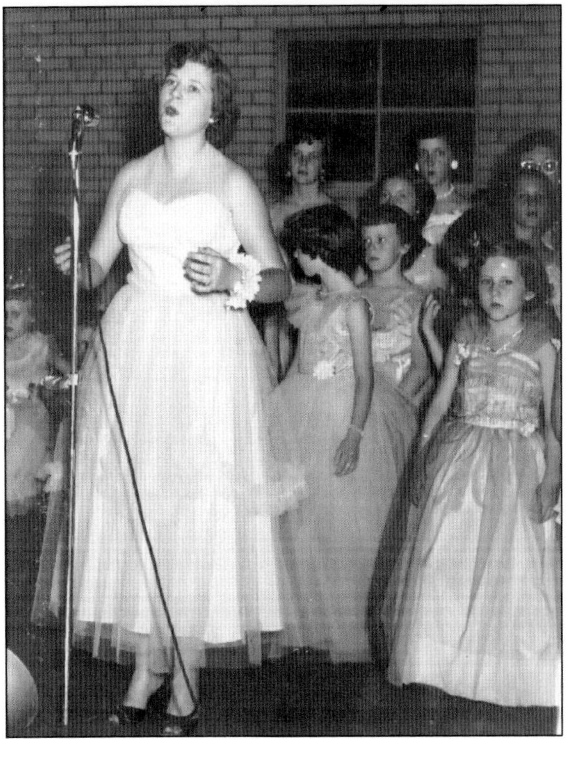

City celebrations ranged from simple get-togethers at City Lake, located north of town, to elaborate parades down Main Street. The 1920s image above features an intricately decorated parade float. From 1938 to 1960 (with the exception of the years from 1943 to 1946), Royse City hosted a community-wide homecoming. In the early days, up to 2,000 people would crowd into the small city for a parade, midway rides, a program that often featured singing and dancing performed by the high school students, and various opportunities for food and fellowship. The tradition was discontinued as the town's population declined. In the photograph at left, Deloris Cross sings at the 1955 homecoming.

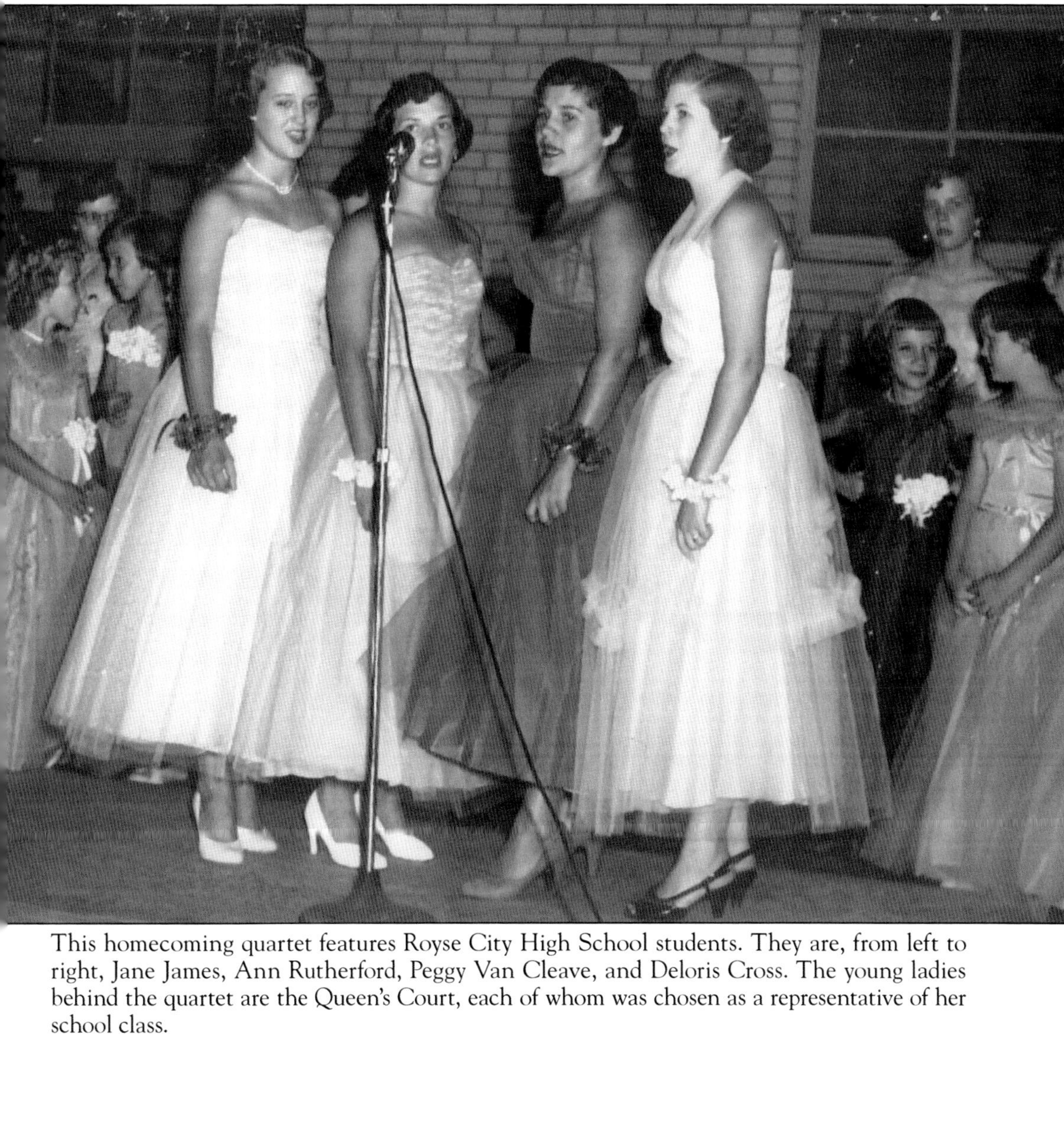

This homecoming quartet features Royse City High School students. They are, from left to right, Jane James, Ann Rutherford, Peggy Van Cleave, and Deloris Cross. The young ladies behind the quartet are the Queen's Court, each of whom was chosen as a representative of her school class.

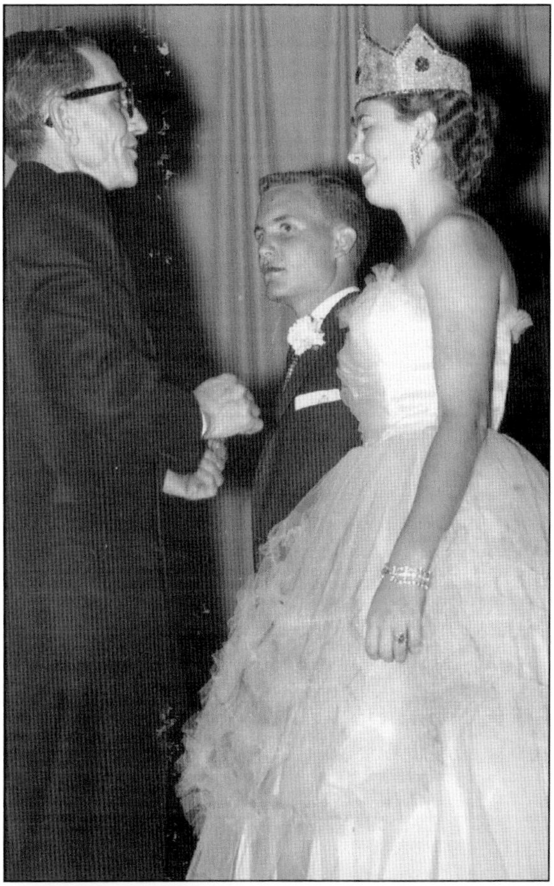

In the image at left, Royse City mayor Yank James crowns Danny "Dart" Davison and Roslynn Browning as 1959 Homecoming King and Queen for the annual citywide homecoming celebration. The king and queen were chosen through the sale of tickets. Each school class had a boy and a girl chosen to represent them, and tickets were then sold throughout the community in order to determine the winners. Below, from left to right, Ann Rutherford, Peggy Van Cleave, Jane James, and Deloris Cross entertain the crowd with a song-and-dance routine at homecoming. The students performed on a stage that was set up at the back of the school building.

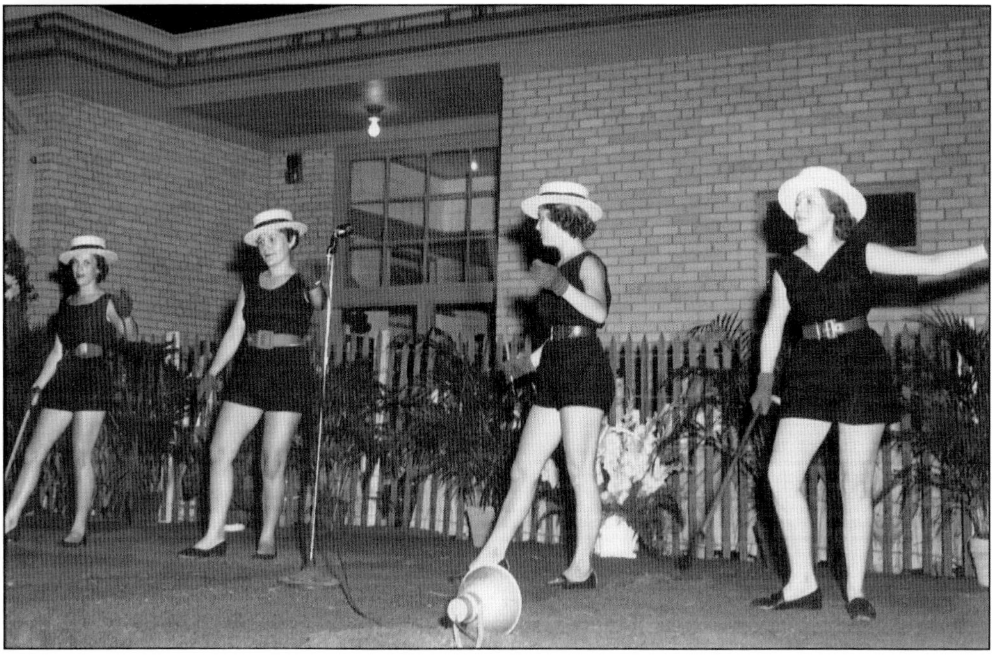

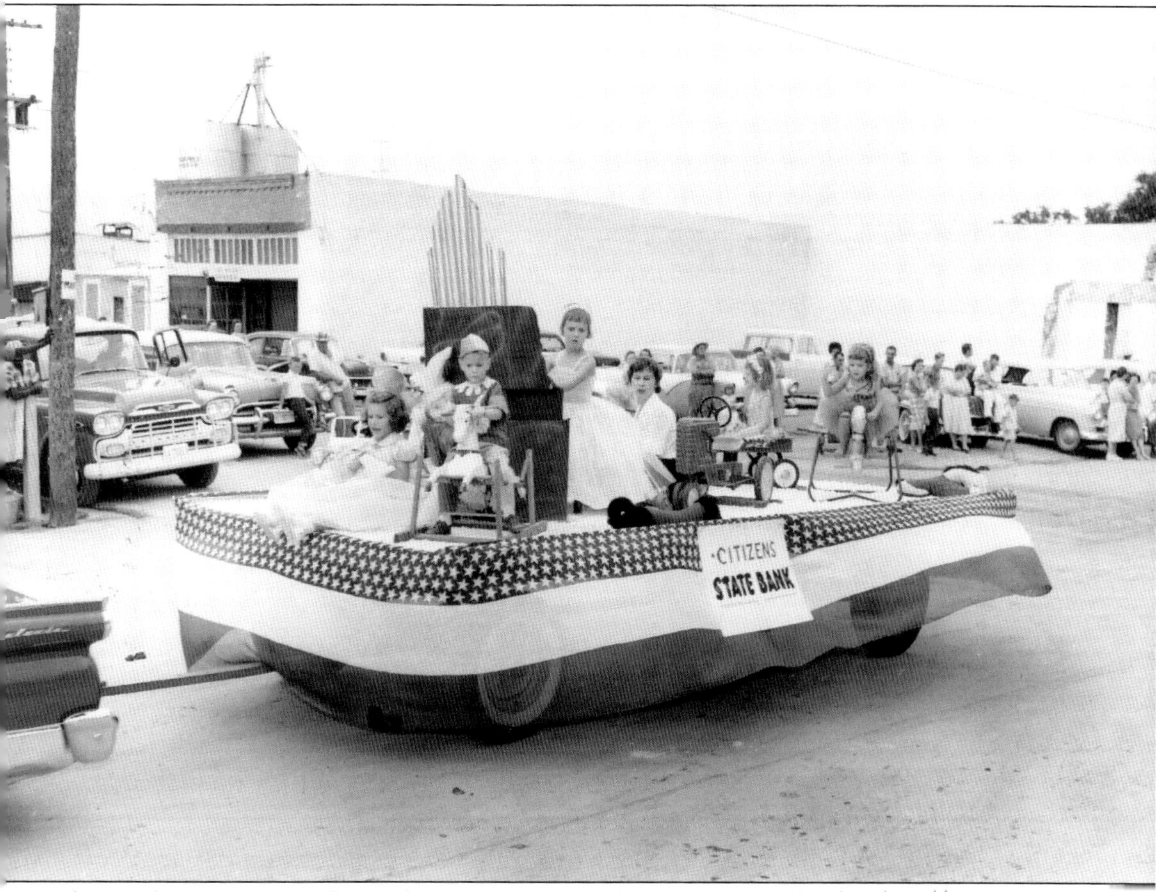

The parade was an essential part of Royse City's annual homecoming celebration. Local businesses and organizations decorated floats, and everyone marched down Main Street. This late-1950s photograph shows the Citizens State Bank float, which features a pint-sized organist and several children on rocking horses and riding toys.

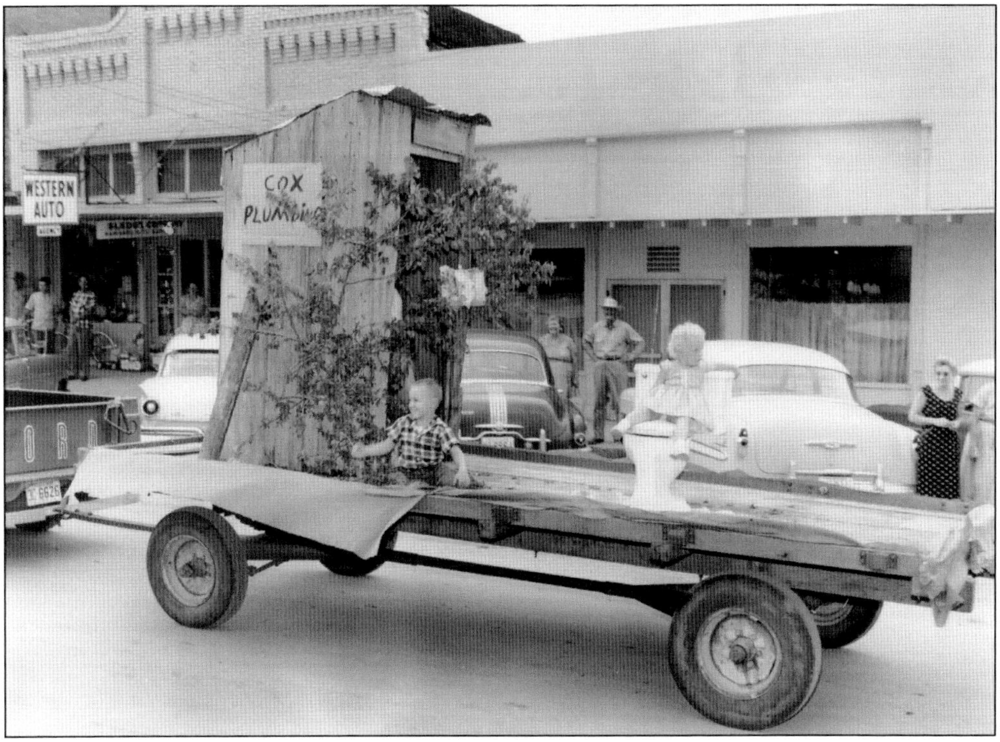

Many Royse City businesses participated in the annual homecoming parades as a way to advertise while also supporting the community. At a late 1950s homecoming parade, the Cox Plumbing float (above) featured an outhouse and commode. The Western Auto store is visible at left; Western Auto franchise stores supplied automobile parts and accessories and were common in small towns. Below, a parade float features a pioneer laundry-day theme with aprons hanging on a clothesline and a sign reading, "Aprons—Buy One and Help the Cemetery Fund."

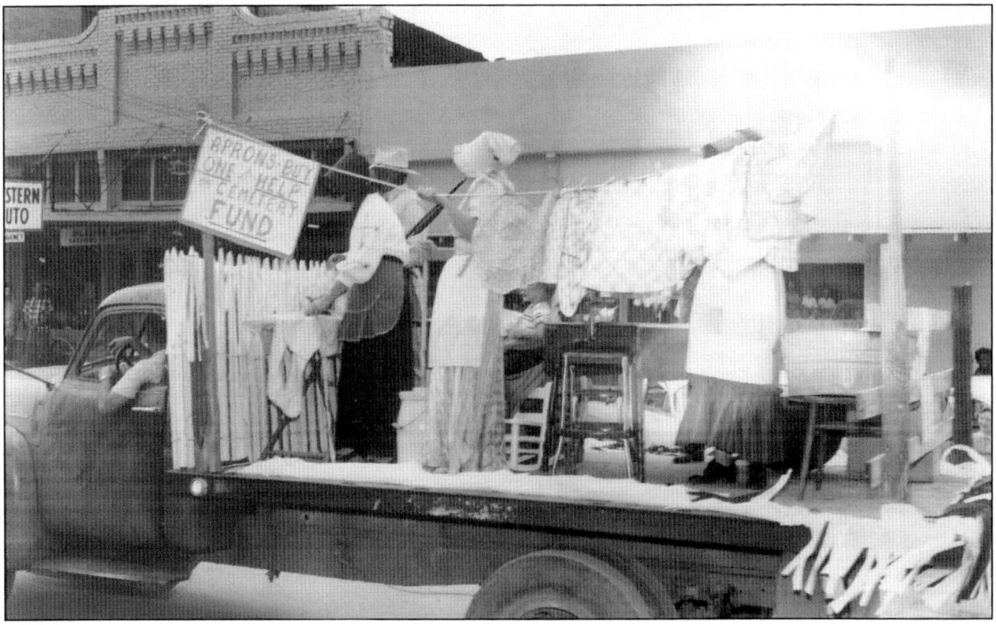

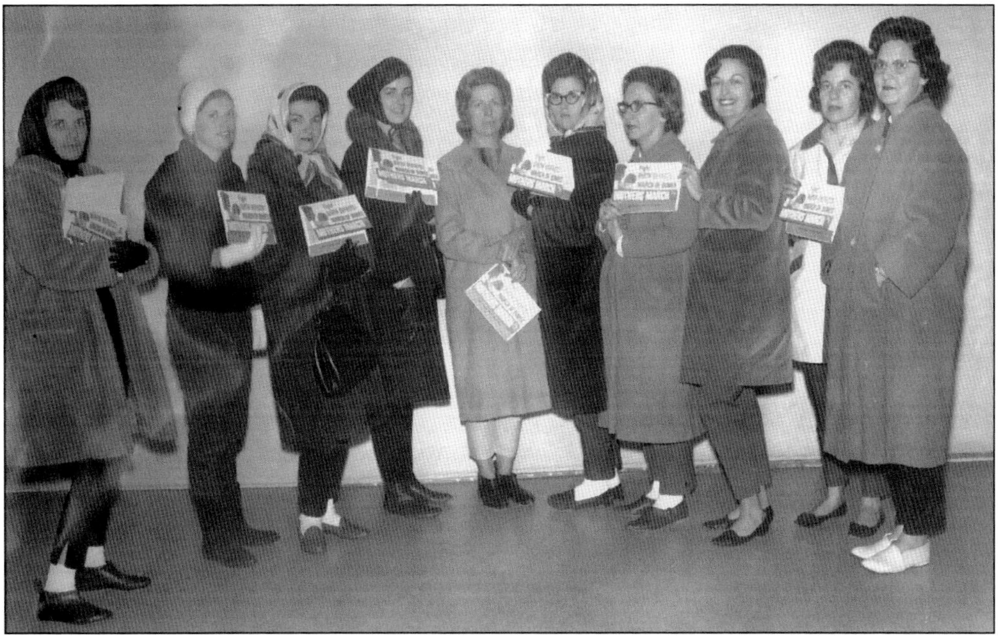

During the mid-1960s, the Jaycees and Jaycee-Ettes were popular Royse City civic organizations. Formally known as the United States Junior Chamber, the Jaycees and Jaycee-Ettes support the community through civic service and business development. Above, a group of Jaycee-Ettes meets on January 18, 1965, to solicit funds for the March of Dimes. The drive netted $210.46. Pictured are, from left to right, Sue Houser, Lee Davidson, Joy Barrow, Connine Pennington, Bonita Houser, Martie Crowell, Pat Paterson, Tommye Clinard, Rogene Pennington, and Betty Mellody. The Jaycee-Ettes also supported the American Cancer Society through a door-to-door campaign. Below, a group of Jaycee-Ettes with American Cancer Society volunteer stickers on their vests prepares for a fundraiser in May 1965.

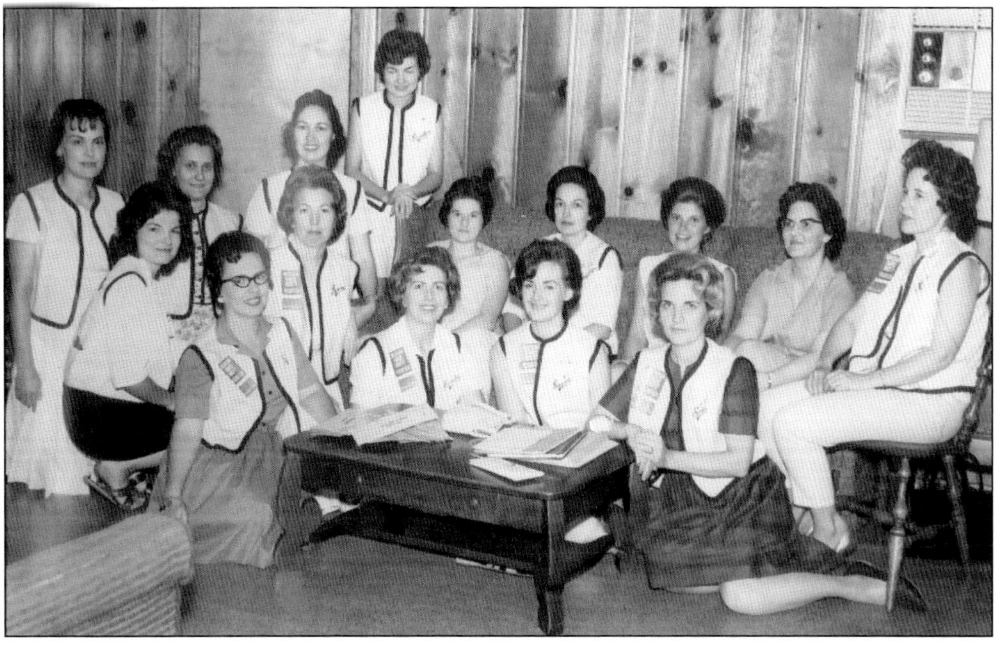

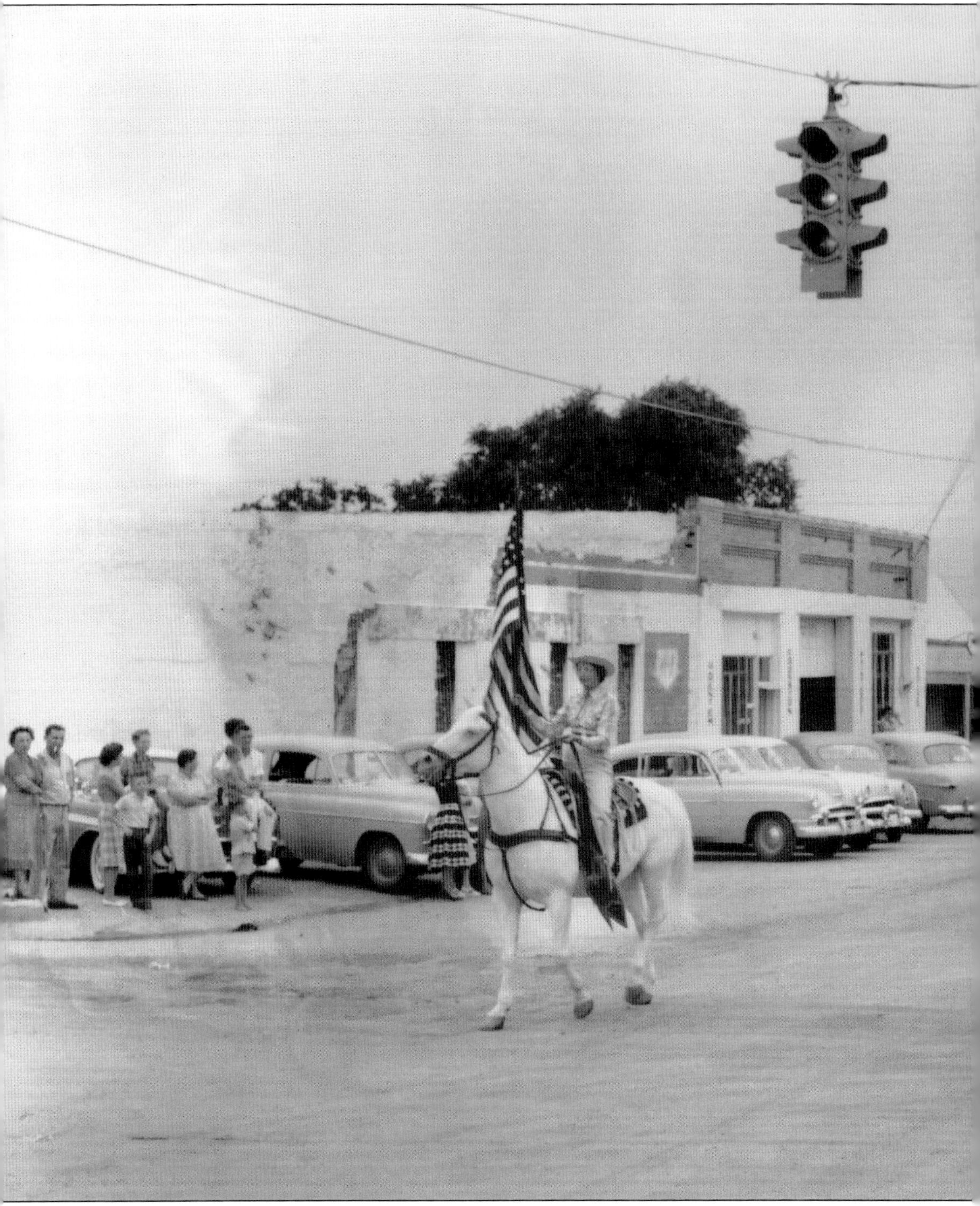

Willie Stodghill (left) and her horse, Snowball, and Woodrow Stodghill and his horse, Whitey, carry American flags as they lead a homecoming parade through downtown Royse City. From the late 1950s through the early 1980s, the Stodghills led parades throughout Rockwall County while riding on ornate black and white saddles with intricate leatherwork. They were members

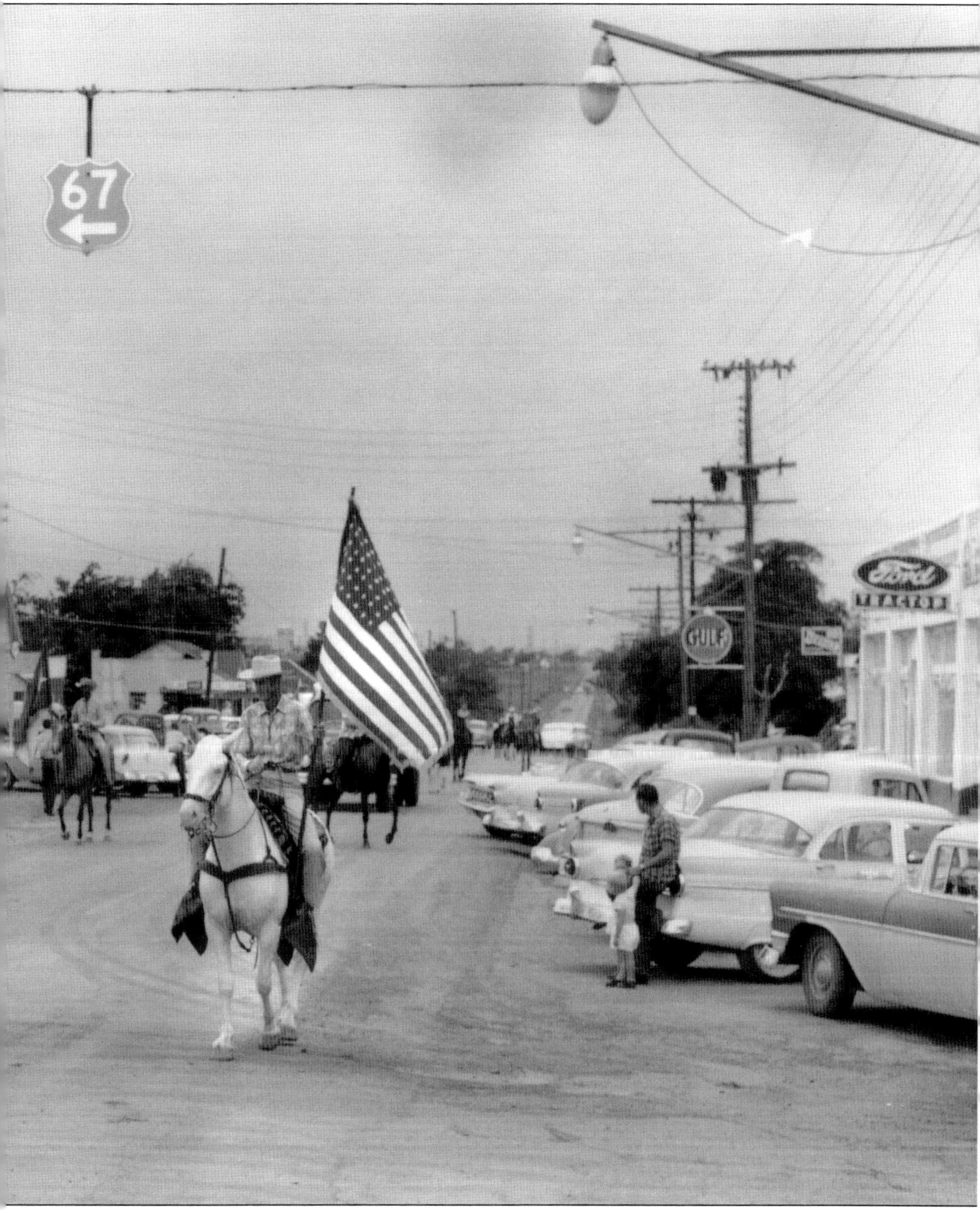

of the Royse City and the Rockwall Riding Clubs. Also visible in the photograph are the Ford dealership and the Gulf Station (right) and the Highway 67 road sign (above center). Today, through Royse City's Main Street effort, numerous festivals and celebrations will bring visitors and citizens into Royse City's historic downtown.

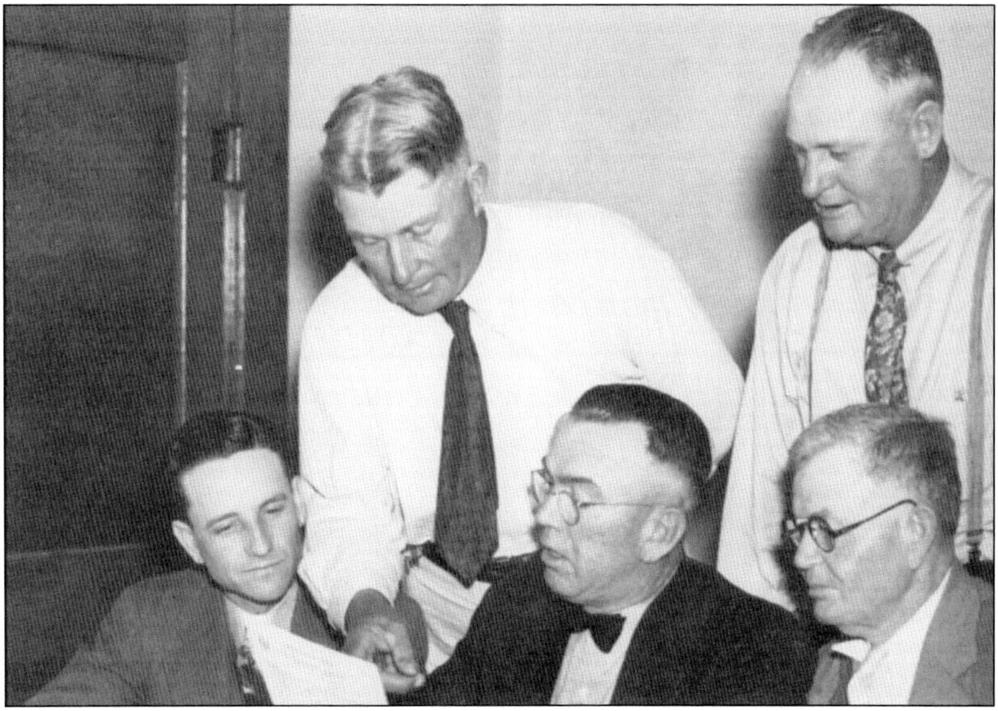

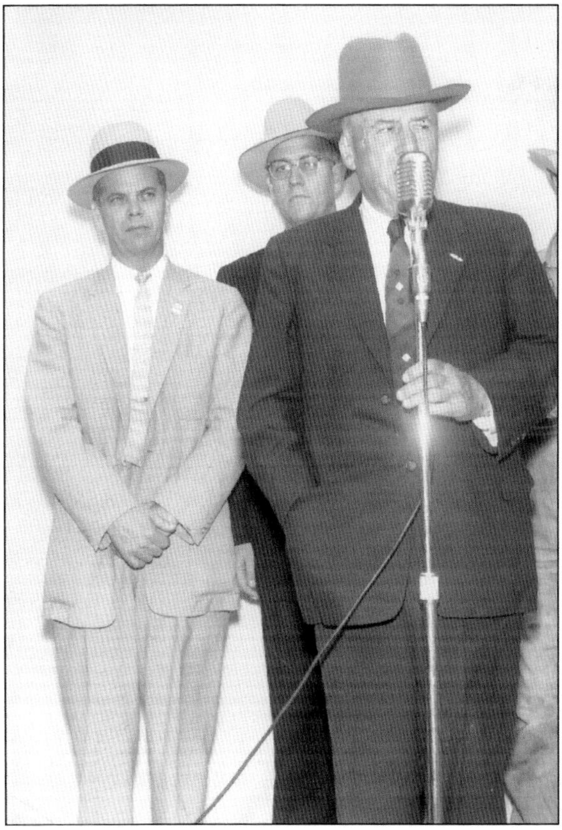

Many prominent citizens served Royse City in elected capacities. The 1938 city council is pictured above. They are, from left to right, (first row) R.M. James, mayor Newt Burton, and T.J. Bailey; (second row) C.R. Allen and P.D. Terrell; councilman H.L. Tay is not pictured. On occasion, Royse City also welcomed well-known guests. At left, US representative Sam Rayburn addresses a crowd during a stop in Royse City. Rayburn was a Democratic lawmaker who served as the speaker of the US House of Representatives for 17 years, the longest tenure of any speaker to date. He entered congress in 1913 as the representative from District No. 4, which Royse City was part of, and remained in office for more than 24 terms (almost 49 years).

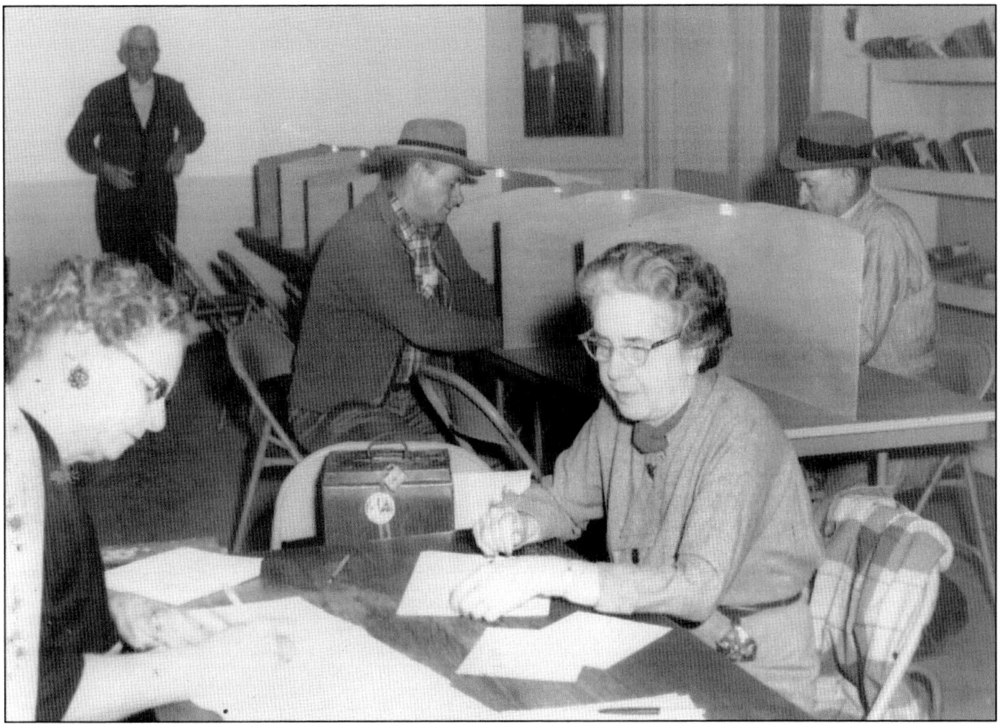

Since the founding of Royse City, the town's citizens have been interested in and involved with the politics of the community. Ermine Burton, pictured above in the right foreground, served as Royse City's voting clerk for many years. In the late 1930s and 1940s, her husband, Newt Burton, served as mayor of Royse City and then Rockwall County judge. Below is J.W. Terrell's poll tax receipt from 1912, which shows a charge of $1.75 for the right to vote. This tax discouraged voting, but it was not completely eliminated at the federal level until the 24th Amendment was ratified in 1964. It was not until two years later, in 1966, that a Supreme Court decision abolished poll taxes at the state level.

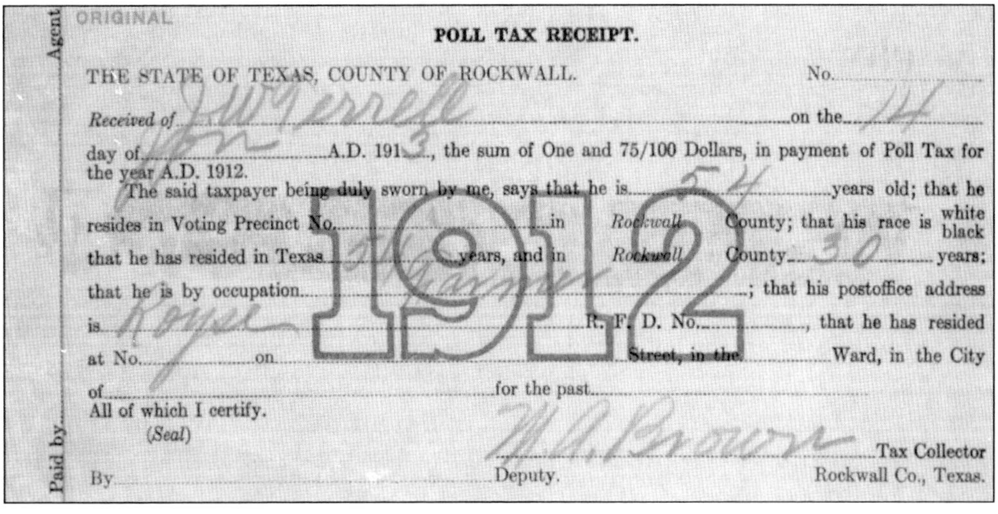

ORIGINAL

Agent

POLL TAX RECEIPT.

THE STATE OF TEXAS, COUNTY OF ROCKWALL. No.

Received of J W Terrell on the 14 day of Jan A.D. 1913, the sum of One and 75/100 Dollars, in payment of Poll Tax for the year A.D. 1912.

The said taxpayer being duly sworn by me, says that he is 54 years old; that he resides in Voting Precinct No. in Rockwall County; that his race is white black that he has resided in Texas 54 years, and in Rockwall County 30 years; that he is by occupation Farmer; that his postoffice address is Royse R. F. D. No. , that he has resided at No. on Street, in the Ward, in the City of for the past

All of which I certify.

(Seal)

W. A. Brown Tax Collector

By Deputy. Rockwall Co., Texas.

Paid by

1912

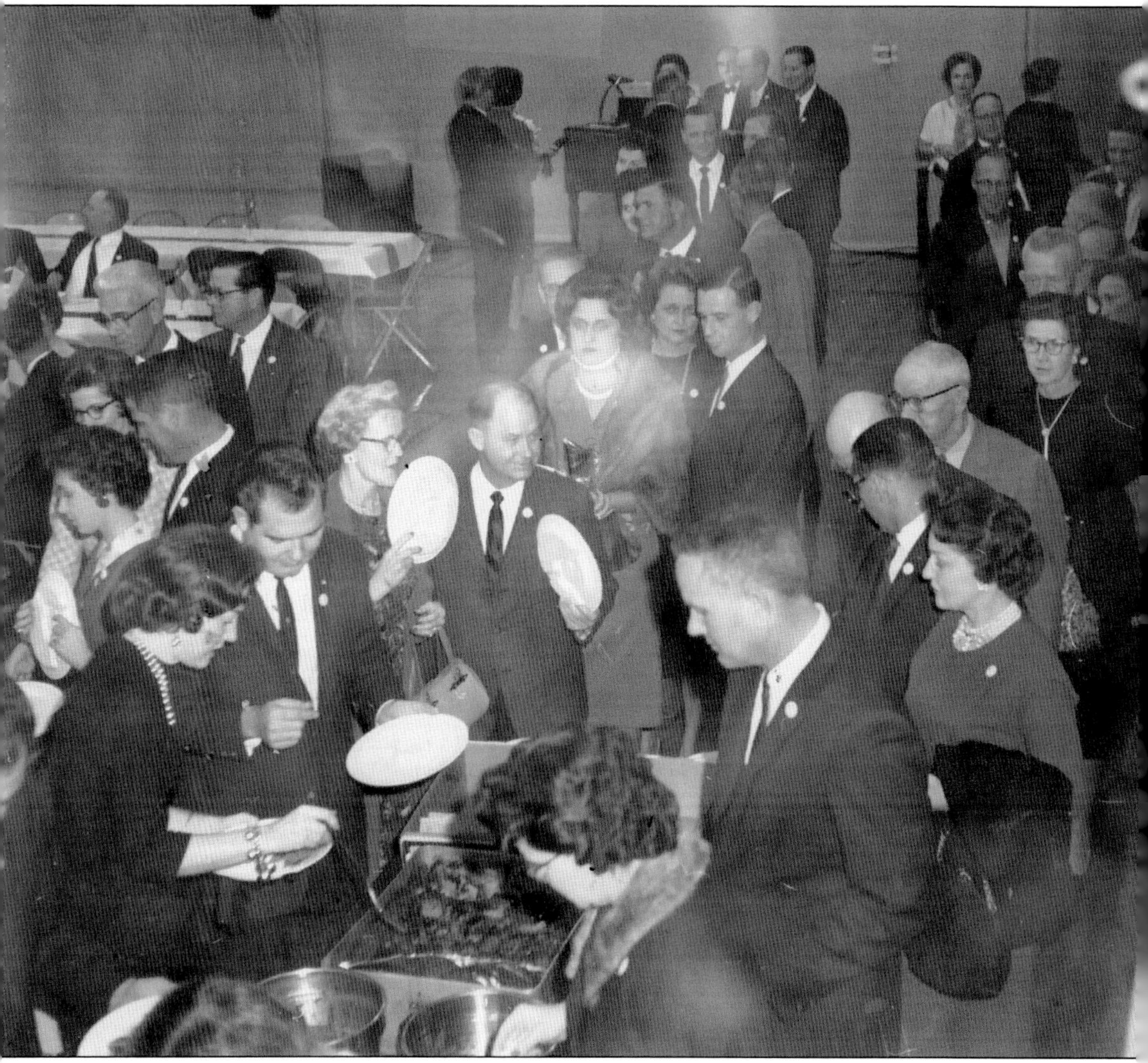

Many longtime Royse City residents might say that the locals were often more like family than just neighbors. Barn raisings, homecoming events, Fourth of July celebrations, school plays, graduations, athletic events, political meetings (such as the countywide event pictured above), and fraternal gatherings have brought residents together for more than 100 years. In a written history of Royse City, lifelong resident Deloris Cross Ballard described growing up in Royse City: "On Saturday, the farmers, along with everyone else, came to town to shop and to visit. People would sit on their car fenders and talk to others as the children played up and down the sidewalks. There was nothing for us to be afraid of . . . the windows were always open and the doors were never locked. . . . Royse City was a great place to grow up, and yes, I would go back and relive those days and times."

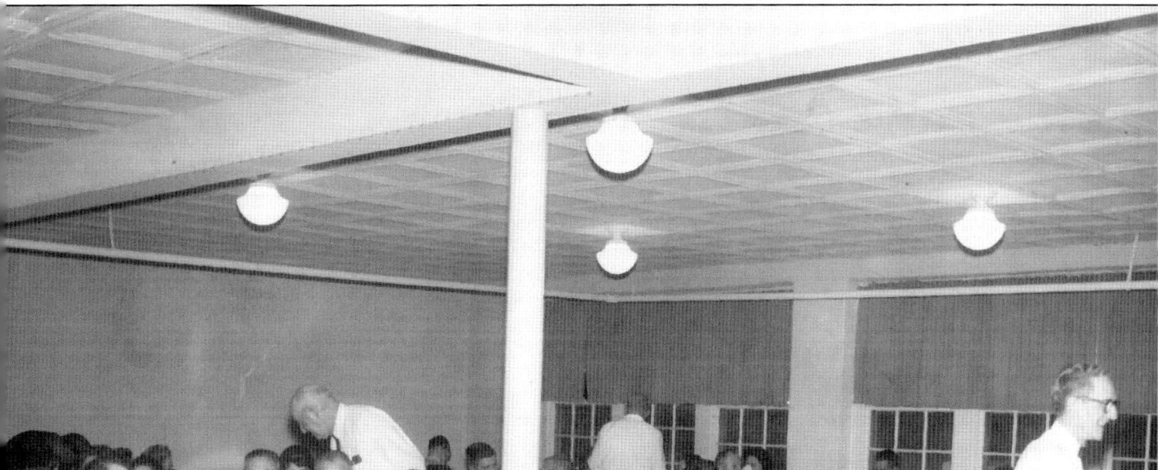

In looking back at the first part of the 20th century, times may have seemed simpler. For example, the lines that separated school, church, and politics were often blurred. The Royse City High School band took its official photograph in front of the First United Methodist Church because it provided a beautiful backdrop, prayer was common in the classroom, and the school cafeteria often hosted political or civic dinners (as shown above). Entertainment was even less complex. "When we were in grade school, we played either hopscotch, jump rope, jacks, roller skates, spun tops, or played in the creek by the railroad," said Deloris Cross Ballard. "We all went to a lot of church gatherings, birthday parties, and school functions. Each summer a traveling skating rink would visit the town, and we loved that. We could also play all over the community riding our bikes until dark. If we did get in any trouble, our parents would know about it before we got home."

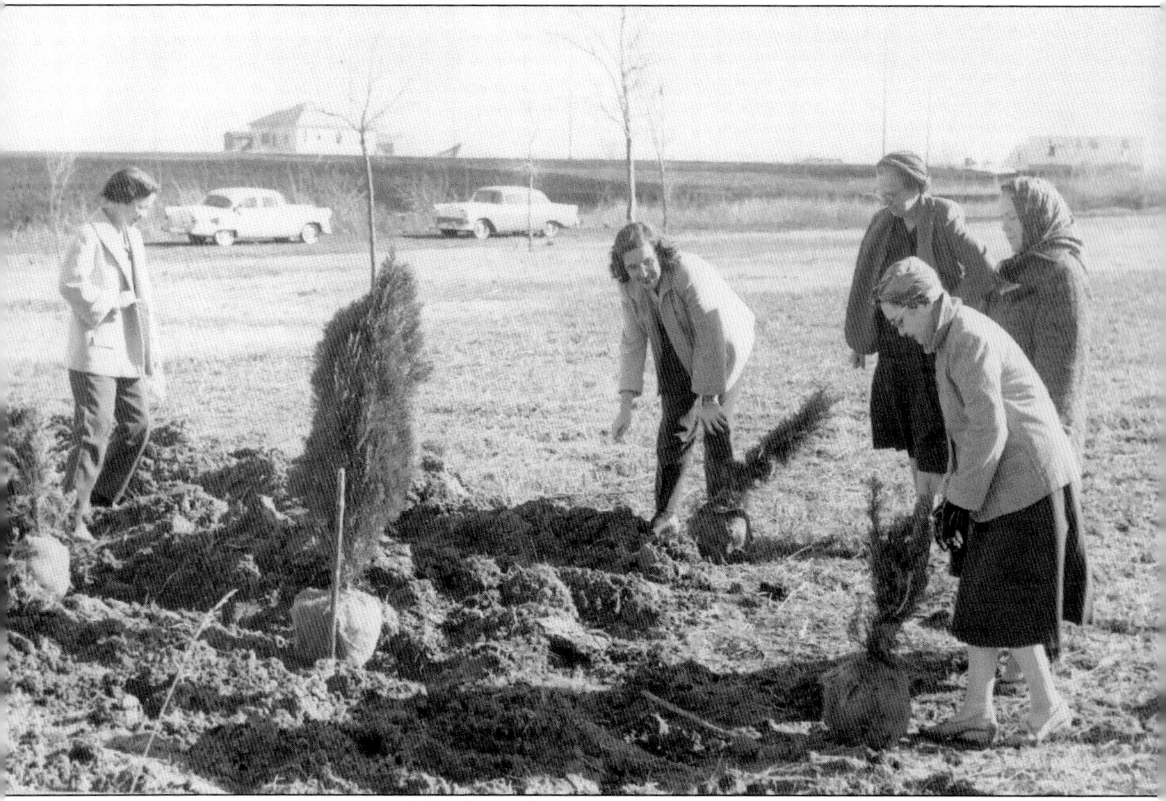

"Keeping Royse City Beautiful" through park improvements and other aesthetic projects has long been the focus of civic-minded individuals in Royse City. City Lake Park, Old Mill Park, Walker-Hawk Splash Park, and Walker-Hawk Sports Complex attest to a community eager to provide amenities for families. Long before the current generation, many local citizens worked diligently to make sure that Royse City was visually appealing to those who call it home and those who are just passing through. In the image above, local Royse City women plant trees as part of a park beautification effort. In a history provided to the Rockwall County Historical Foundation, Lillian Hankins said, "Much respect, honor and appreciation should go into our feeling for those who struggled to make this little city a good place to live . . . the potential for a great future is upon us."

Although the 1950s often produced some differences of opinion between youth and their elders, Royse City was fortunate to have a group of parents and older citizens who adamantly supported local youth in many ways. A strong PTA membership, multiple booster clubs, and mothers and grandmothers who often worked at school events provided a stalwart base of support for the students. In this 1950s photograph, Leslie Jones (center, in the polka-dot dress) is accepting an admission fee.

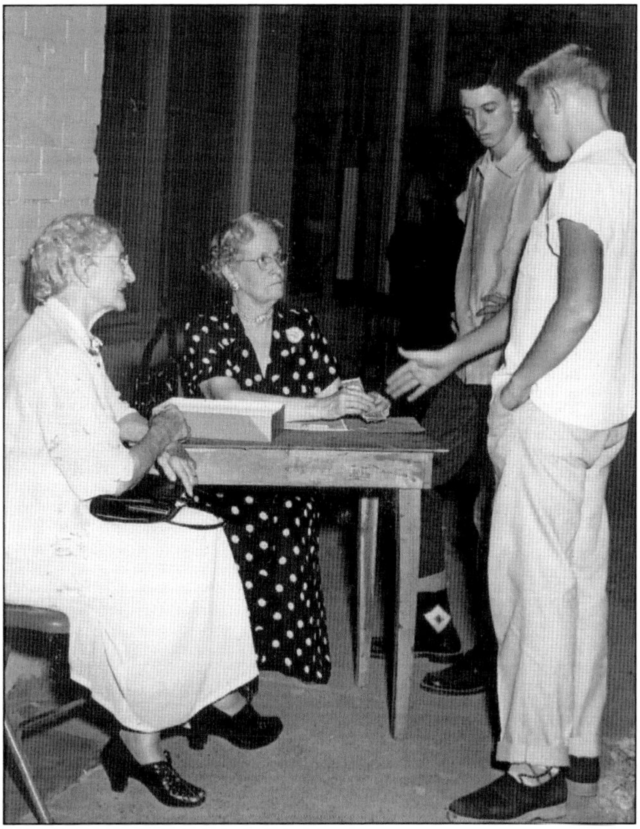

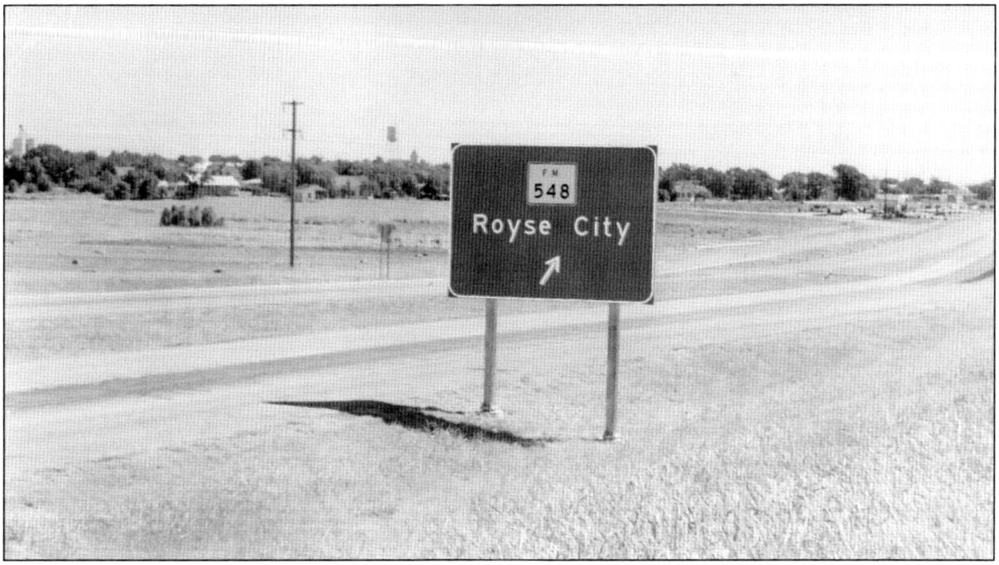

In the late 1950s, a new highway (eventually Interstate 30) was constructed from Royse City to Dallas. By 1962, it went all the way to Greenville. Farmland, houses, an electric line, a water tower, and one business—Fuller's Humble Station—greeted visitors who took this main exit from US 30 into town. At the time this photograph was taken around 1959, Royse City contained around 40 businesses and had a population of approximately 1,300.

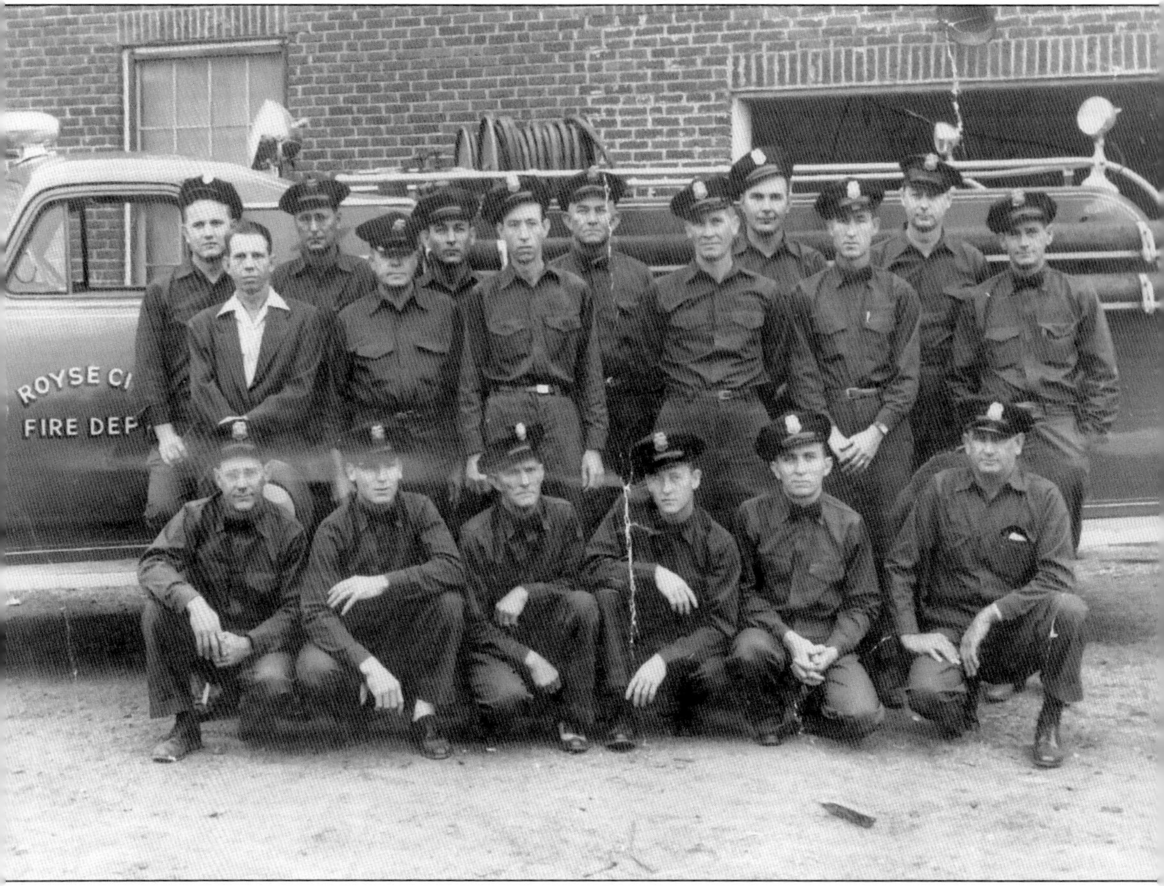

When this photograph was taken in the 1940s, the Royse City Fire Department was housed at 124 Arch Street in the building now occupied by the Zaner Robison Historical Museum. The building (pictured on the following page) was originally constructed in 1925 for the Masonic Lodge and has housed a library and a fire department on the lower floor. The Masons have occupied the top floor since its construction; the city acquired the lower floor in 1941 and made alterations to the exterior to accommodate fire trucks. Pictured here are, from left to right, (squatting) Dean Wester, Cecil Jackson, Cab Dismore, Dick Dickson, Curtis Ratliff, and Clarence Gentry; (standing) Homer Pierce, Gordon Cornelius, Lacy Edwards, Clarence Krider, Irby Campbell, Welby Sherrell, Amon Burton, Ray Tuttle, Doug Jones, Bob Crowell, Carl Edwards, and Lee Smith. The fire department was relocated to a new building in 1980, and the exterior renovations were removed. The building is listed in the National Register of Historic Places.

About the Zaner Robison Historical Museum

The Zaner Robison Historical Museum was founded in 2008 by the City of Royse City and is located at 124 South Arch Street in the only building in Rockwall County that is listed in the National Register of Historic Places. The building was designed by W.A. Kinzey and constructed by J.E. Harris in 1925 to serve as a Masonic Lodge. The city acquired the lower floor in 1941, and the Masonic Lodge still operates out of the top floor. The mission of the museum is: "Educating and providing information about the past and preserving the past for future generations." The extensive collection includes artifacts, memorabilia, printed material, and photographs. The museum is named after longtime resident and civic leader Zaner Benetin Robison. She and her husband, Bob, came to Royse City in 1942 and purchased the *Royse City American*, the city's longest-running newspaper. She also served as mayor and was a founding member of the chamber of commerce. For more information about the museum and its collection, please call 972-635-7438.

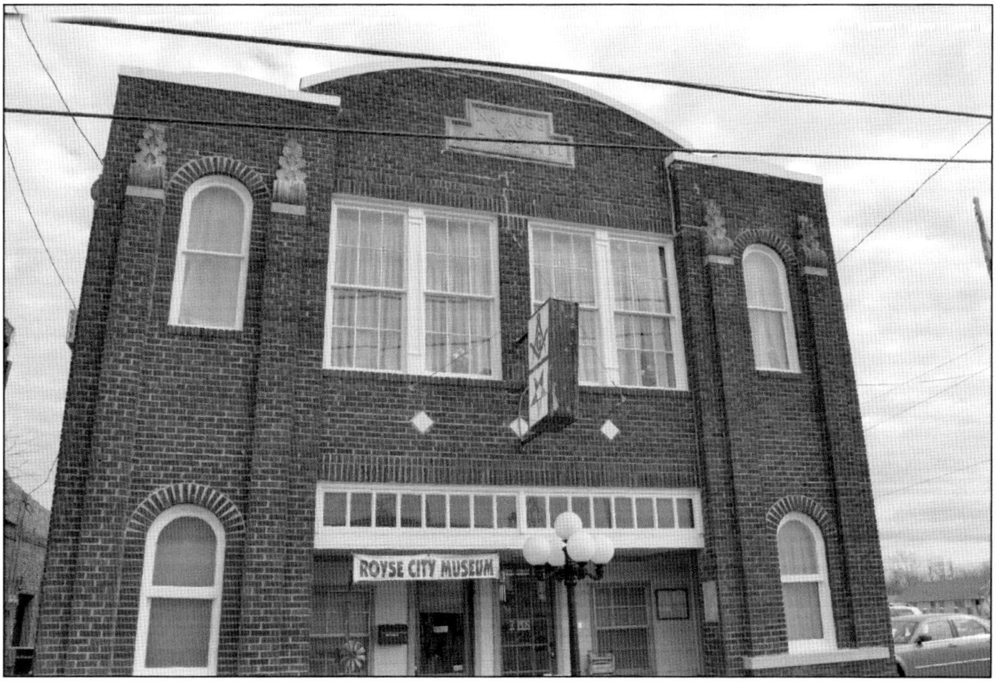

Discover Thousands of Local History Books Featuring Millions of Vintage Images

Arcadia Publishing, the leading local history publisher in the United States, is committed to making history accessible and meaningful through publishing books that celebrate and preserve the heritage of America's people and places.

Find more books like this at
www.arcadiapublishing.com

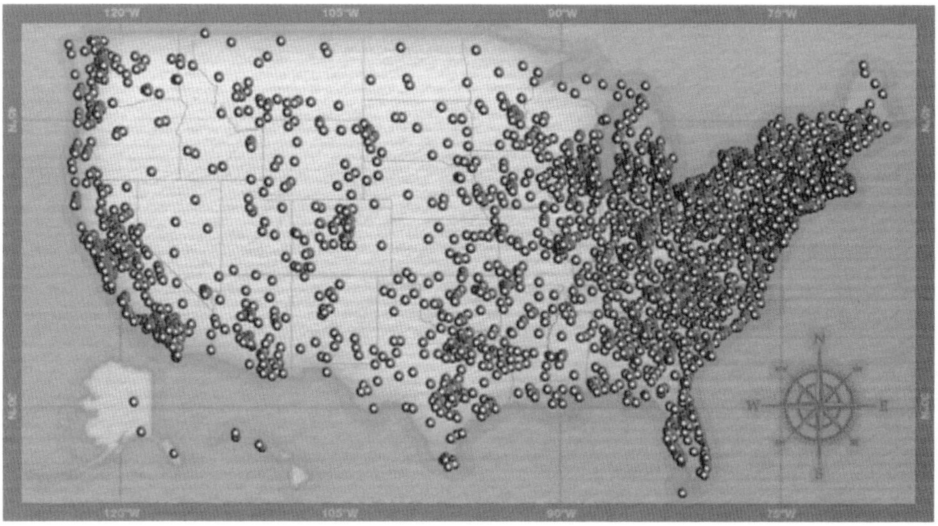

Search for your hometown history, your old stomping grounds, and even your favorite sports team.

Consistent with our mission to preserve history on a local level, this book was printed in South Carolina on American-made paper and manufactured entirely in the United States. Products carrying the accredited Forest Stewardship Council (FSC) label are printed on 100 percent FSC-certified paper.

MADE IN THE USA